Marshall W. Fishwick

Popular Culture in a New Age

*Pre-publication
REVIEWS,
COMMENTARIES,
EVALUATIONS . . .*

"*Popular Culture in a New Age* brings together probing studies by a seasoned cultural analyst on such topics as the Y2000 phenomenon, the impact of the Internet, contemporary symbolism, Disneyfication, the cult of celebrity, African-American popular culture, globalization of culture, and the glut of information that threatens to drown us. The essays are pungent with meaning, distilled over time by original research and original thinking; furthermore, they are written in an eminently readable—indeed, coruscating—style. Professor Fishwick was a teacher of journalist Tom Wolfe (who writes the foreword to the volume); the Fishwick influence seems clear. For example, here is an observation in the Fishwick style: 'Only a few create a new style, while many imitate it. Who can count the number of Petrarchan or Shakespearean sonnets we have endured—or those in our time mimicking Charlie Chaplin, Groucho, Madonna, or Elvis?' This kind of prose evinces a wonderful combination of 'high' and 'low' culture sophistication—a very rare blend that we associate with Tom Wolfe, but that may have had it's origins in a Yale classroom under the influence of Marshall Fishwick.

Whatever the origins of the research and style, *Popular Culture in a New Age* is a wonderful springboard for students and teachers to consider the multiple cultural strands of our time and an excellent stimulator of classroom discussions about where these strands lead into our collective future. Fishwick's willingness to keep his own prejudices and tastes out of the analysis will be welcomed by both students and teachers; the book, while inspiring thought and pointing in various research directions, allows readers the freedom to reach personal conclusions. Finally, this book, while pointed and relevant, does not have an ideological axe to grind—an accomplishment worth noting these days."

Peter C. Rollins, PhD
Editor-in-Chief,
*Film and History:
An Interdisciplinary
Journal of Film
and Television Studies,*
Cleveland, Oklahoma

More pre-publication
REVIEWS, COMMENTARIES, EVALUATIONS . . .

"Widely read and deeply observant, Fishwick has scanned many aspects of our age, shown how it has grown out of life in earlier stages, and speculates where it will end up and why. His is a fast trip from here to there, with pauses along the way to analyze and interpret the phenomena of our culture as it expands into global culture, or as global culture becomes Americanized. Should the earth be renamed Spaceship America? Temporarily it should. What its name will be tomorrow is anybody's guess. Fishwick's probe into the mass is brilliant and entertaining."

Ray B. Browne, PhD
Emeritus Professor
of Popular Culture,
Bowling Green University,
Ohio

"Bam! Pow! Wham! Marshall Fishwick's *Popular Culture in a New Age* takes a fascinating look at the status of myth, symbolism, and folklore at the beginning of the American millennium. Each essay in this collection is a richly rewarding intellectual exploration, but taken together, the tessarae of this particular mosaic form a rich and vibrant image of popular culture that amounts to much more than the sum of its individual parts. From Lord Tennyson to Marshall McLuhan, the printing press to the Internet, folklore to pop lore, Fishwick and his band of merry men (and women) delve into the mysteries of our collective psyche and interpret the meaning of seemingly unrelated political, literary, artistic, electronic, and historical events. What emerges from this compilation is a holistic understanding of our present through the prism of things past.

English, history, art, government, and American studies departments will find much food for thought in these essays. In the words of George Santayana, 'those who cannot remember the past are condemned to repeat it,' and this book goes a long way toward preventing that from happening."

Aldo Bello, MA, CEO
Mind & Media, Inc.,
Alexandria, Virginia

"Marshall Fishwick has again put together an astute and perceptive collection of chapters. Beginning with the assertion that American exceptionalism is alive and well, and that American studies should have a conceptual foundation, he asserts that he would wed conceptual strength to literary power—what he calls sociology written well.

Of course the operative word is 'new,' as in New Deal and new fashion, and so on, in which popular culture plays such a crucial role. The fact is that this book, beautifully put together and well written, wise and very perceptive, is an extraordinarily important assemblage of chapters. *Popular Culture in a New Age* is the pinnacle of syntheses on American popular culture."

Daniel Walden, PhD
Emeritus Professor
of American Studies,
Penn State University,
University Park

More pre-publication
REVIEWS, COMMENTARIES, EVALUATIONS . . .

"In this book, Marshall Fishwick ranges over many aspects of the culture in which we live, and with great insight helps us to understand the forces that shape our common life. He succeeds well in his stated intent: 'I am not attempting merely to compile facts, but to understand a moving process.' Fishwick is particularly helpful in identifying the myths and symbols that we use to give meaning to our times. He does not offer neat analyses or simple solutions, but immerses his readers in the complexities of contemporary life. He does offer a clear message: we must 'change with the times, but never forsake our past,' and 'our best hope lies with our adaptability, our bounceability.'"

Harry B. Adams, MDiv
Acting Dean and Horace
Bushnell Professor
of Christian Nurture,
Yale Divinity School

"If you want to know what *was* and *is* popular culture, read Marshall Fishwick's latest book, *Popular Culture in a New Age*. You will find an amazing distillation of the habits, fads, icons, and heroes of people around the world. Fishwick's analysis is historical, contemporary, and futuristic. It includes an intellectual as well as a down-to-earth approach as he deals with his vo-luminous material. And once again, as in previous publications, Fishwick's new book contains helpful notes and suggestions for future reading for the convenience of students, scholars, and the general public.

His chapter on civil religion in America is full of insights. The importance of attending church on Sunday takes a back seat to watching professional football on television. At the same time, Billy Graham's vast influence is noted and described in a very thoughtful manner.

Fishwick reminds us of the vast impact that individuals such as Walt Disney and P. T. Barnum have had on the people's culture. His discussion of the Civil War and the old South makes one wonder who won the culture war in the nineteenth century, and his many questions about the conventional wisdom of the global village force one to examine the adequacy of that concept.

The variety of his observations includes discussion of black popular culture, the role of celebrities such as Marilyn Monroe and Clark Gable, as well as the influence of Horatio Alger and Harriet Beecher Stowe. Fishwick's analysis will help you understand the roots of popular culture and the significance of Marshall McLuhan and his famous comment, 'the medium is the message.' *Popular Culture in a New Age* is, indeed, pervasive."

Marvin Wachman, PhD
President Emeritus,
Temple University,
Philadelphia

The Haworth Press®
New York • London • Oxford

Popular Culture
in a New Age

THE HAWORTH PRESS
Popular Culture
B. Lee Cooper, PhD
Senior Editor

Popular Culture in a New Age

Marshall W. Fishwick, PhD

For Nancy, the botonisti humanist, good friend of Ann —

With every good wish —

Marshall

Easter, 2003 —

The Haworth Press®
New York • London • Oxford

The Haworth Press, Inc., 10 Alice Street, Binghamton, NY 13904-1580

Parts of the chapter titled "Faith Takes a New Face" have been excerpted from *Great Awakenings: Popular Religion and Popular Culture* by Marshall W. Fishwick. Copyright 1995, The Haworth Press, Binghamton, New York. Reprinted by permission.

Cover design by Jennifer M. Gaska.

Library of Congress Cataloging-in-Publication Data

Fishwick, Marshall William
    Popular culture in a new age / Marshall Fishwick.
       p. cm.
    Includes bibliographical references and index.
    ISBN 0-7890-1297-9 (alk. paper)—ISBN 0-7890-1298-7 (alk. paper)
    1. Civilization, Modern—1950- 2. Popular culture. 3. Twenty-first century. 4. Postmodernism. 5. Technology and civilization. 6. Civilization, Modern—21st century. 7. Popular culture—Forecasting. 8. Popular culture—United States. 9. United States—Civilization—1970- I. Title.

CB430 .F576 2001
909.82'5—dc21

200124338

To all my students
who are also my teachers.

ABOUT THE AUTHOR

Marshall Fishwick, PhD, Professor of Interdisciplinary Studies and Director of the American Studies and Popular Culture programs at Virginia Tech in Blacksburg, Virginia, holds several honorary degrees and teaching awards. In 1998, he was honored by the American Culture Association (ACA) with its Lifetime Achievement Award. Dr. Fishwick is co-founder of the Popular Culture Association (PCA). Having served as Fulbright Distinguished Professor in Denmark, Italy, Germany, Korea, and India, he helped establish the American Studies Research Center in Hyderabad, India, which now houses the largest collection of American books in Asia.

A prolific writer, Dr. Fishwick is the author of *The Hero, American Style; American Heroes: Myth and Reality; American Studies in Transition; Faust Revisited; Icons of Popular Culture; Parameters of Popular Culture; Great Awakenings: Religious Awakenings in America; Jane Addams; Clara Barton; Preview 2001; Go and Catch a Falling Star; An American Mosaic: Rethinking American Culture History;* and *Popular Culture: Cavespace to Cyberspace.* Fishwick serves as advisory editor to the *Journal of Popular Culture* and the *Journal of American Culture,* and is co-founder of the journal *International Popular Culture.*

In 2000, Dr. Fishwick authored a "Millennium Edition" of *Go and Catch a Falling Star* as well as articles about the millennium and the controversial "global village." He is currently at work on a book entitled *Global Village: or Pillage?*

CONTENTS

The dogmas of the past are
inadequate to the stormy present.

—Abraham Lincoln
Annual Message to Congress
December 1, 1862

A Different World

Suddenly the world changed. Buildings vanished, the Pentagon burned, bodies fell from buildings. Airlines stopped flying, the stock market closed, all games were canceled. Our world had seemed safe. Not now.

"Isms" exploded. Terrorism led the way, followed closely by surrealism (was all this a dream?), alarmism, emotionalism. Headlines spoke of DOOMSDAY, APOCALYPSE, END OF THE WORLD. We were at WAR. But this time, we didn't know who or where the enemy was.

A long-dormant "ism" emerged—PATRIOTISM. Our Congress stood on the Capitol steps and sang "God Bless America." In London, the Cold Stream Guards played "The Star Spangled Banner." Strangers hugged. Spectators wept.

A quick flashback: When the British surrendered to Washington at Yorktown, their band played "The World Turned Upside Down." Again? What next?

As the world swirled, the people's culture—popular culture—was thrust into a New Age. Words once used by a few specialists— Taliban, bin Laden, al-Jezeera, al-Qaeda, Northern Alliance, Mullah Omar, President Musharraf, Kandahar, anthrax, biological warfare— were on every channel, in every headline, on every lip. What next?

Fear fought freedom, and fear seemed to be winning. "Security" was the new buzz word. The Bears ravaged Wall Street. Ten mutual funds that were the peaks of 1999 became the valleys of 2001, with lifetime losses of over $4.4 billion. Dozens of happy predictions failed.

Who would pay to help the ailing airlines, get gigantic insurance claims settled, rebuild a shattered New York? How could and would we win a war in bleak Central Asia, fought in the shadows, against the harshest of all generals: General Winter? "You will be sitting ducks," recently defeated Russian generals warned. "There's no negotiations for Osama bin Laden," President Bush insisted. Bombs away.

Unemployment lines skyrocketed, psychiatrists were deluged with frantic patients, companies and magazines (such as the sixty-six-year-old *Mademoiselle*) folded, dot.coms became dot.gone. Gone with the wind.

Flags still flew in abundance, churches filled and overflowed, old "Guts and Glory" movie reruns appeared on television. People were warned they must be patient; polls showed wide support for our allies and policies.

But who could say what might happen next, and when the people would start to sing a different song? Some of us recalled a fine line by the poet John Keats: "There is nothing stable in the world; uproar's your only music."

These were indeed new times, and they would surely upend our popular culture and try our souls.

Marshall Fishwick

Foreword

Do I Dare?

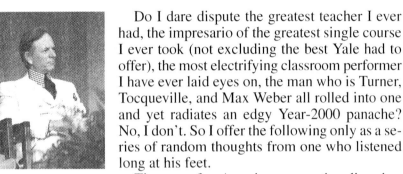

Do I dare dispute the greatest teacher I ever had, the impresario of the greatest single course I ever took (not excluding the best Yale had to offer), the most electrifying classroom performer I have ever laid eyes on, the man who is Turner, Tocqueville, and Max Weber all rolled into one and yet radiates an edgy Year-2000 panache? No, I don't. So I offer the following only as a series of random thoughts from one who listened long at his feet.

The case for American exceptionalism has never been stronger. As I stated in my Year-2000 piece, we are Macedon under Alexander the Great, Rome under Julius and Augustus Caesar, Mongolia under Genghis Khan, Turkey under Mohammed II, England under Queen Victoria. Our military, economic, and cultural might is unchallenged and unique in world history. Just think of our cultural might. Here in America we talk a lot about "globalization." But just ask any European. He or she will tell you, "What you call 'globalization' we call 'Americanization.'" Why is Michael Jordan, giant of a sport that fifteen years ago was about as well known in the rest of the world as curling is in this country today, the most famous athlete in the world? Answer: American television, which now streams into every brain in every part of the world where electricity exists. Why have Germans lost their cradle-to-grave socialized medical coverage? Because the government said, "We can save a fortune doing it the American way—private HMOs." Why do British aristos have to put up with (gnashing their teeth) waiters in the fashionable restaurants who now say, "Hi, I'm Roy. I'll be your waiter tonight. Let me tell you our specials. Tonight we have day-oat Chilean sea bass baked with a red currant and Damson glaze on a bed of fresh-cut kale with whole roasted garlic cloves. . . ." Why? Because the fashionable restaurants in London now cater to all the rich young American investment bankers who are in town knocking down $1,000,000 yearly bonuses and driving up townhouse and apartment prices—and driving the formerly fashionable, now dowdy-looking upper-class Brits bananas.

I could go on, but let us turn to another standard of comparison: social justice. No other nation in the world approaches the United States—even *approaches* us—in accommodating all the peoples of the world peacefully and justly. And we *do* accommodate people from all over the world. This country, according to *EBONY* magazine, now has more than 300 black mayors. Every major American city either now has or has recently had a black mayor. Even Portland, Oregon, which is only 20 percent black, recently had a black mayor. Nowhere else in the world, outside of Africa and the predominantly black nations of the Caribbean, has there *ever* been a black mayor. In America, it is rare that a city's black population is underrepresented on the city council. In Paris, where there is a huge North African population, there has *never* been a North African on the city council, never been a nonwhite face. Eleven percent of America's Army, Air Force, and Marine generals are black, and as everybody knows, we recently had a black chairman of the Joint Chiefs of Staff. No other country in the world has ever had even *one* general who was not of so-called native stock. Even Israel, a nation not even fifty years old that is made up overwhelmingly of immigrants, draws its generals *solely* from native stock, i.e., families who lived in the Palestine settlements before independence—people known as the "*real* Israelites."

The theory of exceptionalism is far from outdated. The United States is more obviously exceptional than ever. We *are* the world's father figure. I'm not saying we *ought* to be; I'm not saying we ought to think in terms of Manifest Destiny. I'm saying that we *are* Rome, we are the world's Big Daddy, and that our destiny, perhaps for the next millennium—the Pax Romana, after all, lasted 600 years—is manifest.

I'm saying it's time to be objective and realistic in American Studies, as objective and realistic as your magnificent course at W&L University was fifty years ago. In your statement of purpose—"New

American Studies in a New World"—did I detect perhaps the tiniest concession to the PC environment of contemporary academics? I hope not. You, egreggio maestro, are too important and masterful a figure for that. You said, "Many of the world's 135 nations seek new dignity and potential power." When did they not? Four desires propel the human beast: to ward off death, to avoid irksome soil, to procreate, and to assert the superiority of "my kind." Not me, but "my kind." Nothing that has happened in over the past 100 years has changed that in the slightest anywhere on earth, as long as you realize that "my kind" is more likely to be an ethnic group or a status group (e.g., "intellectuals," "feminists") than an entire nation.

I entered the Yale program with a strong bias against the social sciences. Despite the fact that sociologist John Sirjamaki was not an exciting teacher, I left Yale convinced that, conceptually, sociology is, or should be, the kingdom in which all other branches of knowledge—even neuroscience—and I am a neuroscience buff—should be the provinces. I won't tarry to argue that point now. For now, I will only argue that American Studies should have a conceptual foundation that is immune to changing historical conditions. Should we expand our purview as conditions change? Of course. Objective scholarship has always done that. But should we worry about what the United States should become or is likely to become? Not for a moment, in my opinion. We should provide the concepts and the evidence, which anyone who cares to can use to argue conceptually as Max Weber (or Fishwick). We should strive to wed conceptual strength to literary power the way Orwell could blend sociology, the literary essay, and vivid narrative—as in "Shooting an Elephant"— and there you've got it: sociology written well. That's what we need. If we have that, changing conditions we'll eat for dinner and smack our lips afterward. Hmmmmunnnnnhhh, changing conditions, do love those changing conditions, like 'em with a red currant and Damson glaze, I do, I do. . . .

Tom Wolfe

Preface

The people are a giant Atlas, carrying the world on their shoulders. How and why do they do it? To ask such questions will always be popular culture's first task.

Marshall Fishwick

Marshall Fishwick, a founding father of popular culture studies, has set the tone and pace of that major movement. This is a splendid summary of what he thinks and knows in our new millennium.

During the turmoil of the 1960s, he was an early pioneer in American Studies, receiving his doctorate at Yale University under Professor Ralph Gabriel. Fishwick began American Studies programs at Washington and Lee University and Lincoln University before joining with Professors Ray B. Browne and Russell B. Nye in 1967 to start the Popular Culture Association, which would both broaden and deepen cultural studies and break down the constricting boundaries of well-entranced departments. The idea caught fire and has burned brightly ever since. Two major journals—*The Journal of Popular Culture* and *The Journal of American Culture*—are the flagships, and scores of books from the Popular Press are the legacy. This book is a distillation of that pioneering and these triumphs.

A graduate of Mr. Jefferson's University of Virginia, Fishwick believes, like Jefferson, that if you give the people light, they will find their way. He also agrees with Horatio Greenough that "it is the great multitude for whom all really great things are done and said." Fishwick also knows there is truth in P. T. Barnum's famous cynical remark: "There's a sucker born every minute." He gives suckers a local habitation and a name.

In an earlier book, Fishwick asked, "Why not put our trust in Electronic Darwinism?" Rather than curtail or restrict information, let it all flow and then trust our great parents, Mother Nature and Father Time, to sort it all out. The silly and stupid must be discarded; the significant will be retained. In a democracy, we must trust the people to judge, as eventually they will. Here, indeed, is an ex-elitist's trust in the people.

Every thinking American is concerned about how media is shaping our daily lives. Too often, the answers of scholars are delivered in jargon-ridden studies that—when closely examined—signify little or nothing. In contrast, *Popular Culture in a New Age* is an entertaining and mature work that will make sense to the college student, the general reader, and the specialist. In the Declaration of Independence, Thomas Jefferson talked about the "pursuit of happiness." At that time and later, there have been varying interpretations of what he meant in that vague phrase. In this direct and informative overview, a scholarly founding father shows how popular culture studies have become a way to understand how ordinary people find meaning and joy in their lives. The result is nothing less than a better understanding of who we are and who we should become. I can think of no more humanistic endeavor—can you?

Peter Rollins
Regents Professor of English and American Film Studies
Oklahoma State University

Acknowledgments

Earlier versions of some of this material appeared in the *Yale Review, Saturday Review, Western Folklore, The American Historical Review, The Texas Quarterly, Virginia Magazine of History, American Heritage, Journal of Popular Culture, Journal of American Culture, Journal of Regional Cultures, The Washington Post,* and the *Roanoke Times,* and is used by permission.

Numerous people have been more than generous in their assistance and suggestions. My wife, Ann LaBerge, tops the list, followed closely by Tom Wolfe, Ray Browne, Bill Palmer, and Patricia Brown. No editor could have been more diligent and astute than Peg Marr. Any errors you find please blame on me.

Introduction

This book is meant as a textbook and trade book, not only a scholarly monograph. What I seek to "trade" are observations and ideas coming from a life of teaching and writing about popular culture. I address the general reader as well as the specialist. Footnotes would be necessary; but I have preferred endnotes, suggesting what sources I have found most helpful and which can lead the interested reader into deeper waters. There is an extensive list for Further Reading.

I try not only to answer questions but to raise them and urge readers to ask new questions for themselves. We live in exciting but confusing times, when high hopes fall prey to false hypes. New technology has upended the old cosmos, as we move from reality to virtual or hyper reality. We find ourselves at the mercy of spin doctors and doctored polls. Popular culture—always close to the people—reflects all this. So it too must be redefined, restudied, and reinvigorated. No task is more important as we enter the new millennium.

* * *

The key operative word in our times is *new*—*new* century, *new* millennium, *new* technology, *new* mergers, *new* wealth, a *new* age. In all these, popular culture plays a crucial role.

We have gone from culture shock to culture meltdown; from modern to postmodern everything. Time and space have come together as time-space. Long distance is short distance—or no distance at all. Long separate tribes and nations are merging into a global village. Night and day have become interchangeable—you can work, eat, sleep, trade, travel, whenever you want. Racial and gender barriers disappear. Men dress as women; women dress as men: gender-merging. Things fall apart; things come together. We have a new mantra: GRE—gender, race, ethnicity. Expect the unexpected. If it works, it's obsolete. These are the new clichés of our newly emerging era.

But haven't other times and epochs felt the powerful tug of *"new?"* Didn't the Chinese, Greeks, Romans, Renaissance princes, Reformation reformers, New World explorers, Old World conquerors, New

Science pioneers, dreamers and dictators, use different words for their version of *"new?"* Can the case for change be matched by the case for stasis? But what makes an age "new"?

Every age is "new" when it opens; every time is "modern" (the word means "just now") when it begins. Americans are obsessed with newness and have been since the first European adventurers came to the New World. One bold leader, Captain John Smith, ventured north from Virginia to discover and name New England, where later settlements were named New Canaan and New Haven. Puritans made a New Covenant with God. Later, colonists created "a new nation under God," named the United States. Surely *that* launched a New Age.

Later on, they wrote a new constitution, set up a new government, and elected a new president. Pushing westward, they named new states, finally reaching from sea to shining sea.

Natives, visitors, statesmen, and salesmen have invoked "newness" for generations. A famous French visitor, Alexis de Tocqueville, asked an enduring question: "What then is the new man, this American?" This newness was constantly renewed by millions of immigrants seeking a new life. Shakespeare called us the "Brave New World." Politicians always promise newness: Wilson's New Freedom, Roosevelt's New Deal, Kennedy's New Frontiers, Clinton's New Globalism. A new president rephrases the idea.

This book is about old themes set in new circumstances. Trained as a historian, convinced that the past is prologue, I shall attempt to attach branches of our New Age to a tree with old roots. No Buck Rogers speculation or dabbling with futurology in these pages—the one thing we know nothing about is the future. We shall not engage in pop astrology.

I will not propose remedies for dilemmas and problems that beset us. My aim is to examine and diagnose, not to reform and remedy. There are many who try that. I do not attempt to write political, social, or diplomatic history. I am interested in a new area, not taught in my student days and still an academic orphan—popular culture. I do so because I think the "culture of the people," more than some older and more formal disciplines, holds the mirror up to humankind in our postmodern, multicultural democracy. Reflecting sudden and dramatic changes, the mirror also suggests some recurring similarities, patterns, motives, and meanings.

We have moved from cave space to cyberspace, but we are still only human, with the dazzling and dismaying traits that no one has described better than long-dead English poet Alexander Pope in his *Essay on Man*. He was the epitome of newness and popularity in the eighteenth century, and his words ring true today:

> Created half to rise, and half to fall;
> Great lord of all things, yet a prey to all;
> Sole judge of truth, in endless error hurled;
> The glory, jest, and riddle of the world.

This is the paradox of popular culture, which has intrigued humans ever since they could be called human. It thrives on surprises and serendipity. Emotion overtakes reason. A love affair sparks a major war; a Trojan horse defeats mighty Troy; Japan's surprise attack on Pearl Harbor moves America into world dominance; a chance White House encounter between a young intern and the President leads to Clinton's impeachment. What next? If the past is prologue, how does it illuminate and explain the role of popular culture?

Let's begin by turning back the clock—not just years or centuries, but millennia. The word "popular" is derived from the Latin *populus,* meaning people. As long as there have been people, they have had stories, struggles, and culture.

My comments on the long dim history of popular culture are not an attempt to be inclusive, scientific, chronological, or thematic. This is a personal interpretation, growing from years of teaching, traveling, and writing. I am not attempting merely to compile facts but to understand a moving process. By examining specific movements, icons, and trends, I hope to give the effect of a zoom lens rather than a panoramic shot. To the historian, nothing is insignificant—particularly in popular culture. This might make it possible to evaluate our "New Age" from within and without, macroscopic and microscopic.

My text mainly will be about recent centuries and Western civilization, adhering to a central theme: the parameters of popular culture should be expanded and explored. I hope to refute those who think popular culture is peripheral to the human drama, that it is only electronic, or that it sprang up in the 1950s and 1960s with beatniks, hippies, new journalists, pop artists, and celebrities.

Popular culture is as old as humanity itself. Culture has always been "popular," thriving on formula, archetypes and stereotypes, fads and follies. It is cyclic, repetitive, and powerful. Here today and gone tomorrow; just wait, it will be back in the next year, next decade, or even next millennium. We like to think of ourselves as inventing mass production. Yet the Sumerians were mass producing funeral effigies centuries ago; so were the Egyptians, Tibetans, and Chinese. Most "new" ideas are old.

We are in a new Space Age, but we are also neo-Victorians in many ways. The French had it right: *Plus ça change, plus c'est la même chose.* The more things change, the more they stay the same. Yet we never know just when, why, or how change will come about.

One notable recent change is the overuse of the word "culture," derived from the Latin *cultus,* meaning to work or cultivate the earth. The word makes sense to farmers who own a cultivator. But in our time it has become the label of choice for shifting beliefs, actions, and prejudices. The 2000 edition of *Books in Print* uses up four columns in small type to list books about "culture," including the culture of anthropology, astrology, childhood, crime, corruption, Congress, complaint, drug addiction, computers, television, science, war, Microsoft bashing—the list seems endless.

Still, dominant ideas or themes fit well with "culture." Many of them emerge when we prefix it with "popular," as we do here. In our time *these linked words* mean one of these four things:

1. *Vernacular, folksy, earthy.* Talk shows, Disney World, chat rooms, guy bars, country music, and barn dances appealing to "good ole boys" and "good ole girls." We still "hang out" and "pass the time" when we can.

2. *New, faddish, "in."* On the charts, a best-seller, a blockbuster, a "top-ten," a pace setter. Most visible in style changes, such as sports bras, blue jeans, and grunge. As I write this, many of my students, male and female, wear their baseball caps backward. Who knows why? It's popular!

3. *Electronic, global.* On the Web. Part of the new Information Age. Surfing the Internet. To be popular is to be online. This definition shows how quickly the concept of culture changes. Not many years ago, only a few advanced scientists would have followed what was taking place—computers were made mainly for the military, not the average citizen. We are electrified and computerized.

How to encompass all these and the many other definitions? If we are to deal with life stretching from the prehistoric to the postmodern, we must pick and choose from the unlimited feast set before us, hoping to bring new insights from our selections and interpretations. We must be pragmatic, not dogmatic—as open-minded as Oscar Wilde, who said, "All definitions are wrong—including this one."

* * *

So much for definitions. Which ones, and which frameworks, does one follow? Both the content and style of my writing reflect a deep debt to my friend, the prince of pop-think, Marshall McLuhan. Working with him left indelible marks on my thinking and writing. He helped me to understand what his mentor, Harold Innis, taught him.

Innis, McLuhan points out, discovered how to arrange his insights into patterns that resemble the art forms of our time: He put those insights in a mosaic structure of seemingly unrelated and disproportional sentences and aphorisms. He presented his finds in a pattern of insights that are not popular but obtuse. He needed a McLuhan.

This "mosaic structure," McLuhan demonstrated, is well suited to our age and our popular culture. In doing this, he became one of the most controversial and "popular" critics of our times. In mosaics, separate pieces create a complex multilevel awareness. The glory of past ages is crucial to our new electronic perceptions. The television, movies, celebrities, fads, fancies, and the Electronic Revolution can be seen and studied as tesserae in our mosaic. I work and write on this premise.

But do we confront a "faded mosaic" in our New Age? Christopher Clausen states the case in his new book *Faded Mosaic: The Emergence of Post-Cultural America* (Chicago: Ivan R. Dee, 2000). He argues that America's native and immigrant cultures have vanished; that we have neither one big culture nor many small ones—only a dizzying mixture of freedom and nostalgia. I shall try to show that this is an interesting but flawed diagnosis. Far from vanishing, our native and immigrant cultures are becoming mainstream in the United States. Instead of fading, our mosaic is expanding and flourishing. Let me elaborate.

Certain insects have what biologists call "mosaic vision." They have compound eyes made up of independent units, so that objects viewed are not seen in isolation but in patterns. We can learn from them.

We also have "aerial mosaics," which involve matching up aerial photographs, to show a continuous representation of an area. Can we create an aerial mosaic of popular culture to illuminate our New Age? Did it work in other ages? What do we know of "people's culture" long ago?

* * *

Of those who lived before recorded history, we know almost nothing; and of those who lived in the historic past, we know very little. Histories of civilizations tend to concentrate on political and military leaders, thinkers, and artists. Who spoke or wrote for workers, women, slaves, criminals, outcasts, ordinary soldiers, and peasants? They were the inarticulate, the ignored, the oppressed. Popular revolutions brought them briefly on the scene of history, but they were largely ignored. Many still are.

In recent years, using new techniques, anthropologists and archaeologists have cast much new light on the prehistoric past. We enter the twenty-first century with much greater understanding and sympathy for those countless centuries from which *Homo sapiens* finally emerged. How did thay learn to communicate—perhaps the single major element that made them "human"?

Communication, derived from the past participle of the Latin word *communicare,* means to impart, to participate in. Communication is the most human of all skills; the stuff of which relations are made; a source of power; the process of creating meaning. Survival, popular culture, and, eventually, civilization depend on it.

We know very little about our distant beginnings and the great revolution of speech. Complete communication is impossible, because each of us lives in a reality essentially composed of our own ideas. It changes with the context: no word means the same thing twice. All five senses are involved. When we change the delicate ratio or balance of the senses, we change the message. Our senses engage in a data reduction system. We select patterns and details, which allow us to comprehend and survive.

Formal communication studies began with what the Greeks called rhetoric (from the verb *eiro,* "I say"). For them, rhetoric involved the art of speaking or writing effectively. The great "masters of rhetoric" have included Plato, Aristotle, Homer, Cicero, Christ, Buddha, Mohammed, and Shakespeare. Popular culture has developed its own rhetoric, especially in the field of music, where terms like Motown, bebop, hip-hop, rap, and ragtime compete for popularity. Slang, slurs, and clichés keep reoccurring.

All this laid the foundation for our Electronic Revolution and today's global popular culture. The world is wired for sight and sound. Technology has altered our psychic landscape. What is the difference between folk, popular, and mass culture? Will cyberspace develop its own unique culture? Has popular culture entered a New Age? Has the new flood of information produced new knowledge? If so, what does this portend? Where is it taking us?

How do we make our aerial mosaic? It should be an interesting experiment, but we don't know where it will take us or what we will see. We begin in the year 2000 A.D.—a new millennium. Let's get in our popular culture spaceship and see what was happening on January 1, 2000. Fasten your seat belts and we will get underway. It should be a fascinating voyage.

Millennium Merrymaking

Ring out, wild bells, to the wild sky!
Ring out the old, ring in the new!

Alfred, Lord Tennyson

On January 1, 2000, the whole world began a great unprecedented global celebration. Millions of dollars supported parades, light shows, special editions, concerts, extravaganzas, and fireworks, which lit up the skies from Fiji to Fredonia. For the six billion humans alive in 2000, this was the supreme moment of merrymaking—and apprehension.

After all, no one alive had ever welcomed a new millennium before; and no one will live to see the next one in 3000 A.D. The chance of a lifetime! Ring out wild bells! The opening of a New Age!

Nowhere was the celebration more long-lasting and lavish than in the United States. "We pulled out all the stops," politicians, pollsters, spin doctors, ad men, and media moguls agreed. Hollywood, eat your heart out. This was the blockbuster of all blockbusters. Hype, hype, hurrah!

There was a flip side to the ecstasy: a sense of destruction and doom. The computer flaw that would "read" the new year not as 2000 but as 1900 (known as the Y2K bug) caused worldwide alarm, even panic. The Red Cross and FEMA recommended stocking supplies in case of emergency. Primers on Y2K predicted everything from the breakdown of electrical systems and airline flights to global thermonuclear meltdown. Sensing the hysterical interest, journalists cashed in on it. Books flooded the market with titles such as Karen Anderson's *Y2K for Women: How to Protect Your Home and Family in the Coming Crisis*. *Time* magazine went further, warning its millions of readers about "The End of the World As We Know It." Who among us took what now seems like meaningless anxiety seriously? An estimated one-third of the American public stockpiled water, cash, food, and other supplies.

Now we are well into the new millennium. Dire predictions of doom have dispelled and the Y2K bug has been exterminated—what can we say about the new millennium? How does it illuminate our chosen topic—Popular Culture in a New Age? From what old roots did this spectacular new branch sprout?

The millennial myth originated in ancient Hebrew and Christian apocalyptic writings. Key elements are tribulation, armageddon, the Messiah, and the millennium. These ancient and powerful religious symbols have great flexibility, adapting easily to changing cultures and technologies. In nineteenth-century America, groups such as the Oneida Community, the Shakers, the Millerites (later to become the Seventh-Day Adventists) and the Jehovah's Witnesses flourished. The most successful attempt to build an earthly millennial paradise was the Mormons, today one of the fastest-growing churches in the world.

The ancient symbols have blossomed again, finding new life in a "pop apocalypticism" which has swept over today's America—New Age consciousness, messianic cults, extraterrestrial believers, "Constitutionalists," witchcraft (Harry Potter made his first appearance—read on), teenage suicides, cyberpunk, grunge rock bands and apocalyptic films (such as *Apocalypse Now*), American television, films, pop music, toys, and games prove that interest in the occult, the sinister, and the catastrophic permeate our daily lives. Supernatural beliefs and practices mushroom: astrology, out-of-body experiences, channeling, ufology, the healing power of crystals, pyramids, and channeled spirits are heralded. Shirley MacLaine is our extraterrestrial spirit "Ramatha," and Laurie Cabot is our "official" Salem witch.

There is a dark side to all of this. Punk is the look of mass oppostition. White supremacists meld with paramilitary antigovernment extremists and we get the covenant, the sword, and the arm of the Lord. Former President George Bush used apocalyptic language to lead us into the Persian Gulf War—so we could preserve a "New World Order"—which took on new life and form in the growth of militias and the "America First" platform of Pat Buchanan. Winning the 1996 New Hampshire presidential primary made Buchanan the flavor of the month. He still represents a burgeoning political and cultural force, which is becoming a nationalist movement: Praise the Lord, abolish affirmative action, and stop abortions—the barbarians are at the gate!"

Fundamentalism—the fiery voice of imminent fear—has rushed out of the churches and into the streets, the media, and popular culture. There is much talk of the beast, the dragon, armageddon, and the Antichrist. Such terms find a place in our talk shows, tabloids, magazines, and television miniseries. They build on a trail of blood worldwide through acts of terrorism—not only in New York, Paris, and Jerusalem, but in Oklahoma, through Amtrak derailments and in rural Scotland. But nothing could have prepared us for what happened on September 11 (9/11), 2001. The attacks on New York and Washington, D.C., killing thousands and stopping the world's "Number One Super-Power" in its tracks, would thrust the whole world into a new uncharted era. Empires crumble, alliances weaken, holes puncture the ozone layer, bandits defy the United Nations, and AIDS spreads—the worst epidemic on record. What does it all mean? Can one doubt that things seem to be falling apart?

The survivalists don't doubt it for a minute. Like punk, theirs is a philosophy of mass destruction and death. Survivalist ethic and millennial beliefs merge and attract myriad followers. Survivalists believe that a nuclear war (or another major social disaster) is inevitable, so they stockpile food and weapons and learn to practice survival strategies. They believe it's their only chance.

Messianic movements crop up, such as the Moonies, the People's Temple, or the Branch Davidians. Tokyo subways are flooded with poison gas. What are most alarming are not these offshoots, which occur in every age, but religious and secular movements and cults that are entering into mainstream American culture. The impact of a billion Muslims is felt on every level of our culture. We are in a new war. They are becoming as "American" as Mom and apple pie.

They are using effective public relations ploys to make a buck. There was the opportunity, for example, to join the Millennium Society, which promised a global extravaganza to welcome in the new millennium. They booked the *Queen Elizabeth II* to transport members from New York to Alexandria, Egypt, then on to seek new light in front of the Great Pyramid of Cheops in Giza. How much to join the tour? $10,000.

What powers the millennial myth? Novelty, publicity, hype. It provides a worldwide picture—a frame of reference—about our place in the universe and the passage of time. It draws on the stories of apocalyptic myths and interprets current events through them. When survivalists, militias, "patriots," or soldiers of fortune use apocalyptic language and imagery to describe current events, they are transforming the secular into the sacred.

The myth sends prophets and futurists into a frenzy; it titillates our paranoia and curiosity. The flames are fanned by the unprecedented social and cultural changes that are literally turning the world of many upside down, invading and sometimes even dominating our mass media and popular culture.

Widespread social, political, cultural, ideological, and technological changes are suggesting the shape and form of a "New World Order." The love affair with high technology is flourishing. No one knows where our dash down the Information Superhighway will take us. We seem lost in a labyrinth of undigested facts and factoids, numbered by statistical blizzards that bedevil and befuddle. Different codes, protocols, and command languages lock us in our Tower of Babel. We may drown in disinformation.

What is new is the changing scope of change itself. What is unprecedented in the early 2000s is that most things we see, buy, wear, and use are more short-lived than we are. Time is out of joint. Purchase, plunder, pave, and rush forward: but just where are we going?

Traditional jobs vanish and bureaucracies flourish. Bureaucrats armed with computers are the virtual legislators of our age; they are a terrible burden to bear. Computers not only work—they direct work. They have little value without something to control. What is the grand prize they offer to good boys and girls? More computers. Turn on your television and see some being installed in elementary schools. A new utopia!

But already there is trouble in Utopia. What has quashed the merrymaking? Is the party over? Remember the comment of Napoleon's mother as she watched her son crowned Holy Roman Emperor: "If only it lasts!" It didn't.

To make our optimism last, we might expand it beyond our own borders and share with the world. That would involve taking less and giving more, sharing our excesses with those who have too little. Most of all, it would mandate putting our *own* house in order. Unless we do that, our long-range optimism is doomed. What are some problems we must address?

We have become too self-indulgent. Credit card debt tops one billion dollars and bankruptcies soar. Congress and the White House play hide-and-seek with millions of campaign dollars. The gap between the rich and the poor widens. Crime goes down, but our new prisons fill up.

We are losing things that are more precious than the mighty dollar. We pay a price for our new wealth: it takes time to make money. We are running out of time—overwhelmed with tasks at home, at work, at school—even at play. New ads show a man or woman on the beach or golf course, talking on a cellular phone, staring at a laptop computer. "Time's winged chariot," Andrew Marvell wrote, is "hurrying near." In the 2000s, that chariot isn't drawing near; it's roaring past.

Time has become a thief, stealing our leisure and dulling our pleasure. Dinners are interrupted by unwanted phone calls, mailboxes are jammed with junk mail. What was once called the "leisure class" has become the leisure mass. The time crisis crosses class, race, and gender lines. Even play has become work. Our pleasure seekers are like Dante in the meadows of Paradise: Guilt-ridden strangers in a heaven of their own design. A little voice haunts us. "Shouldn't you be back on the job?"

Our average work schedule has increased 170 hours per year—which has added a full month—and 23 percent of the population gets or takes no vacation. Parents spend 40 percent less time with their children than a generation ago. Half of the working mothers say they don't have time to prepare regular meals for their families.

"What is the good life?" Plato asked. We must ask that question again, make up our minds about the answer, and act. We have made tremendous gains in recent years. The United States has triumphed on many fronts. We live in a beautiful part of the world and have good reason to be optimistic. But much more must be done, many more problems must be solved. That is the real challenge. How we meet it will determine whether the New Optimism will be a legacy passed on to future generations or a short-lived phenomenon which will be gone with the wind.

In the new century, the great world divisions are not only national but also political, economic, and cultural. Like it or not, mass culture is a crucial key to survival. It is everyday culture, and everybody has everyday experiences.

The millennium is here; we can make of it what we will. So long as some Christians accept the Bible text as the literal word of God, and as long as many others search for a better and more humane world, the millennial myth will evolve, adapt, and endure. It is part of our new cultural age.

Our job, then, is to humanize that culture—to make it our servant, not our master. As we move forward, we must look backward, identifying the wellsprings of energy, the heroic actions, and the sense of community that made us a great and vibrant nation, the envy of the world. Ben Franklin was right: we must all hang together or we will hang separately. We are, and must remain, the *United* States. We have a goodly heritage. The time has come to study it, seize it, revitalize it, and move forward.

What to conclude about the millennium year, 2000 A.D.? It arrived as "the greatest global celebration ever" and ended with the greatest power, the United States, trying to figure out how to elect a president. As for the rest of the world? Much of the optimism and joy seemed to disappear. The Middle East was in shambles, with blood covering the ground where the Prince of Peace once walked. NATO and the West failed to bring any workable truce in the equally bloody Balkans. The weary peacekeepers were anxious to go home. AIDS, ebola, corruption, and tribal outbursts swept through Africa. Stock markets around the globe plummeted, as the bears chased the bulls out of Wall Street, and high-tech stocks reached all-time lows. Still, most Americans seemed pleased with the past decade of prosperity and expected it to return quickly. Two somewhat bland and centrist candidates spent much of the year campaigning for the 2001 presidency—George W. Bush and Al Gore. Millions of dollars poured into both campaigns, much of it to be spent on television ads. An alarming problem was soon to occur.

The Great Quandry occurred on November 7, 2000. Based on exit polls, the major networks first estimated that Al Gore had beaten George W. Bush. However, they were forced to retract their statements and later declared Bush the next president. Gore prepared his speech accepting defeat, only to have the networks recant: the premature announcements were again wrong. Bush wasn't elected! Whoops. Later on that night we learned that the presidential race hinged on a few thousand votes in Florida, and that neither man was yet president.

Then followed days of wrangling, claiming, and denying. The race was so close that the final decision in Florida would elect the president. Unwilling to let the process proceed under Florida law, lawyers flooded the state, abandoning fair Harvard and big-money accidental injury cases to work for fame and fortune in the Florida sweepstakes. What did the numbers really prove? We soon found out that no one could say or agree.

Counts and recounts were demanded. New words popped up—chads, for the tiny bits of paper emerging from hole-punched ballots, and dimples. When was the punch really a punch? New terms were coined: dimpled chads, pregnant chads. Al Gore's effort to convince Florida election officials to count dimpled chad ballots ran contrary to all jurisdictions using the punch-card system.

Run, lawyers, run! Back and forth from one court to another, finally ending with the Supreme Court. December came: the battle continued. What a way to end year one of the new millennium!

The presidential election was finally determined at 9:00 p.m. EST, on Wednesday, December 6, when Al Gore conceded the election to George W. Bush. After the endless flurry of activity by lawyers, pundits, courts, and historians, it had come down to the nine votes of the justices of the Supreme Court. That vote was five to four, which only added to the anger and frustration. Being awarded Florida, Bush was ahead by a single electoral vote. Many Florida votes remained contested, and postelection probing would surely continue the bitter feuding. The predictions for the federal government: deadlock.

The idea that the new millennium would be a time of grand reckoning and harmony got off to a poor start. This was to be the moment for exciting dreams about the future and triumphant reevaluation of the past. We had hoped to free the imagination to make for a better future, which now seemed like a fading utopian dream. Could and would popular culture help to revive and reawaken that dream in a new age? That, indeed, was the question.

As the year 2000 passed, many wondered if all the hype and hurrah had worked. Had "The Year That Was" turned out to be the year that wasn't? The endless blather about Y2K, the trivial debate of whether the new age really begins in 2000 or 2001, and the worry about the champagne supply were hallmarks.

The time of grand reckoning didn't come. What had the most powerful nation on earth left to mark the moment? The Dawn of the Millennium never saw the sun rise. The nasty political bickering never ended. Politicians and pundits claimed "history was in our hands." If so, we dropped it. The government of, by, and for the people ended up the government of, by, and for the lawyers. They talked the year into oblivion. Our artists, visionaries, and thinkers were never mobilized or consulted. The failure of the imagination was all too obvious. We began 2000 with colorful confetti and ended it with pregnant chads.

The whole situation found a kind of minimodel in the 2000 season of the highly hyped Washington Redskins football team. Everything in their saga was *big*. The price tag was big—owner Daniel M. Snyder spent $110 million in salaries and bonuses to get the biggest and best players. The resulting names were big. The press coverage was enormous. Ticket sales were big. Expectations were big. So was the collapse. The team slated to be number one fumbled and bumbled and didn't even make the playoffs, let alone the Super Bowl. What they delivered was a Super Bust.

Perhaps, when things settle down, and the sound and the fury subsides, we won't say the same thing about the year 2000. But the four-word conclusion of a former Redskins quarterback, Joe Theismann, may well stand the test of time. "We expected too much."

In the long-anticipated new millennium, tired old themes dominated the news. Bogeyman communism returned with a tug-of-war with Castro over a six-year-old Cuban refugee, Elian Gonzalez. Cold War espionage cropped up with Taiwanese-American scientist Wen Ho Lee and missing nuclear secrets at Los Alamos. Horse-and-buggy crawling traffic clogged interstate highways, and scores of people died or were injured before 6.5 million faulty Bridgestone/Firestone tires were recalled.

Back home, we watched people eat rats on *Survivor,* the number-one-rated television program, while others chatted, saw porn, and enjoyed bad taste on the Internet. High tech faltered while low-tech voting machines fouled up the presidential election.

A final staggering blow occurred as the year ended. On December 31, a gigantic blizzard and ice storm, 150 miles wide and 500 miles long, covered the East Coast. Further west, thirty-seven people died in storm accidents, which devastated much of the Southern Plains. Hundreds of thousands had no electricity or heat. Arkansas was hardest hit: the governor likened the result to a nuclear attack. The year did not go out like a lamb, but a raging bull. Only the bull market refused to join in. All told, we had the millennium blues. What next?

Many years ago a hysterical doom-sayer rushed into Emerson's study, shouting: "How can you sit there and write your books? Don't you know the world is coming to an end on Thursday?"

Emerson looked up, smiled, and answered, "I can get along without it."

On to the new millennium!

What to Make of the Millennium

Mary Lee McLaughlin

The first year of a new era. As the year comes to an end, we can finally let out our collective breath. That breath can entail several scenarios, depending on your stance. Many feel relief that the human race survived yet another year in this world. Others are wondering why so much hype was placed on the event in the first place. With so many discrepancies in historical records, are we even sure that we have the real millennial date right?[1]

I can sum up my feelings on the past year quite simply: overload. Perhaps an equation would better serve the purpose: technology overload = information overload = confusion and indecision.

All these ideas immediately come to mind when contemplating the future of the United States. To many, the United States is the greatest superpower, a world leader in economic standards, medical facilities, technological advances, and implementation; many could not envision a better place. Without any real hardships facing U.S. citizens, life is favoring the sunny side of the street.

But what if the worst is yet to come? Are we taking life in the fast lane for granted? Studies show that Americans today are more depressed than ever before. How can this be, with all the advantages an American has today? Often I wonder if, in our relentless pursuits to live and succeed, we are losing sight of the core qualities of life.

What is the meaning? A question proposed in a lecture class, designed to propel student thinking about the future of humankind, the catchy phrase replays in almost every aspect of daily pondering. Life, education, economy, work, career, love, future, government: what is the meaning?

Mary Lee McLaughlin is a senior undergraduate at Virginia Tech University, Blacksburg, Virginia.

The wake of the millennial mayhem seems to have left the country spinning. This explains the state of affairs concerning the 2000 United States presidential election.

As a first-time eligible voter, I was determined to make the best decision after careful consideration of each candidate's platform and promises. With a diverse educational background, including a minor in mass media communications, I decided I would be able to decipher the message behind the spin. This task itself was comparable to contemplation of the millennium itself: what is the meaning? What does this time, this era, this state of being, this election, mean to our future well-being? Bombarded with news flashes and media commentaries, one hardly has time to conjure up an original opinion on life itself, let alone a presidential candidate. An article "reporting" the latest campaign developments seemed little more than a well-versed opinion written to persuade the public.

Apparently neither candidate succeeded in this task, because the entire nation was divided in its choice for the next president of the United States. Polls showed support wavering in majority support for each candidate. This election will go on record as the closest in our history. Uncertainty seems to be a common theme.

I wonder if the cross-platforming nature of mass-media-generated society has impacted our presidential candidates' contemporary platforms. Exponential leaps in technology have come about since earlier presidential elections. Previously, distinct communications media, such as television, radio, newspaper, magazines, and video each had their own reason for existence and unique method of delivering information. But with the widespread use of the Internet, these media are being integrated into a single smorgasbord of active information. Schizophrenic computers now act as news messengers (newspaper Web sites, informational Web sites), interpersonal communicators (e-mail), audio entertainment systems (CD players), video entertainment systems (DVD players), live entertainment (Web broadcasting), and, of course, data management.

Interestingly, this election's presidential candidates cross-platformed comparatively. George Bush, the GOP's revered nominee, did not follow traditional Republican political stances on issues such as education and government spending.[2] Likewise, Al Gore had a more conservative platform than traditional Democratic candidates. Many

Americans had trouble distinguishing the different party lines in this situation.

With all the uncertainty and debate centered around the presidential election, I wonder if the worst is yet to come. Is this situation a precursor to the fate of the United States as a world leader? Are we in such a media-dominated society that all of our debatable national issues must be sensationalized, scandalized, and dramatized to captivate the audience at large? More likely this is a test of our will to succeed as a unified, democratic nation.

Perhaps 2000's election situation is a check to humble the inflated egos found throughout our governmental establishment. Is this democracy at work? A civics lesson to refresh the memories of all U.S. citizens? A reminder that we are not as invisible as we might believe?

I believe the scrambled state of governmental affairs will ultimately have a positive outcome. The American public, who, as a general whole, lacks faith in our government, must be convinced that its votes do count. This is the ideal time to communicate this message, while stressing the importance of the United States' position as a leading democratic nation.

The entire country now debates the American electoral system; everyone has an opinion. As a student in my fifth year as an undergraduate, I can attest that during the 2000 presidential election, there was little heated debate among campus coeds. However, recently, everywhere I turn more people are tuned in to current events, particularly concerning the recent presidential election. Are we experiencing an awakening of the American public, a realization of the importance of public awareness and voting to implement the causes in which one believes? Events we experience as a nation, such as the tumultuous election, encourage public debate about key contemporary issues.

The current debate about the efficacy of our electoral system is a surface issue covering more serious questions facing our society. For example, the Florida vote recount raises several questions. If the recount there revealed new election results, where else were the election results miscalculated? Which system is most accurate? Which do we distrust the least: human or mechanical judgment? But, more important, what does this reflect about our faith in human integrity? Do we suspect corruption in manual recounts? Will we entrust our future elections to a machine that unintentionally misconfigured could change the results of the entire election?

The state of the American political situation during the election cirise encourages speculation about the history of the United States. How will historians record that uncertain time? Considering the extreme changes in technology and their effects on public interpretation of current events, this era will have a profound effect on American Studies. The media institutions today are both a cause and effect of popular culture. The presidential campaign is a test of which candidate can understand contemporary popular culture and harness public opinion.

Scholars often debate the longevity of American Studies and Popular Culture curricula. I fail to see a question; popular culture is a function of our daily lives. By the nature of the media-intensive, technology-driven, communication-oriented society we live in, popular culture is a means to define today's society.

As the indecision concerning the 2000 presidential election might suggest, we as a nation are facing an identity crisis. Technology plays an important role in defining American culture today. The government takes great strides to ensure the academic enrichment and technical education of all U.S. citizens.

But where are we going with this technology? Will we be doomed to confinement indoors, facing a computer screen, sitting helplessly as the remnants of our personalities slip quietly into cyberspace? Perhaps we the people, destined to rule the world in the new millennium, should focus more on educating ourselves overall and extending an intellectually fortified hand to those less fortunate in our communities and abroad. In doing so, leaving some of the electronic entertainment to which we have become so accustomed behind us could help regain lost culture.

Surrounded by my present educational environment, my thoughts drift with the spring breezes that playfully tease as they send spirits soaring and papers flying. What a day to be alive! A day to dance, a day to play, to rejoice and revel in the fresh air of this mountain community. This area uniquely blends technology and creativity. Located in the technological corridor of Virginia, Virginia Tech boasts the most advanced technological developments in the country. Projects such as multimedia software creation and building of electronic cars put Virginia Tech on the front page. Furthermore, Blacksburg has the reputation of having more people per capita "plugged-in" to the

Internet than anywhere else in this land of the free. Hence, Blacksburg's new recognition for being the premier electronic village.

But we must ask ourselves, as we head down the technology corridor, are we still in the land of the free? How long before our lives are consumed by the technology that ironically advertises liberation? Technology is a double-edged sword; as we propel ourselves further and further into cyberspace, faster than the speed of light, we lose sight of our roots. Perhaps since the United States lacks the history of other civilizations, we, its citizens, feel the need to continue conquering unknown frontiers in order to compete with other nation's contributions. Every great civilization has their time to rise and fall. Since the beginning of time, the same repeated mistakes throughout history caused empires to fall. In order to salvage what is left of our culture, I believe we must look to our past in order to create a better future.

What is our direction as we enter a new millennium? Will we retreat from our sunny, tree-lined streets to the electronically illuminated confines of cyberspace via the World Wide Web? Oh, the places we will go, the people we will see, from our Internet connections. With this technology one can visit distant lands, previously accessible only in our dreams: Got family in Nepal? Siberia? Guatemala? No problem. Reach out and touch a friend or, rather, a computer whose Internet-based messenger service can instantaneously deliver news, video, and photos.

But what is the price of this faceless communication? Have we made a Faustian bargain? As we eagerly accept all the new toys technology has to offer, are we trading our humanity for fifteen minutes of cyberspace? Or rather fifteen hours, as the case may be with Internet connections becoming the same means for escape that television has in the past.

I know this is a somewhat pessimistic point of view and that technology has allowed opportunities for many students to take learning to another level. I enjoy learning and applying new technological knowledge. But there must be a limit. We cannot all be programmed to live the same life.

In fact, with the new millennium in full swing, many scholars recently analyzed the social evolution of patterns throughout the past 1,000 years with special attention to current public sentiment. One scholar of social trends in the United States, John A. Hague, investigates the public's self-opinion. Based on research after the 1992 presidential campaign, he documented a significant percentage of Americans as being unhappy with themselves.[3] Hague proposes various reasons for unhappiness, the self-centered depression that plagues our society. One major factor lies in the American dream.

Americans catch on early that the goal is for individuals to find the golden road to the American Dream. From day one, young Americans learn the importance of being an independent individual: stand out! Make your mark! From school slogans to commercial and fashion advertising, the individual spirit is no longer a desirable personality trait; it is a personal attribute necessary for success in today's society.

With a positive embrace of the subject, Barbara Grizzuti Harrison enthusiastically outlines the joy to be found in oneself in her article "The Incubator of Dreams." She describes the intimate discoveries possibly only with a strong sense of self: "It is only in solitude that introspection and art flourish. . . . " Harrison, like Virginia Woolf, reinforces the importance of having a room of one's own, a "refuge and retreat."

> Without the private room, a gift of the Renaissance, it is almost impossible to imagine the flowering of the self. . . . it is a cavelike retreat that insures the vast inner open field of privacy and saves the soul from the tumult of the head.[4]

Perhaps with a positive outlook we can make the best of fragmented society, realize the beauty of our cultural differences, and revel in the irony of their juxtaposition in a technology-bound global community. Maybe we will take our cultural enclaves and share knowledge (through technology, even!) to embark upon a present-day Renaissance. Take Michelangelo.

Michelangelo remains one of the most famous Renaissance men ever. An accomplished humanist, Michelangelo flourished in several disciplines and his artistic contributions will be forever celebrated. Born in 1475 in Caprese, a Tuscan village, Michelangelo was exposed to the Renaissance spirit from an early age because of his father's prominent position in Florentine government.[5]

Michelangelo's talents began to emerge during his early apprenticeship to Domenico Ghirlandaio, a leading fresco painter in Florence. But his true talent emerged with Lorenzo de Medici, "Il Magnifico." The ruler of Florence requested that Michelangelo come to work for him at the palace in 1490. This was significant because it gave Michelangelo freedom from the craft guilds that regulated and dominated every aspect of artists' careers at this time.

This creative license granted to Michelangelo allowed him to give one of the greatest gifts to the millennium. Without Michelangelo's art, the world might not have seen such concentration on figure studies. Michelangelo's passion for the human form overtook his art. His fame extends to sculpture and architectural media, as well. Michelangelo's move from painting to sculpture had an element of "universal genius."[6] Contemporary scholars and art lovers alike study his famous *Pietà* and *David* sculptures today. Michelangelo's technical ability extended into the architectural realm; he redesigned the plan for the new St. Peter's cathedral at the Vatican in Rome. Michelangelo's innovative changes influenced high Renaissance architects as well as later architecture students.

Michelangelo's permanent place in history presents great competition in terms of accomplishments for the next millennium. Some think that every useful invention possible has already been invented. But those living at the turn of the nineteenth century shared that thought, and the following 100 years brought more technological advances than ever. So, what direction will history take next? Will our self-absorbed culture communicate only through their laptops? Perhaps we should take a break from our fast-paced technological world and reflect on past contributions from a time when people interacted daily as a means of making progress. I relate more to Walt Whitman's idea of reveling in oneself, of celebrating oneself in a positive way.[7] I am a Renaissance woman; we might all be subjects of a present-day Renaissance to embrace the future and create a livable, enjoyable millennium for years to come.

In an environment where fast-paced technology is constantly outdating itself, we should simultaneously embrace the fundamentals of humanity. These ideals brought forth by liberal arts have transcended the test of time since their emergence in early Roman civilization. They endure for a reason. With all the excitement surrounding new inventions and technological advancements, one can easily lose sight of the broader perspective. It is important to remember how we came to be as Americans and the ideals on which we base our country. This is especially important to consider now, as many Americans are skeptical of the government and question public process—such as the voting process and the electoral college.

As a recent inductee to the Phi Beta Kappa honor society, I am a fierce proponent of a strong liberal arts foundation in any education, whether it be fine arts or mechanical engineering. A member of Phi Beta Kappa recently wrote an essay to the organization's newsletter on the subject. It is proven that a diverse background in the liberal arts will carry you throughout life, whereas technology drops you off when it becomes outdated and replaced. The ability to self-identify and communicate effectively through traditional methods of speaking and writing will never be obsolete. For this reason, the printed word will never die, and the arts will always flourish. People need to experience life without being plugged in, because one day the electricity might go out.

As long as we can take time to remember the fundamental dreams for a better existence on which our forefathers founded this nation, we can have faith in our ability to lead and influence the global community. In doing so, we can unite as a country in times of crisis so that we might avoid the controlled chaos experienced with the recent presidential election. With careful thought and consideration, I have faith in our ability as a nation to overcome system glitches and sustain as an empire throughout the next millennium.

Popular Culture: The Beggar at the Gate[1] of Our Public Schools

Katherine Lynde

Overcrowded . . . apathetic . . . standardized . . . incompetent . . . drugged-up . . . underpaid . . . stressful . . . violent. These are but a few of the current buzzwords associated with American public high schools. Unfortunately, people using these adjectives and working outside of education find themselves tuned in to and turned on by media just dying to update them about atmospheric conditions in our hallways and in our classrooms. Behind sensationalized news broadcasts, daily talk shows, outlandish sitcoms, and touchy-feely evening dramas—somewhere within all the hype—the truth exists.

Many of my colleagues seek this elusive truth from our national media. We become part of the viewing mass, expecting eventually to be treated to something remotely similar to what we experience when we step into our hallowed realm every day. Often, it's no such luck. Instead, for us there is anger, disillusionment, disappointment, and the realization that so many children, parents, and alumni see this as the current state of secondary education. It's frustrating no matter how much it is deemed as entertainment.

Within the school system for which I work, Montgomery County Public Schools in Virginia, there are strict qualifications, dedicated teachers, orderly classrooms (for the most part) and eager students. In fact, Blacksburg High School, where I teach English, has recently been acknowledged as being one of the top one hundred high schools in the United States.[2] It may sound ludicrous in comparison to what is frequently being portrayed through the media, but our students are thirsty for knowledge, ready to understand the world, and capable of

Katherine Lynde is an English major from Virginia Tech University, where she first encountered courses in popular culture. She teaches all levels of American and British literature; her special interest is Advanced placement.

questioning their existence and their place in the scheme of the universe.

For these young people, the new-age technology of the twenty-first century presents more information at their fingertips than generations before them could imagine. They are spending more time at the computer than at the movies, at the mall, at their friend's houses, and at the family dinner table combined. My students can access anything that strikes their fancy—instantaneously, in any form and from any source, simply by typing in a single word—an opportunity that presents wondrous possibilities and realistic dangers. What sites are they accessing? What should they trust to be accurate? Discernment is the key. But who is teaching them the skills necessary to recognize the difference?

For the past several decades, colleges and universities have been offering classes that examine what popular culture guru Marshall Fishwick calls "people's culture." The onslaught of evolving technology, Fishwick warns, "makes people's voices heard." These college courses analyze what appeals to the masses and, more important, how these appeals achieve that status. Evidently, institutions of higher learning recognize the relevance of preparing students as participants in global conversation.

Not only do my high school students live in the global village of the United States, they are also able to "connect" with individuals, groups, and cultures around the world—all for less than $10.00 a month. What a bargain! This should require that high school educators step up and incorporate the study of the vehicles that drive our culture and the sources that inculcate our tastes and opinions into their curriculums.

While obtaining my undergraduate degree in English at Virginia Tech I fortuitously enrolled in popular culture electives, decisions that caused electrifying changes in my perspectives. Suddenly, integrating classical elements from history, literature, and art with the constant waves of cultural phenomenon made perfect sense. More often, classmates seemed to be discussing intertextual relationships between such writers as Chaucer and Baudelair and John Grisham and Bob Dylan. Old does more than meet new—it relates to it. I wanted the same revelation for my future students. However, the high school classroom was my desired destination, and, as quickly as our cultural tastes change, ironically, revolution is a slow process in public education.

For any teacher hoping to gain tenure, the first years are spent being careful. That about sums it up. New teachers cannot be *too much* of anything—except hardworking. I practiced what I believed to be important for my students, however different it was from my colleagues' conceptual view—but on a small scale—and I learned quickly that it had to be done on a nonthreatening level. This became easy when I was assigned to teach Advanced Placement Language and Composition, a course equivalent to the first semester of college freshman composition and whose focus is on American literature. It required that I include a few modern texts on the substantial reading list. This did not mean novels written in the twentieth century; it meant novels written in the last decade.

The first novel added to the reading list was *Into the Wild* by Jon Krakauer.[3] It was chosen for three solid reasons: (1) it was and still is on the bestseller list, (2) it contains high-interest themes for high school/college students, and (3) it is filled with connections to classical literature. Krakauer recounts the real-life story of Christopher McCandless, a young man who leaves everything behind to live a Tolstoyan, bare existence in the American wilderness, an attempt that ends with his death in the backcountry of Alaska. My Advanced Placement students are immediately drawn to this novel because McCandless was raised in the upper-middle-class environs of Annandale, Virginia, a demographic similar to their own, and he experienced an overwhelming sense of wanderlust all too familiar to young people longing for independence and freedom. But there is more. McCandless read. In his backpack he carried sacks of rice, and books—well-read, highlighted, dog-eared books. Students taste Tolstoy, Thoreau, London, and others while vicariously sharing McCandless's vision—*Walden* to the extreme. It's the pioneering spirit. It's romantic. It's from their lifetime.

Later, Stephen Chbosky's *The Perks of Being a Wallflower* [4] made the list after a student suggested we read it together as a class. The often-painful, epistolary style account of sixteen-year-old Charlie reaches students as no other novel has to date. One of my students put it best in her essay this year:

> The novel embraces a storyline that high school students can relate to, as many of them are probably presently facing the same

situations as those that are occurring in the book. The main aspect that makes a novel enjoyable to the masses is its ability to create a personal connection between itself and the reader. Not only does it connect the reader to the novel, but it also connects the reader to fellow readers who also connect, providing a web of understanding. If the general intended audience of a novel cannot relate to the story, the novel will become a vacuous mass of pages and words.[5]

Like McCandless, Charlie is an avid reader. In *Perks*, Charlie mentions his readings of *The Fountainhead, The Catcher in the Rye, To Kill a Mockingbird,* and many other novels revered in English classes across America. How can anyone fault novels that endorse reading?

After I loaned one of my copies of *Perks* to a colleague, he referred to it as the MTV generation's bastardization of J. D. Salinger's *The Catcher in the Rye.*[6] Maybe he missed some of *Perks'* finer points while sizing it up against his generation's identification with Salinger's protagonist, Holden Caulfield. Haven't lifestyles changed drastically since Holden's prep school world a half-century ago? An article in one of this year's issues of *Parents* magazine claims that our nation's preschoolers are experiencing stress disorders. Our teenagers face more, know more, and do more. My colleague should not find it so insulting that they have more in common with Chbosky's Charlie. It is also important to note that I teach the two novels as companion pieces. In any event, many students were carrying the small novels with spring green covers along with their textbooks, and a significant number of those students were not in my class. This fact indicates that students were reading out of sheer intellectual curiosity. That's the point of education, isn't it?

C. S. Lewis wrote, "Every age has its own outlook. It is specially good at seeing certain truths and specially liable to make certain mistakes. We all, therefore, need the books that will correct the characteristic mistakes of our own period. And that means the old books."[7] No teacher would dispute Lewis' statement, but that does not eliminate the intriguing dialogue constantly occurring between the old books and the current bestsellers being purchased by our students for their own reading pleasure.

Secondary education has built its curriculum on Lewis' idea, and it holds firmly to it—so firmly in fact that many English teachers do not adequately scratch the surface of later twentieth-century literature.

The average high school junior possibly advances to the twelfth grade believing that worthwhile literature has not been written since the 1950s. Far worse, the average senior leaves high school and cannot confidently claim that anything of literary merit has been written in England in the last one hundred years.

Let's make no mistake—there are more hurdles to being innovative than merely breaking away from the canon. Teachers generally prepare for three different levels of classes and teach five sections every day. After school, papers must be graded. If a teacher decides to incorporate something new into his or her routine lesson plan, it means conducting research, producing new handouts, and creating new assignments. Familiarity breeds comfort. Unfortunately, comfort leads to lack of motivation. Some teachers still continue to use quizzes and tests copied from mimeographed originals. Unfamiliarity can breed contempt. Coincidentally, these same teachers tend to frown upon popular culture in the classroom. Even though teachers cannot escape being the students of and being educated by popular culture, some of these same educators set up the blockades that prevent it from being used openly by others.

When Virginia adopted the Standards of Learning (SOL)[8] for its public schools, it guaranteed an accreditation process for the system, but it also closed out opportunities in the classroom. Courses have detailed guidelines. Although the guidelines are not too specific, the emphasis is on breadth not depth. Teachers are frantic to cover material, administrators are concerned about test scores, and students are lost in the fray. Where is the time for the here and now?

The accompanying SOL test in May is not the only pressure for faculty and students. There are Stanford Nines, LPTs, ACTs, SATs, APs, midterms, and final exams. For testing purposes, there are IEPs[9] and special accomodations. Montgomery County is also the inclusion capital of the United States.[10] Many of our students participate in extracurricular sports and academic activities, and most of our students have jobs. More than 90 percent of our students go on to college, and the upperclassmen must make college visits. By June, everyone is burned out, and students have not had a chance to discuss the world in which they live.

In the sections in which the majority of my students are not pursuing higher education, we have had valuable experiences studying advertising propaganda. The SOLs require that students learn methods of persuasion. Perhaps the best way of incorporating popular culture and meeting the standard is by examining what companies employ to empty our pockets. The syllabus course description states:

> You will become aware of the persuasive influences that the media enjoys in our culture and of the power that these forces have on your life. By the time that the year comes to an end, you will be able to analyze and evaluate persuasive messages and limit the power that these forces enact upon your preferences and decisions.

Even the most reluctant students enjoy this unit. And why shouldn't they? One thing is immediately obvious—relevancy is not irrelevant to teenagers.

I have tried to reconcile myself to the fact that electives are few and far between in secondary education. We have journalism, drama, and even psychology. On the other hand, many educators do not believe that electives are worth our time. "Give them what they need, and let them go!" But I believe they need more choice. It goes with the predominating idea of their age—unlimited access.

For students, there is an amazing gap between the number of high school years attended and the number of credits necessary for graduation. Four years of high school @ seven classes per year = twenty-eight credits. A high school diploma requires twenty-four credits. What happens to the other four credits? Some students enroll in the few elective courses available. Some students enroll in an additional vocational course. The rest of the students opt to leave early during the school day, or they become library aides, office aides, guidance aides, or teacher aides (because they have an empty class period in the middle of the school day).

I have offered to teach electives. I have drafted a proposal for Contemporary Media. I have discussed Literature and Film. I have started the process of instituting dual enrollment Creative Writing. When I mention a possible elective, my colleagues always ask the same question: "Which of us is going to take those students who would be in your fifth English section?" Simply, there are not enough teachers for the regular sections of English.

Besides the five sections that full-time teachers are assigned, there is one planning period and one duty period. During the duty period, the teacher must work for the school in a nonteaching capacity.

Duties range from clerical jobs (copying, typing, phoning absentee students' parents) to lunch duty (watching students eat). What if a teacher wanted to take on a sixth section elective? Been there; tried that! Only a handful of teachers are able to teach a sixth section because they must be paid an additional percentage for that section, and the funds are limited. Volunteering is not welcome. I tried that, too. If you think about the whole situation for too long, your head begins to spin.

We are busy people; this cannot be denied. The pace that we have chosen for ourselves and for our children leaves little time for contemplation. While studying Plato's "The Myth of the Cave," I used to ask my students where they retreated to escape reality. I am not sure they have time to visit caves anymore. It is much scarier to imagine that our busy schedules *are* our caves. The message we impart to our high school students is that we are so concerned with studying our past and with preparing them for their futures that we do not have time to look at the world as it exists for them right now.

Now is a good time for popular culture studies to trickle down from the upper echelon of education. If there are not enough resources for elective courses, at least teachers could attempt to blend the "people's culture" into their lesson plans. They do not have to go far to find it. They live it! If they truly believe that the best literature is ageless and that its themes are universal, then connections must be all around them—on the tube, on the screen, on the stereo.

For next year, I have taken on a new challenge—British Literature. I will continue to teach my usual Advanced Placement class, including selections from the bestseller list of course. But the prospect of helping seniors discover twentieth-century literature excites my blood. True, even the oldest literature from England, *Beowulf,* is well worth study. Near the other end of the spectrum, C. S. Lewis wrote some good stuff worth reading, too. For instance, while stressing the importance of reading old books, Lewis also advocates the regulated reading of new and old literature. It might be much to students' surprise, but there are playwrights currently living and writing in England.

Perhaps after finding a good foothold in the twentieth century, I can pull my students into the world of both twentieth- and twenty-first century British pop culture. In 1914, Fernand Leger stated that "a modern man registers a hundred times more sensory impressions than an eighteenth-century artist."[11] Imagine how that figure has multiplied in the last century. Education must keep up. Professor John Fiske, Department of Communication Arts at the University of Wisconsin, boldly claims that students cannot study British literature without studying its popular culture. Since the majority of my high school students will never choose to enroll in an English elective while at a college or university, my classroom must provide the proper forum for Fiske's proposed synthesis.

Writer Aldous Huxley knew a good line when he read it. He used it to shape his novel published in 1932, *Brave New World,* in which he predicts our present world with chilling accuracy: "O brave new world / That has such people in't."[12] Bravo, old chap! We realize this is not utopia, but it's the best we have at the moment. Wish me luck.

The New Gold Rush

Time will run back and fetch the Age of Gold.

John Milton

Is anything "as good as gold"? The very word excites and delights us. Thomas Hood echoed it:

Gold! Gold! Gold!
Bright and yellow, hard and cold.

History glitters with stories of gold rushes, most of which faded as quickly as they surfaced. Some did not. The great California gold rush of 1849 helped change the face of America. But no one living then could have guessed that a century later a much different kind of gold rush would dwarf all our earlier ones.

Beginning in the 1950s and increasing with every passing year, the new gold was not in the ground but in small silicon chips. America's future would be quickly changed by our revolutionary computers.

The first computer, rushed through to aid the war effort in the 1940s, was called ENIAC, and predated today's computer chips. Built at the University of Pennsylvania, it occupied a whole room and involved thousands of working parts. Half a century later, a much more efficient machine was small enough to be called a laptop. The gold rush increased in intensity, and seemed about to consume American society. Utopia was here, now. Get in on the action!

The Romans were right. *Caveat emptor*—let the buyer beware. What happens when the goose refuses to lay more golden eggs—or when the eggs were not golden in the first place?

Here the historian can be helpful, pointing out earlier examples of failed gold rushes and bubbles that burst. A fine example is the South Sea Company, which flourished in eighteenth-century England. The market value of South Sea shares increased tenfold in a few years. (Think Nasdaq in our day.) Vying to cash-in on selling stock shares, promoters organized bogus companies, an insurance company to insure female chastity, and a company "for an undertaking which shall in due time be revealed." (Think of the Mafia invading Wall Street in June 2000.) But in September 1720, British stockholders panicked and began to sell. Soon, the whole unstable structure collapsed. The British Parliament passed the Bubble Act, allowing only companies chartered by the government to raise capital by selling stock. So much for one of history's spectacular gold rushes.

Closer to home, we have the well-known story of the collapse of the American stock market in 1929, which led directly to the Great Depression of the 1930s and a new national theme song: "Brother, Can You Spare a Dime?"

Now the cry is, "Brother, can you share a silicon chip?" In the same California where the 1849 gold rush began, another rush of far greater proportions is taking place in Silicon Valley. Now the "workers" go not into streams or caves, but to new buildings filled with electronic wizardry to "pan for gold"—or, in their terms, "push for high tech." Leading the pack is Bill Gates, our new J. P. Morgan, the multibillionaire who presides over Microsoft, where all the original employees (so the story goes) are millionaires.

That there are millions of instant millionaires whose new fortunes are based on silicon and not gold no one disputes. Surely the new wealth has revolutionized the economy of many other nations around the world—especially Japan. From goldlore to cyberlore—this may be the most appropriate title for our new century.

So we might pause and find out how "cyber" got into our culture and how it is changing our world. Cyberlore came down on us like a wolf on the fold. There were no computers in the world when World War II began. During that war, we developed one for military purposes—a monster weighing fifty tons—to speed up ballistic calculations. Pandora's box was opened. It will never be closed again.

"Cyber" is the Greek word (from *kybernetes*) for *helmsman* or *guide*. Cybernetics is best defined as the scientific study of those methods of control and communication which are common to living organisms and machines—especially the analysis of the operations of machines such as computers.

The word has expanded like the computers that are its trademark—into our offices, factories, homes, schools, economy, and mythology. To many, they are symbolic and iconic. To others, they are a threat—

perhaps even diabolic. To everyone, they are a consuming new element of the New Age.

Like many others, I struggle to place "cyber" into perspective and to measure its impact. I am writing this chapter on my computer, and my publisher will want it on a disk. If we need to "talk," it may well be by e-mail. Surely high tech will be involved in producing the book, and orders for it will come in electronically. Like it or not, I am adrift in the cyber sea.

American culture and our popular culture have gone through dramatic and traumatic changes. The stratosphere has been joined by the datasphere; the Interstate highway, by the Information superhighway; consumer technology by computers, palm devices, video cameras, fax, satellite, television, photocopiers, and the ever-flowing "new gadgetry." They have transformed our social environment and hence our society. Media-fed and media-driven, we are suddenly in a world that few could have imagined a generation or even a decade ago.

Some say my World-War-II generation is getting old, brittle, and resistant to change. This is the future versus the past, and we are mired in the past. Our reply: we are not talking about technology but cosmology; about moving from the real physical world to an unreal "virtual" world; mistaking the shadows on the tube or computer screen for the real world.

We call this infiltration media virus—the instant introduction of icons, ideas, and images into the culture via the media. A good example is the O. J. Simpson trial, which put not only the man but the whole justice system on trial. Other media events come to mind: the Willie Horton ad campaign, the Tonya Harding skating scandal, the Jack Welch book advance, the untimely death of Princess Diana, the Clinton impeachment, the Elian Gonzalez melodrama, FBI blunders—all "top pop stories." Such events, often overblown or transient, quickly snowball into national or even international obsessions. Where does the news end and the hype begin?

One complication is the belief in and dependence on two powerful buzz words: *research* and *statistics*. Certainly both are vital in today's culture, but many who depend on them have come to question them.

Consider research on the Internet. For many students (including mine), it tends to replace the research in books and journals. Since anyone can say anything on the Internet—and not identify themselves, their sources, or their motives—research often is uninformed gossip. There is no verifier.

The more reliable research and polling, authorized and properly identified, have other problems. Labeled "meta-analysis," they may depend on a few hundred queries and lack the necessary scientific controls to make solid conclusions. If the research is industry funded, will it automatically result in industry bias? Edward Miller, former editor of the *Harvard Educational Letter,* writes: "The research is set up in a way to find benefits aren't really there. Most knowledgeable people agree that it isn't valid. . . . Essentially, it's just worthless."[1]

Worthless research? Is that what we are calling the glitter without the gold? Are we mining the wrong veins?

All gold rushes have a similar problem: how to distinguish the real from the phony—from what miners call fool's gold. But this time it *is* real: haven't we created a million new millionaires since 1997? To say nothing of the billionaires? Doesn't every statistic prove that this is the longest boom in our history? Isn't the data the final proof?

No one can oppose the accumulation of data; information is always better than ignorance. The crucial questions are: what does it mean? How can it be used? Surely we should employ a second "in"— interpretation. Even that isn't enough. The third essential "in" is inspiration—the human facility to move forward to the higher plateau of knowledge. As Francis Bacon realized centuries ago, knowledge itself is power. Nor should we stop there—there is a greater place still, which we call wisdom.

Surely the accuracy and utility of material in this Information Age varies greatly. Some of that information is more precious than gold; one wonders, how to get the gold from the dross?

Some demographers are like people who take Polaroid pictures: instant, glossy, persuasive. But when are they misleading, even deceptive? All that glitters isn't gold. As that great American showman, P. T. Barnum reminds us, there's a sucker born every minute. We shall take a look at Barnum in a later chapter—and see how his humbuggery has turned into twenty-first-century hype.

Folk/Fake/Pop

A few simple fables will suffice
to gild millions of lives.

Anatole France

Folklore is the country mouse talking. Taken to the city, cheapened by charlatans and opportunists, folklore became fakelore, as the mass took over from the folk. To some, the tale ends here. But wait—there's another mutation. Using new urban material with its chrome and kitsch, imaginative artists, ad men, and scriptwriters are developing a poplore which is as true to its environment as was folklore to an earlier one. Call it poplore.

Folklore is material passed on by tradition, oral or active; by mouth, practice, or custom, folk song, folktale, Easter eggs, dance steps, or knocking on wood. To try for an eloquent oversimplification: Folklore is oral history transmuted into poetry. Scholars will accept no short definition, of course. In fact, the more one investigates, the more convinced he is that they won't accept any definition. The *Standard Dictionary of Folklore, Mythology, and Legend* lists twenty-one. Key words in the twenty-one "standard" definitions are "oral," "transmission," "tradition," "survival," and "communal." But there is no central agreement or emphasis. Experts have filled more than seventy volumes of the *Journal of American Folklore* without agreeing on just what their subject is.[1]

We do know when the world "folklore" was introduced into the English language—W. H. Thomas suggested "a good Saxon compound—Folklore" in the August 1864 issue of the London magazine *Athenaeum*. He coined the word which would deal with "popular antiquities or popular literature from olden times." By folk, Thomas meant unlettered peasantry. He wanted to preserve "fast-perishing relics," especially in rural areas.

The word was quickly adopted in many languages and launched the field known as "the science of folklore" worldwide. The great early achievement was Sir James Frazer's monumental *The Golden Bough* (1890, expanded in 1902 to twelve volumes), which gave numerous examples of parallel beliefs and ritual all over the world. In the United States, the subject was especially appropriate for studying the Native Americans, whose culture included folk interest in star, plant, and animal lore. Accompanied by poetry, music, and dance, Native American "folklore" made an ideal area of research.

If we have trouble defining folklore, we can say where it is found—among isolated groups who have developed their own distinctions and stability. This isolation may not only be spatial, but occupational, religious, racial, linguistic, or a combination of the five. The enclave of provincial culture may be in the Kentucky mountains, among sailors, the Pennsylvania Dutch, Gullah blacks, or French-Canadians. A family might be the crucial, isolated unit, as with certain ballads. The central thread is plain; they are essentially rural and religious. Behavior is traditional, spontaneous, and personal. The sacred prevails over the secular. Status, rather than the open market, determines the economy. All folklore is orally transmitted, but not all that is orally transmitted is folklore.

The connection between genuine European folklore and American variations is well documented and convincing. "Barbara Allen," a ballad, crossed oceans and mountains with ease. The essential tale is that of a young girl who scorns her lover, Sweet William (or Willie, Sweet Jimmy, Young Johnny, or Jimmy Grove). Samuel Pepys praised a rendition by the celebrated actress, Mrs. Knipp, in 1666. He would have been surprised to know that generations later Americans were singing:

> Way down South where I came from
> Is where I got my learning.
> I fell in love with a pretty little girl
> And her name is Barb'ry Ellen.

The Twa Sisters became "Sister Kate" in the New World. A jealous girl pushes her younger sister into a millstream for stealing her suitor. The European version has the miller, who recovers the body, perform magic on various parts of the corpse; in America, this aspect was dropped and the story became a children's game. Magic was transformed into merriment.

In "The Gypsy Laddie," a fair lady gives herself to a roving gypsy. Her lord returns, finds her gone, chases after and rescues her, and hangs fifteen of the gypsies. In adaptations that have come to light, the retribution and hanging are omitted. Instead, the lady decides to cast her lot with the roaming vagabonds—a decision that might well have appealed to the hard-pressed trailblazers moving into frontier territory.

> How can you forsake your house and land
> How can you forsake your money O?
> How can you forsake my sweet little babe
> To go with the gypsy laddie O?
>
> O, I can forsake my house and lands
> O, I can forsake my money O,
> O, I can forsake my sweet little babe
> To go with the gypsy laddie O.

"The Three Ravens" was revamped on this side of the Atlantic into "The Three Crows." In the Appalachians you might still hear the macabre song, which moves forward with the bareness and directness that marks enduring Folk ballads:

> There were three crows sat on a tree
> As black as any crows could be
> One of these crows said to his mate
> "What shall we do for food to eat?"
> "There lies a horse in yonder land
> That has been only three days slain
> We'll sit upon his bare backbone
> And pick his eyes out one by one."

Vestigial remains of Old World folklore fascinate scholars. The English expert Cecil J. Sharp tramped through the Blue Ridge Mountains in 1918, finding a community in which singing was as common and almost as universal a practice as speaking. Sharp's groundbreaking collection was published in London under the title *English Folksongs in the Southern Appalachians.* A decade later, Harvard's Francis J. Child assembled a five-volume collection of migratory *English and Scottish Popular Ballads,* while A. K. Davis Jr., was finding fifty-one British ballads still sung lustily by woodchoppers and whiskey makers. Visiting isolated mountain pockets, Vanderbilt's George Pullen Jackson was able to show that white spirituals were the progenitors of many black folk tunes.[2]

Early America had a glorious folklore, full of shouts and screams and wild adventures. Heels clicked by day and glasses by night. Tales grew by the telling. Boastful demigods fought in the grand manner:

> They fit and gouged and bit
> And struggled in the mud;
> Until the ground for miles around
> Was kivered with their blood,
> And a pile of noses, ears, and eyes
> Large and massive, reached the skies.[3]

After the Civil War, patterns of folk culture changed rapidly. The day of the folksinger and folk hero passed; the publicist and huckster took over. Folklore was supplanted by jokelore and fakelore. After the 1860s, the homespun yarn never again became nationally available. Instead, an event in 1869 would usher in a whole new era and attitude.

FROM FOLK TO FAKE

A famous 1869 hoax pointed to the new day. Workmen in the little town of Cardiff, New York, "discovered" a buried petrified figure over ten feet tall, weighing 2,990 pounds. Carved secretly in Iowa, buried in New York by George Hull, the Cardiff giant electrified the media and the people. Phineas T. Barnum offered $60,000 for three-months' rental. Oliver Wendell Holmes called the giant a "wonderful anatomical development," and Ralph Waldo Emerson found it "beyond my depth, very wonderful, and undoubtedly ancient." Even when Hull admitted it was a fake, people still rushed to Cooperstown, New York, to see it. They still do. The Golden Age of Fakelore had begun.

Richard Dorson claims to have coined the word "fakelore" in an *American Mercury* article, March 1950, to refer to the contrived efforts of hucksters and jokesters who hid behind the word folklore. Imitating ballads and folktale thrived in the eighteenth century, but Heinrich Heine, Rosetti, Wordsworth, and Meredeth wished their imitations to be accepted as literature. Fakelorists wished their work to pass as folklore.

Exploiting folklore is no new thing; the Grimm brothers found a good market for their "fairy tales." What we now call fake style saw pseudo-Roman buildings sprouting up everywhere, and artsy-crafty movements (such as those sparked by John Ruskin and William Morris in England), which allowed a whole Victorian generation to become romantic medievalists. Gilbert and Sullivan produced a brilliant satire of Victorian fake style in *Patience,* in which the Duke admits:

> It's clear that medieval art alone retains its zest
> To charm and please its devotees we've done our very best.

Old culture was vanishing, and a new one emerging. Sentimental nostalgia set in. Instant new cities made fortunes and destroyed folklore. Old myths retreated into memories; new fake style preserved the form but not the substance of earlier days.

A good word to use here is bogus—counterfeit, spurious, sham. The "bogus" (or counterfeit) problem: once we have accepted it, we try to pass it on to someone else. Just as bad money will drive good money out of circulation, bogus lore will drive genuine lore off the scene. Anyone who is a regular television viewer knows this works.

Our folk heritage has been cheapened; the word *kitsch* best describes its shoddy current manifestations. But do not think folklore has disappeared. Instead, it has taken on manifestations—levels of meaning—not associated with traditional folklore. These new forms are so much a part of our cultural landscape that we seldom isolate or evaluate them. What *others* believe is "folklore." Our *own* beliefs we give a different label—"the truth." Witch doctors no longer wear black masks. They have moved in from campfires to offices. Now they wear white jackets. Voodoo dolls are declassé; but psychiatric couches are very much in style.

Just how much of our current science smacks of folklore or fakelore future historians will have to decide. Consider this whimsical platitude of leading physicists: On Monday, Wednesday, and Friday light seems to be corpuscular; on Tuesday, Thursday, and Saturday it's undulatory! The staggering thing about nature is not how much, but how little, we know about it. When we say we have outgrown our folklore, we merely demonstrate how we are dominated by later and current manifestations.

It is part of contemporary folklore to say that folk culture is finished. This vast body of knowledge, handed down by mouth, practice, and custom, is still very much with us. Folklore is first cousin to mythology. Patterned on common experience, indigenous and indelible, it feeds and sustains popular culture. The demos are all individuals, despite massification; each has his or her pride and prejudice, customs, songs, and idiom. The sap and savor of a people endures.

That is why our young, strumming their electric guitars, yearn for the attachments that the industrial urban environment has denied them. They dream of pink cherry blossoms and a sow that got the measles and died in the spring. Amid the siren screeches they reaffirm that "never did hoof beast go down on a lark's nest." The ecology crusade is another manifestation of our folk longings. One of the Old Boys who keeps attracting the young is Henry David Thoreau; a newer model is Ralph Nader.

The creative thrust in folklore studies today is in environmentalism and the "folklife movement." Adapted from the Swedish term *folkliv,* the word implies an analysis of folk culture in its entirety. By limiting themselves largely to literary aspects of folklore, scholars have tended to slight other aspects and to take the material studied out of context. In Sweden today over 400 communities maintain "outdoor museums." The first such venture in America was in Decorah, Iowa, in 1925. The most spectacular was Colonial Williamsburg (begun in 1926). Despite good work at Cooperstown, Sturbridge, Shelburne, and Dearborn, we still know and see far too little of folklife. Professor Don Yoder, a leading advocate of the folklife movement, lists things we should study: folk names, agriculture, architecture, cookery, costume, crafts, medicine, music, recreation, religion, speech, transportation, the folk year. Back to the plow and the flail, the husking peg and hominy block, the schoolhouse and the meetinghouse![4]

Knowing more about settlement patterns, games, song, dance, clothing, and customary behavior, we might see folklore as an integral part of the total range of traditional behavior—and hence of popular culture. To illustrate: long isolated Scottish-Irish farmers in the Ozarks are so deeply Calvinistic that they still refer to bulls as "gentleman cows" in mixed company. Yet they send maidens to dance in the apple orchards each spring and encourage couples to "jolly themselves" in newly planted fields, thus helping seeds to germinate. In the ritual for sowing flax, Vance Randolph reports, the farmer and his wife arrived naked in the field at sunrise. The woman walked ahead as the man sowed, chanting a rhyme which ended, "Up to my ass, and higher too!" The man threw the seed against his wife's buttocks, singing and scattering as he planted. Then they laid down on the ground and had a good time.[5]

A less delicate local informant told us, in his own words, what took place at turnip planting: "When the boy throwed the seed, the gals kept hollering 'Pecker deep!' When they got done, the whole bunch rolled in the dust like wild animals. Ain't no sense to it, but they always raised the best turnips in the creek!"

In my own quest for genuine folk songs, I spent many days trying to track them down in Virginia's Blue Ridge Mountains, in isolated areas such as Irish Creek. There I found people who could sing about "Old Joe Clark," a legendary figure whose six-horse team was still alive in local memory.

Taken to the city and twisted to make a fast dollar, folklore can become fakelore. Nor does the story end there. Taking genuine urban material created for mass consumption, artists and admen are creating a body of material that is as true to its city environment as folklore was to the rural one. We can label it poplore.

Imitating genuine ballads and folktales (if that is the essence of fakelore) is no new enterprise. Elite artists did not hesitate to exploit the folk heritage, as already noted. They imitated, but they wanted their imitations to be accepted as literature. The people who "made up" Paul Bunyan, on the other hand, tried to pass him off as a genuine folk hero, created by oral tradition.

The poet Carl Sandburg asserted that Paul Bunyan was indeed authentic folklore, that this remarkable and authentic creature was in fact as old as the hills, young as the alphabet. Actually, the Paul Bunyun most Americans knew was younger than Sandburg's *Chicago Poems.*

"Maybe the scholars have been following a false lead," Bernard De Voto wrote in *Harper's* of June 1955. "Maybe popular literature isn't a folk art at all." By then factory-made folklore had blazed a trail across American journalism, advertising, and entertainment like a jet plane racing across a cloudless blue sky.

Many other manufactured folk heroes and villains have sprung up in America, including Pecos Bill, Annie Christmas, Tony Beaver, Whiskey Jack, and Bowleg Bill. Thus does fakelore hide as folklore. In the age of television and mass media, another substitution takes place: celebrities are put forth as heroes and heroines. Rock musicians and sports high-scorers strut acrss the stage, but tend to fade like falling stars. It is a new variation of the old Gresham's law: counterfeit money (or personalities) tend to drive the genuine item out of circulation. Poison tastes so sweet that we choose it over plain food. Of our fakelore creations and overhyped clebrities, we end up saying: "I'll never forget old what's his (or her) name." They are already forgotten.

FROM FAKE TO POP

The transition from fake to pop was less of a move than a merger. So many of the leading "pop movements" of today—environmentalism, animal rights, peace "crusades," antiadvertising, diet frenzies— prove the point. Is the "return to nature" and all that implies real or romantic? Perhaps both.

What we tried to describe and define as "pop" on the preceding pages, generated by a highly urban, technical, democratic society, such as contemporary America, is pop style. It serves as a mirror held up to today's society.[6]

This America is "into" Oriental politics, African sculpture, prehistoric caves, Zen scriptures, and the click-clack of computers. Artists see—like their precursors, the surrealists—things as beautiful as the chance encounter of a sewing machine with an umbrella on an operating table.

One key to popstyle is coalescence. Time, space, and tradition have been so wedded that all of the old barriers are burned away. Things from "the distant past"—astrology, witchcraft, acupuncture— are as up-to-date as the morning newspaper. Welcome to the eternal Now. All the past is now; so is all the future. Gone forever is the chicken-and-egg argument. The chicken was the egg's idea for getting more eggs.

Gone too is the country-rhythm, nature-centered world that made folklore and folk style central. When the literate Greeks abstracted visual order out of oral chaos, they called their artifact "Nature" *(phusis).* But in today's electric world (as Marshall McLuhan points out), man has come to see this "nature" as an extension of himself, just as he is an extension of nature. To this extent, nature itself has dropped out, and reality gives way to virtual reality.

We look at the present through a rearview mirror, and march backward into the future. In Marshall McLuhan's apt comment, "Suburbia lives imaginatively in Bonanzaland."7

What he did in his erratic but provocative books was to admire folklore, reject fakelore, then discover poplore. He went through the whole cycle, which is just what America is doing now.

The new poplore is not the antithesis of traditional folklore. Pop is not slick but savage; in musical terms, it avoids the chromatic scales of the nightclub and uses the old Greek musical modes. Both folklore and poplore avoid sentimentality; reject the "arty" approach for the earthy; draw from primary materials, colors, and emotions. The line of force connects more with the stomach than with the cerebellum.

The world has changed, and the young are moving out into realms their parents will never enter. The young have always done this, only to return and occupy the stable, conservative positions they once decried.

The folk/fake/pop division is no neat thing; bits of data do not fit the pattern. Much genuine folklore and folk music remains, for example, in distant valleys. Perhaps factories and computer centers will create a vigorous new folklore of their own; the notion that folklore is dying out is a kind of folklore.

Poplore may lack both the vitality and significance I attribute to it—only time will tell. But I am convinced that pop artists (especially Andy Warhol and Claes Oldenburg), pop politicians (especially Bill Clinton and Ralph Nader), and pop performers (especially Oprah Winfrey and Bill Gates) have helped change the course of our culture. Once online, we will never really get off.

Movie and television producers have gone postmodern and adapted a new idiom. Advertisers and spin doctors led the way and now hold us captive. Their victory may eventually be global.

Having been dominated by classical forms and European models for decades, they broke out in the 1960s as traditional lines and barriers were pushed aside. Instead of scripts, actors ad-libbed. A kaleidoscopic variety of subforms sprang up in the arts, and the street itself became a stage. This was the world of *poplore.* Some of it, the artificial lore, left its mark. Probably only 10 percent will survive, but can we ignore gold nuggets because they are found amid tons of fool's gold?[8]

Power plus structure equals a life of being. The poplore that sprang to life was pointing to something much larger than publicity—perhaps to a new ontology. We are much too close to put forth any final judgment. We can record only some manifestations and let history take over:

FOLK	FAKE	POP
Oral	Verbal	Multisensory
Traditional	Nostalgic	Experimental
Realistic	Romantic	Psychedelic
Earthy	Sticky	Tart
Front porch	Nightclub	Singles bar
Homespun	Factory-spun	Polyester
Continuity	Transition	Explosion
Improvised	Ersatz	Electronic
Cowhand	Buffalo Bill	Luke Skywalker
Community sing	Folk festival	Disneyland
"Old Timers"	Baby boomers	Gen X

One land, three lores, or is it a case of three in one? Beneath the surface, aren't folk, fake, and pop part of the same tradition? What do they have in common? These are the questions we must try to answer.

Sacred Symbols

The war of icons and symbols has long been underway.

Marshall McLuhan

Icons are admired artifacts, external expressions of internal convictions; everyday things that make every day meaningful.[1]

They are also cultural ciphers. With them we decipher or unlock our attitudes and assumptions. They operate on an emotional level, objectifying deep mythic structures of reality, revealing basic needs that go from age to age, country to country, generation to generation, media to media. In the Information Age, our icons have been updated. Consider the iconic power of the computer, satellite, or the Internet.

Where can we look for icons in our time? Online, on MTV, in malls, in new car showrooms, and in funeral parlors. They pop up on billboards, bumper stickers, televison commercials, and magazine covers. Many old icons hang on. Automobiles may still have a Virgin Mary on the dashboard—artifact, image, symbol, icon, plastic piety brought into the twenty-first century.

The iconic Virgin Mary doesn't speak to us as she did to people in the thirteenth century. The swastika does not motivate German youths today as it did in the 1940s. Many observers think our flag, Old Glory, had lost much of its iconic power in the past decade; a national crisis has brought it back. The American landscape is blanketed with "Old Glory".

Scholarship on icons in the West has centered on Byzantine Christianity, when icons played a major role in transmitting messages to the masses. In addition to figures of God, Christ, and Mary, frequent use of fruits, birds, and animals were used. Difficult to decipher or appreciate now, they were popular in their day and are still powerful in modern-day Greece and Russia.[2]

Icons were powerful in the cultures of Egypt, Africa, China, and the Mediterranean area long before the Byzantine Era. All cultures create icons. The mind is not so much a debating society as a picture gallery, and icons inhabitat that gallery. We look with our eyes, see with our minds, make with our hands. The word becomes flesh and dwells among us.

A long record of sacred meaning-bearing objects goes back to the dawn of humanity. To the sophisticated eye, the small crude figures of prehistoric humans hardly seem human at all. Discoveries made by Heinrich Schliemann when he excavated the ancient strata of Troy permit us to follow the development from formless stone to human figure.[3] Findings have allowed scholars to date early figures in the period from 30,000 to 50,000 years ago, the best known example being the so-called Venus of Willendorf, coming from the Aurignacian culture around 24,000 to 20,000 B.C. Female obesity, which exaggerates the lower part of the body denoting fertility, dominated these statues, which were diffused through the whole of Europe in the relics of primitive statuary.[4]

Vitality is the prime attribute of early icons, including those found in ancient tombs and on walls, showing the isolation in time and space of painted animals. Here we have representations of awesome natural animated power. Eventually, Herbert Read notes, such symbolic imagery tends to be "conventionalized, systematized, and commercialized."[5]

Studies in classical Greece and Rome confirm this. Ancient Pompeiians made their domestic house shrines a gathering place for traditional memory, tutelary powers, and gods, using conventional canons and rigid postures.[6] Yet color, detail, portrait, quality, and execution made each one different. What David Pye calls, "the workmanship of risk" helped to attain a vital, if irregular, ritual group of icons.[7] Similarly, as we shall see, the pop icons of today are constantly being evoked and evolved, redesigned and reshaped, as our high-tech society seeks to revitalize our icons.[8]

Images as well as icons fascinated the early Greek philosophers, especially the Stoics. Images have always been central in the Judeo-Christian tradition. In Genesis, the Bible begins with God's saying: "Let us make man in our image, after our likeness" (1:26). And a bit later it adds: "When God created man, he made him in the likeness of God" (5:1-3).[9] Arguments over how God could or could not be depicted rocked religion for centuries; and what about sculpted and painted images of the saints? How could the Eastern religious concepts of spirit meld with Western ideas of material culture? "We do not say to the Cross or the Icons, 'You are God,' " wrote Bishop Leontius. "For they are not gods but opened books to remind us of God and to His honor set in our churches and adored."[10]

Eusebius, Bishop of Caesarea in Cappadocia (265-340 A.D.), claimed to have seen a great many portraits of Christ and of Peter and Paul. The catacombs were iconic enters, both for the demos and the ecclesias. But the battle over icons raged, especially after Islam prohibited them.[11] Leo III (717-741 A.D.) tried to abolish the image of Christ in the church. The resulting schism caused a major crisis, partially resolved in the Second Council of Nicaea (787 A.D.), which ruled that "the honor which is paid to the image passes on to that which the image represents, and he who shows reverence to the image shows reverence to the subject contained in it."[12] Ever since, the word *icon* has been banded with ringlets of magic; key words have been *legend, belief, sacred object,* and *veneration.*

Icons are associated with age and class groups. They demand a cult, a lore, a spot of veneration. "All sacred things must have their place," Claude Levi-Strauss notes in *The Savage Mind.* "Being in their place, even in thought, the entire order of the universe would be destroyed."[13] As the old order has changed, yielding place to the ever-new, the sacred spots for icons are no longer churches and monasteries but, in the new venues of man's beliefs and aspirations, on superhighways, television screens, and in discotheques. Wherever they are placed, the icons objectify something near man's essence.

This is why, in the late Roman Empire, the emperor became god on earth, the apex of order and stability, master of a symmetrically structured state hierarchy. The emperor image (icon) became a devotional focus. He became a "holy type," and his form and function changed little from one ruler to the next. So it was that Ammainus Marcellinus could say of Constantius II, "The emperor was not a living person but an image."[14] Can we not say the same thing centuries later about Michael Jordan, Ronald McDonald, Darth Vader, and the cowboy?

We can, I think, because icons are symbols and mind marks. They tie in with myth, legend, values, idols, and aspirations. Because of the great stress placed on icons by religion, some would limit icons to conventional religious images typically painted on a wooden panel. I reject this idea and seek instead to revitalize the word and relate it to popular culture.

Every age is compulsively creative. With each, mythology is transformed into history, history into life, and life into icons. Concepts and emotions finally become creeds and images, as Plato's ideas, Kant's categories, Jung's archetypes, and McLuhan's media all illustrate. Pop icons are created by and mirrored in twentieth-century life, as they have been in the life of all centuries.

We need to devise new criteria and categories for intrinsic meanings. Profiting from Erwin Panofsky's creative work, we should apply the same serious analysis to the current American Renaissance that was used for the Italian and French period. This would involve not only surface data (identification, description, authentication) but interior qualities (evaluation, interpretation, significance).

Most of all, it would involve an intensive reappraisal of the thingness of things (for our purposes, the iconness of icons). Filling the space-time continuum, haunting our dreams, things determine not only our lives but also our fantasies. Primitive man wrestles with life's raw stuff, stone and wood, until he develops technology. And as cultures have technology, so do they have history.[15]

Thus objects in general and icons in particular are the building blocks of reality. They are sensitive indicators of who we are, where we come from, where we intend to go. Long after an individual has died and even his language and culture have disappeared, artifacts remain. By digging into the earth, men and women known as archaeologists uncover the stories of the past. Artifacts form the solid basis of our understanding and concern for the millions of human beings who preceded us. Archaeology plus imagination equals historical insight.

Dynamos, telephones, cameras, film, printing presses, compact discs, picture tubes: Are these icons not the essence of popular culture? Have they not shaped mass media, which carries the message?

The thingness of things has fascinated the liveliest intellects since Aristotle's time. A conscious interest in how things work has been such an obvious major factor in history that one posits and predicates it in every period, event, sequence. Yet how few people in the academy know how to deal with—even to describe or classify—the artifacts that make things go.

There is ample evidence to support Professor Harold Skramstand's article "American Things: A Neglected Material Culture."[16] Some readers were surprised to find him single out "New Journalist" Tom Wolfe for special praise, since Wolfe "demonstrates how insights

from a study of new artifact forms are able to increase our understanding of present day American civilization."

Discussing icons with my former student, Tom Wolfe, we agreed
that they dot the American landscape. Sometimes one man or woman
can be largely responsible for inventing and marketing an icon. Consider the case of Florenz Ziegfeld Jr., whose "Ziegfeld Girl" flowered
for three decades in the early twentieth century.

Ziegfeld (1867-1932) was the P. T. Barnum of the theater. For him,
choosing a beautiful young girl (usually blonde, slim, with small lips
and a straight nose) was only the beginning; then the hype and humbug were applied.

Women couldn't possibly be as beautiful, desirable, and breath-
taking as that. Yet they were, under the Ziegfeld master touch of illusion.

Marketing, rather than invention, was his genius. He had a formula
for show business: one-third glamour, one-third merit, and one-third
advertising. Properly blended, they were almost sure to work then—
as they do now. Welcome to American popular culture.

Ziegfeld was a choreographer of racial, sexual, class, and consumer desires that were deeply rooted in American culture. He turned
away from the loftier ideals of his father, who presided over the Chicago Musical College from 1876 to 1916, and turned to the earthier
popular entertainment. His "Ziegfeld Follies" were staged nearly every year from 1907 to 1931. They featured two things central to
American hype: huge budgets and outrageous one-upmanship. They
became, in the phrase of the day, a "national institution."

They were cultural icons—products and representatives of a white,
upscale, heterosexual national ideal. Along the road, the icons had
names: Anna Held, Fanny Brice, and Bessie McCoy, for example.

In recent years, showgirls have been centered in Las Vegas. As Las
Vegas slowly becomes a theme park, showgirls compete with water
slides as tourist attractions.[17]

A far more pervasive icon, originating in America but belonging to
the world, is Coca-Cola and the Coke bottle. Coke is, as we all know,
"The Real Thing." How long will it be with us? "Always."

Colas are flavored with extracts from coca leaves and kola nut. The
"Pause That Refreshes" both cools us off and freshens us up. Critics
have pointed out that the Coke bottle looks like a breast, which psy-
chologists say might be significant. Coke is also one of the few safe

things to drink in many countries; drinking it is being progressive and "American." So far, it is more than a mere drink.[18]

Craig Gilborn made interesting observations in his essay on "Pop Iconology: Looking at the Coke Bottle."[19] He points out that Coke attracted the attention of pop artists and advertisers everywhere. The first "pop" depiction of the bottle was Robert Rauschenberg's "Coca-Cola Plan," a sculptural construction created in 1958 incorporating three bottles. Among other early treatments was Andy Warhol's large 1962 piece illustrating 210 Coke bottles. The bottle's unparalleled success as a commercial and cultural symbol is suggested by a still-life painting of an egg and a Coke bottle done for the author by Jonathon Fairbanks. The sacred and the profane are confounded by these juxtapositions, in which the mysteries of art are appropriated by the clutter of everyday life.

The Coke bottle is the most widely recognized commercial product in the world. Only one person out of four hundred was unable to identify a photo of the bottle in a product recognition study undertaken in 1949.[20] The bottle is one of the few truly participatory objects in the United States and in much of the world. Presidents drink Coca-Cola; so do sharecroppers. Usage cuts across nationalities, social and occupational classes, age groups. The bottle, unlike most other objects which might be regarded as symbols *par excellence* of American culture, is singularly free of anxiety-producing associations. It is regarded with affection by generations of young Americans who congregated and socialized in gasoline stations, boot camps, and drugstores and evokes pangs of nostalgia when Americans gather in the cafés of Europe, Africa, and Asia.

The Coke break cuts across nations, classes, races, and sexes. The company has its own archives and a curator who has spent all his working life collecting and preserving the history and memorabilia of Coca-Cola.[21] Craig Gilborn has undertaken a detailed study of the Coke bottle and has shown how the latest anthropological techniques can be applied.[22] This study is important not only in itself, but also as a model for the many other studies we must undertake if we are to quantify and organize the study of popular icons.

How the Coca-Cola Company itself has expanded and exploited this phenomenon is an elaborate and intricate story not yet fully told. The amount spent on advertising, and the items involved, is staggering. Beginning with calendars and outdoor signs, the company has become involved with trays, change receivers, dishes, coasters, mirrors, clocks, periodicals, posters, cardboard cutouts, signs, blotters, bookmarks, bottle caps, stationary, emblems, coupons, menus, games, toys, openers, ice picks, thermometers, pocket knives, pens, pencils, pencil sharpeners, music boxes, paperweights, radios, smoking paraphernalia, jewelry, and more—like the sorcerer's apprentice, there seems to be no way of stopping the iconic flow. Nor has the company hesitated to purchase the endorsement of athletes, movie stars, writers, politicians, and war heroes. Legendary figures are cultivated too. "The Coca-Cola Company," Cecil Munsey writes in his official history, "has made one of the largest contributions to the legend of Santa Claus." He then documents how this was done, stressing that every year since 1930, Santa Claus has appeared on posters, billboards, and magazines promoting Coca-Cola.[23] All this, plus the multimillion dollar campaign on television.

The Coca-Cola Company started the same year the Statue of Liberty was unveiled—1886—showing how two very different icons can serve the needs of an expanding culture. The "Lady with the Lamp," standing at the entrance to New York harbor, has become one of the best-known and revered objects in the world. The statue itself, by Frederic Auguste Bartholdi, resembles the output of dozens of other sculptors and monument makers of the period. Bartholdi's conventional art was meant to turn our attention to myths, not museums. In fact, the statue resembles a Pop Art gimmick or toy, since visitors look out from its row of windows as through the eyes of a giant, thus *becoming* the colossus. Marvin Trachtenberg has written a book on this icon, which has aroused more intense emotion than any other work of art in the New World. He points to the symbolism of the torch, the history of female figures of liberty (including the central personage of Delacroix's celebrated "Liberty Leading the People"), and the placement of the statue just when the floodgates of immigration were opened.

Taken together, he suggests, the symbols of liberty were reshuffled into a new icon. "If the significance of the Statue of Liberty has in our day again been altered, it remains constant in the memory through its association with America's grandeur as Mother of exiles."[24] Restoring it for its centennial in 1986 became a popular crusade.

If icons are old, ways of using them are constantly changing. A new field of iconic communication has developed since 1965, when a group at Johns Hopkins University began research with computer-generated films. Iconic communication deals with nonverbal communication through visual signs and representations that stand for an idea by virtue of a resemblance or analogy. How do films, for example, communicate visual messages to human beings? No one approach or discipline can answer that question. Relevant information from psychology, perception, anthropology, education, popular culture, computer graphics, and other fields must be considered. We are only on the threshold of this new frontier.[25]

Consider this: now we can generate moving pictorial images with computers. The ability to convey concepts through moving images and symbols is a radically new genre. Instead of expressing concepts in the traditional static symbolic forms of natural languages or mathematics, we can contrive modes of expression using dynamic visual imagery.[26] Soon there will be a science of iconics. How will it affect the humanities?

Icons are pictorial, and everyone "understands" pictures. "Iconic" implies a mode of communication using primitive visual imagery, relying on the ability of people to perceive natural form, shape, and motion, rather than relying on alphabetic symbols defined in terms of arbitrary conventions.

Language must be taught. Iconic images and structural information about the three-dimensional world are acquired merely by maturing. Will that be the hope or the despair of the world?

Our technology and cosmology always change, but they cannot replace icons; we simply invent new icons. Sigmund Freud called them optical memory residues—things as opposed to words. The mind is not so much a debating society as a picture gallery. Form and formula fuse. The word becomes values, idols, and aspirations. Because religion stresses icons, some would limit the word only to religious images. But this overlooks that fact that we confront icons in malls, discotheques, used car lots, and funeral parlors; on billboards, computer screens, television, and in chat rooms.

Objects are the building blocks; ideas the cement that holds them together. Postmodern men and women must give meaning to the Information Age. What they find most acceptable are images more fragmentary and illusive than those of the past. However fleeting they may be, they still have great iconic power over us.

In secular times religious icons sometimes return in a different guise. In a much-discussed book called *The Secular City* (New York: Macmillan, 1967), Harvey Cox argued that biblical faith desacrilized the secular and echoed the old idea that "God is dead." The special power of the church has been transferred to the Internet. Instead of being on our knees, we find ourselves online. But is that not a new form of worship?

Living in the world of virtual reality, we must create a new psychological environment. We may reach a "posttime"—postmodern, post-Marxian, post-Newtonian, posthumanist. Over a century ago, the French poet Baudelaire invited friends to flee from the old world of romance and nostalgia to seek the new. That is what we are beginning to do, when films are "reel" illusion and real life is becoming more novel than fiction.

We must not be awed by newness. Putting the adjective "new" in front of a noun does not cancel connections with the old. The search for new icons may end up exalting the old. In the Middle Ages, all experience found philosophical unity and visual unity in a single metaphorical system. Will this be true in the new century? Might this be the place to look for a new unifying factor? Is this, and not the Global Village, our best bet?

The Man and the Mouse

We just try to make a good picture. And then the professors come along and tell us what we do.

Walt Disney

As the twentieth century closed, a great debate began: Who was the greatest American of the century? Many factors influenced many answers: race, gender, ethnicity, region, politics, age, economics, religion, and occupation. There is no consensus.

Who dominates popular culture? Who left the deepest imprint on the popular imagination? My choice has two faces, two personalities. He is both Walt Disney and Mickey Mouse. Together, they helped reorient the world.[1]

Why not Henry Ford, who put America on wheels? Or Thomas Edison, who electrified us? Or Eisenhower, Kennedy, or Reagan? They all left deep marks, as did many heroic women, such as Helen Keller, Eleanor Roosevelt, Amelia Earhart, Rachel Carson, and Gloria Steinem. They also left souvenirs and playthings—Ford at Dearborn and Edison at Menlo Park, the presidents in their libraries, the women in suffrage, feminist, and human rights crusades. But only one left a new cosmos. Disney World is a unique shrine, moving beyond life to imagination.

And we have the much-beloved mouse. Anyone who lived and fought in World War II knows that most of the training films were made by Disney. The films trained millions. Who knows how much they contributed to our victory?

Ford, Edison, and Disney had much in common: modest educations, immodest ambitions, incredible work habits, and puritanical lifestyles. You crossed them at your peril. They were lords of their own kingdoms.

The story of Walt Elias Disney's life is well documented.[2] Born in Chicago in 1901, his family moved to a farm in Marceline, Missouri, in 1906, where he got his inspiration for the Main Street, USA, to appear later at Disneyland and where he observed the animals that would become his trademark. A lonely child, with an abusive father, Walt had a drab childhood. He did not do well in school. The farm failed, the family moved to Kansas City, and Walt worked in a jelly factory. During World War I, he joined the Red Cross Ambulance Corps and served in France.

Once back in the United States, he took art lessons and drew illustrations for farm magazines. He wanted to create movie shorts and did a series of fairy-tale films. When his distributor failed, he decided to perfect a new medium: the animated animal cartoon. He studied animation, but there was no market in Kansas City. Always ready to follow his star on short notice, Walt left for Hollywood with forty dollars in his pocket. That decision would change his life, and the course of popular culture.

There were animated pictures long before the movie days by flipping booklets in one's hands. Sir John Herschel had worked on animated visions. Georges Melies had established an animated film studio in France before 1900. *A Trip to the Moon* (1902) was a classic. Russia's Ladislas Starevich did La Fontaine's *Fables* and released his full-length *Tale of the Fox* before World War I. America's Winsor McCoy turned out *Gertie the Dinosaur* (1914) and *Felix the Cat.*

But no other animated character could ever match Mickey and the family Disney created to support him. Some of them—like Donald Duck, Pluto, and Minnie—became superstars in their own right. Over the years, Mickey's fame grew, exported on tons of drawings transferred to miles of film. The Man and the Mouse became crown jewels in the popular culture collection.

World War II greatly enhanced Disney's role in American life. At his new studio in Burbank, California, completed in 1940 and outfitted with 1,100 employees, Disney produced hundreds of training films during World War II. The skills learned and applied to Mickey helped thousands of Americans to fight in and win a war.

Always looking for new ventures and adventures, Walt began to dream of an amusement park different from any other, called Disneyland. His biggest coup was getting ABC (the American Broadcasting Company) to buy 34 percent of Disneyland's stock, in exhange for which Disney would produce a weekly hour-long television program for seven years called *Disneyland.*

Now the construction crews could get to work. In the summer of 1954, the park took shape on a 160-acre plot in Anaheim, California; in the fall, the television program *Disneyland* went on the air. It quickly rose to the top of Nielson ratings and set a trend that has continued ever since. The park was completed and opened in 1955, featuring five worlds joined by a central plaza: Main Street USA, Adventureland, Frontierland, Fantasyland, and Tomorrowland. In six months, over 3 million "guests" enjoyed Disneyland; the 25-millionth came in July 1965. By then attendance had come to equal a quarter of the total population of the United States.

What explains this enormous popularity? Main Street is not so much a memory as it is an archetypal ideal—a universally true Main Street where everyone wants to live. The visitor moves in one direction, from frame to frame, enjoying the well-kept perfection. Here life is bright, clean, and poignantly beautiful. Suddenly time has stopped. That is the magic. Both the past and the future are rosy. The present is ignored.[3]

Then there are Disneyland's innovations in a field named audioanimatronics. This involves creating three-dimensional figures with sound and movement, operated by electronics and computers. Each figure costs approximately $6 million, not including the computer—more magic.

Disneyland is dreamland—an idyllic place where there are no problems, no violence, no responsibilities, no need to work; a release from everything connected with suffering. It is the Promised Land, and people from all over the world go to enjoy it.

Of the many studies of Disneyland, the most detailed analysis is Michael Real's *Mass Mediated Culture* (1977), which presents it as a total, ideological universe. Disney, Real believes, recast the older contours of collective recreation into something new: a landscape which revolved around consumption. Another important book, Herbert I. Shiller's *The Mind Managers* (1973), argues that there are distinct concealed social and political messages in all of Disney's seemingly innocent productions. Disneyland, both Real and Shiller believed, was a reinforcement for the status quo.[4]

Visitors to Disneyland also comment on the "cult of Walt," which has taken place of the earlier creative atmosphere. Everything ended up on his desk. In Ford's empire, they were afraid to call the top man Henry. In Disney's, they dared call him nothing but Walt.

But Disneyland was not big enough for Walt. He wanted a whole world—made to his specifications. He dreamed it, planned it, but did not live to see it take full shape. In a sense, he built it from the grave.

In the summer of 1964, his agents began purchasing parcels of swampland and citrus groves in southern Florida, on the outskirts of Orlando. By October 1965, they had acquired 27,443 acres—nearly forty-three square miles—for a total cost of just over $200 an acre. Meanwhile, Disney had made a deal with Florida officials, giving him "absolute control" over the east tract. On November 15, 1965, Florida Governor William Haydon Burns confirmed plans for the building of "Walt Disney World Resort (WDW), near Orlando, Florida." The game was afoot.[5]

And what a game! Engineers had to drain the swamps, build canals for continuous drainage, ensure flood-control, conserve the water table, and construct sixteen self-regulating dams and various other structures. Walt was building a state within a state—the Vatican City of entertainment; a vast theme park with hotels, resorts, boating, tennis, golf, bird watching. Walt himself planned and supervised all of this, preparing general directions for the whole complex. He laid out plans for a City of Tomorrow. But fate intervened, and his tomorrow would pass on to other hands.

On December 15, 1966, Walt Disney died of lung cancer, six months before the first earth-moving equipment began work on Bay Lake. The body was cremated and there was no funeral. But myth set in: some said his body lies in a state of cyrogenesis, preserved for possible future resuscitation. What if Walt returns?

This was acknowledged to be the best-planned, most efficient city in the world. The Magic Kingdom was built on top of a vast utility basement with a network of tunnels through which employees traveled, not disturbing the "guests" above. All the water, sewer, and electric lines were there, out of sight, along with storage areas and computers, laundries, and offices. An energy-efficient monorail system moved people effortlessly, monitored like most things by computers. That was part of the magic. Disney World was nearer to what people wanted than anything architects had ever given them, and they flocked to Florida to enjoy it. It seemed eons, not merely decades, from the push-and-shove Coney Island days.[6]

Everything in Disney World is bigger and grander than Disneyland. One still enters through Main Street USA and goes on to

Adventureland, Frontierland, Fantasyland, and Tomorrowland. There are new additions: Liberty Square, Mickey's Birthland, and a much more elaborate Cinderella's Castle. There are thrill rides, a Haunted Mansion, and a Hall of Presidents. On October 1, 1982, EPCOT Center was opened—the Experimental Prototype Community of Tomorrow. American corporations were partners in the $900 million venture, interested in image enhancement and product promotion. The 600-acre center contained a Future World and a World Showcase. Historians noted that a trip to WDW has replaced visits to religious shrines, such as Mecca, Rome, or Canterbury; people come not to affirm religion but to experience corporate capitalism. And come they do.

The two major Disney ventures overseas carry the American pattern with them. They have the four basic elements: a castle, a Main Street, and two American parks. Tokyo Disneyland, which opened in April 1983, is on a 114-acre site of land about ninety miles from Tokyo. It has been a huge success, with over 14 million visitors per year. It appeals to such Japanese passions as order, cleanliness, service, and technical wizardry. Its future in the new century looks bright.

The story was far less favorable in Euro Disneyland, built on 138 acres twenty miles east of Paris. Opening on April 12, 1992, it was denounced by French critics and intellectuals as a "cultural Chernobyl" and by the French unions, angry at the "fascism" of the company's hiring policies. In Britain, London's *The Sunday Times* relished Disney's problems in France. A London *Times* headline for December 6, 1992, read: "Hi ho, hi ho, it's off the cliff we go."

Led by elitist French intellectuals, Europeans called Euro Disney, the vaunted bid to export an American pop culture icon, a spectacular flop. The reported loss for 1993 was over $100 million. Officials admitted the park had not even generated enough cash to meet interest payments on its debts.

How could this be? America's Disneyland and Disney World flourish, and Disney movies are blockbusters. Ever since his first cartoon in 1928, Mickey Mouse has delighted the world, and become, like Uncle Sam himself, public property. For a whole generation Mickey was a prefabricated barometer of popular culture.

He was wholly, but not merely, American. Abroad he was Topolino, Michel Souris, Miki Kuhi, Mikki Hirri, or Mikel Mus. Inspired by Mickey Mouse, Walt Disney wedded art and mass media, revitalizing fantasy for our times. How dare the French send Mickey packing?

The fault was not all Mickey's. A severe economic recession had crippled Europe, and Euro Disney was an expensive luxury. It opened in 1992 when there was real tension between France and America over trade policies, and France blocked any efforts at compromise. Indeed, French farmers even blocked the road to Euro Disney. In December 1993, the French movie industry held up the GATT trade treaty, insisting on subsidies for their film industry, which was swamped by American imports. There never has been a harder time for us to win friends in France.

There are other reasons. The French are highly sensitive over losing their former cultural dominance in the arts and world affairs. The world art center has shifted from Paris to New York. What did French intellectuals call Euro Disney? A cultural Chernobyl.

Then there is the basic concept of Euro Disney. It depicts a totally American sugar-sweet world of castles, talking animals, princesses, and kings. All this delights America, which, as Mark Twain noted, is "fresh out of kings." Not so for Europeans, who wrote the book on such things and fought to get rid of them. (Even Britain's ancient monarchy is under attack.) We carried the wrong message to Europe, packaged as a super-American sales campaign.

Hence, many Europeans saw it as a cheap reproduction, a cultural intrusion, an overkill. "This isn't better than Europe's real thing—it isn't even close," they said. And it was expensive. Yankee, go home.

But Euro Disney has some old Yankee virtues—if at first you don't succeed, try, try again. Some obvious decisions were made. Change the menu. Funnel in money from America and from any foreigners who are willing to help. Most important: stay the course. As the century ended, Mickey Mouse had recovered in France. He would always have his enemies there (as does anything American), but he picked up new friends in a new generation and went on his merry way. Even in France, he is holding his own in the new millennium.

There are scores of books about Walt Disney—the cartoons, films, and worlds he created. Academics tend to scorn him, but ordinary people love him—and the money keeps rolling in. Having read many of the books and visited the sites, I maintain Walt Disney is popular culture's Man of the Century. Here are my main conclusions:

1. Walt's was a kind of Horatio Alger Jr. success story—out of obscurity into fame and fortune, a self-made man.

2. He was a complex, difficult person who drove himself and all those around him almost to the breaking point. For every friend, he made two enemies. His obsession was ceaseless work—trying to create an idyllic illusory childhood he himself never had. This required total control of space, mood, and movement, at which he was a master.

3. Yet he clung to his American dream, rooted in small-town Kansas (a *Wizard of Oz* comparison?) and made that dream a reality for millions of people. His theme parks became themes of the twentieth century. The Disney park concept created a new growth industry, which now blankets the Global Village. The parks are an antidote to ordinary life.

4. Walt Disney had a precise and intuitive identity with ordinary Americans. He was literally the king of popular culture. Walt Disney World is his enduring kingdom.

5. Walt and those who followed him thought big and took risks. They made mistakes, corrected them, and thought bigger. They captured the admiration not only of the American public but also of corporate America and wedded entertainment to family, patriotism, and profit. They whistled while they worked.

6. Walt has gone, but Mickey Mouse survives. You can see him daily at Disneyland or Disney World, where ageless King Mickey presides over a Magic Kingdom. Visitors get a free bumper sticker that reads: "Vacationland for the World."

When the Federal Telecommunication Act of 1996 opened the door for deregulation and merger, the Magic Kingdom quickly changed into a media giant. The little mouse became Mr. Big.

The expansion—and its implications—are staggering. Disney's holdings in 1999 included six film production companies, theme parks in America, France, and Japan, 530 Disney stores worldwide, 100 magazines, seven record companies, a hockey team, a baseball franchise, and two cruise ships—scheduled to dock at a Caribbean island owned by Disney. The ever-expanding giant not only owns a Disney television channel, but is partners with other channels such as ESPN, A&E, the History Channel, and Lifetime. Also, it has formed a merger with Capital Cities—ABC added ten television stations and twenty-one radio stations, including the nation's largest radio network.

The dynamic CEO of Disney, Michael Eisner, has perfected a system called "cross promotion," which has allowed these various enterprises to assist and promote one another. Hence, a popular actor such as Tim Allen could move from "one of our TV shows" to "one of our movies" to a book published by "one of our publishers." The left hand definitely knew what the right hand was doing and lent a helping hand at every turn. Eisner also popularized a Disney buzzword, *synergy.* Derived from a Greek root (*synergia,* joint work) it advocates joint action, a combination of individual effort. In short, it justifies big mergers and Mr. Big.

Other giant conglomerates sprang up like mushrooms and raised disturbing questions. Was the day of the independent producer and entrepreneur drawing to a close? Was the name of the new game "Winner Take All?" And where were the rate deductions that were promised with the mergers? Instead of going down, many prices went up. Rates for the largest cable company, for example, TCI, went up 21 percent in 1996, with another 6.8 percent increase in 1997. My old dime-movies can cost eight dollars today.

Pondering these questions, I remembered where I had first heard of Mr. Big—in an article by Frank Lloyd Wright, America's greatest architect-philosopher. Back in the 1940s, Wright warned against a gigantism that would change forever the Jeffersonian family-farm dream and American democracy. But who, half a century ago, could have imagined moving from the American village to the Global Village? And who can say what will happen to everything local, regional, or national in the new global economy? Have we thought through the meaning of the malling of America?

Much more is at stake than booming profits for capital-intensive companies. Will quality be ousted by quantity? Will profit ignore aesthetics? Will robots replace people? Will long-cherished handicraft, diversity, and regional appeal vanish in a mass-produced entertainment society? Are we (as Neil Postman suggests) entertaining ourselves to death? Has Mickey Mouse become Monster Mouse?

Will the ever-growing Global Village become the kind of cloned colorless regimented place Aldous Huxley imagined in *Brave New World?*

Baruch Spinoza said the big fish eat the little fish by supreme natural right. But what would the sea—in our society—be like without little fish? My little Mickey Mouse is little no more. He doesn't squeak. He roars.

I miss my little mouse.

Carnivals—Old and New

Eat, drink, and be merry.

Luke 12:19

Carnival: a merrymaking, feasting, masquerading; an organized program of entertainment or exhibition. The carnival spirit seems inherent in human nature and surely in popular culture. Eat, drink, and be merry, Were not Adam and Eve feasting on the apple in the Garden of Eden?

All ancient cultures had their ways of celebrating. Some (such as the Chinese) continue today. The Greeks had their various festivities (including the Olympics) and the Romans their Saturnalia, a ten-day winter solstice holiday which began on December 17. We borrowed the idea and called it Christmas. Roman Catholics have always had festive days for many saints and martyrs and enjoyed pilgrimages to Canterbury or Lourdes. (We go now to sports events or Disney World.)

A medieval English monk named Rahere, a former jester to King Henry I, organized Bartholomew's Fair outside London in 1133. Ben Jonson's play, *Bartholomew Fair,* first performed in 1614, tells of jugglers, fat women, genetic "enormityes," and other freaks. We have the receipts of the 1828 fair, which give the money made from the pig-faced lady, the fat boy and girl, and the Chinese juggler. Pimps, pawnbrokers, bawds, jilts, jockeys, and thieves flourished. Seven centuries after its inception, overrun by unruly mobs, the Lord Mayor of London closed the last Bartholomew Fair. Now the mobs descend on soccer matches and political rallies.

Festivals on the continent of Europe fared better. There, carnivals invade both public life and artistic literature. Venice became the City of Carnival. Crowds still flock there to enjoy the special flavor of a city devoted to fantasy and pleasure. New Orleans, with Mardi Gras, serves the same function in the United States, although its vulgarity and exploitation have created detractors.

Other "pleasure gardens" sprang up in England and Europe. London's Vauxhall Gardens opened in 1661, Ranelagh Gardens in 1742. In his book on *The London Pleasure Gardens of the Eighteenth Century* (1896), Warwick Wroth lists sixty-five. Here working people could escape the smoke and soot of the Industrial Revolution, walk in the woods, and enjoy concerts, plays, balloon ascensions, and fireworks.

On the continent, Emperor Joseph II gave his Vienna hunting ground "to the people of Vienna" in 1766. The resulting Prater Park became known as Wurstelprater, the Sausage Prater, because good food was there, as well as carousels and "up-and-downs" (now known as the Ferris wheel).

By 1776, the American colonies were thinking revolution, not sausages. Still, there were carnivals and pleasures—picnics, barbecues, family gatherings, hoedowns, horse races, tavern brawls, fairs. New York's Central Park became a carnival center. As late as 1912, the merry-go-round in the Park was operated by a single slow-moving mule.

The most spectacular American carnival, the 1893 Chicago World's Columbian Exposition, was staged to honor the 400th anniversary of Columbus's discovery of the New World. Here we got our first midway and Ferris wheel (named for George Washington Gale Ferris), which 1,453,611 customers rode for the then-extremely high price of fifty cents, bringing in $726,805.50.[1] The era of American carnivals began with a patriotic landmark.[2]

Another carnival center was Coney Island. In our New Age, it's hard to recreate the aura and wonder of nineteenth-century Coney Island. From the 1870s until Disneyland in the 1950s, Coney Island was our magic kingdom—the "pyrotechnic insanitarium" that released millions from the crowded, drab urban areas and immigrant ghettos. For one brief moment, fantasy and fun met. Richard Le Gallienne summed it up in his *Human Need of Coney Island:* "Coney Island is all the wonders of the world in one pyrotechnic masterpiece of coruscating concentration—strange Isle of Monsters, preposterous Palace of Illusion, gigantic Parody of Paradise."[3]

Earlier, Coney Island had been an idyllic ocean shore and clam beds stretching five miles near Brooklyn. Seventeenth-century Dutch settlers called it "Konijn" (rabbit), for there were hordes of them on the dunes. The rabbits left and humans took over. In 1875, a railroad was built from Coney Island to Brooklyn, and the fare was thirty-five cents.[4]

Three large Coney Island hotels were built between 1877 and 1880. "Boss" John Y. McKane, who was the one-man government of the fast-booming area, allowed con artists, gamblers, and prostitutes to settle in for a fee in a section of the beach known as "the Gut." For awhile, McKane prospered, sporting a diamond-studded police badge and a gold-handled cane. His luck ran out and he ended up in Sing Sing Prison in 1894.

The power vacuum was filled by George C. Tilyou, who opened Steeplechase Park on Coney Island in 1897. Fascinated by new technology, he encouraged La Marcus Thompson to build his Switchboard Railway Coaster on Coney Island, and Paul Boyton to build his Sea Lion Park a year later. This was our first enclosed amusement park with an admission fee. As the century ended, Coney Island flourished. Rockets flared, concessions grew, and trainloads arrived on the hour from the steaming cauldron of New York City.[5]

Between 1900 and 1930, organized amusement zones sprang up in cities across America. Lakeside, between Roanoke and Salem, Virginia, was the Mecca of my youth. The "Thriller" promised to throw us out into the local brambles, the "Whip" to break our necks. We went, rode, survived. Things slowed down around America for the Great Depression and World Wars but picked up quickly in the postwar years, when a building boom doubled the number of amusement parks.

Estimates vary from 1,000 to 1,500 for the number of amusement parks operating at the end of World War I. The trolley car, invented by Charles J. Van Depoele, made the spread of street railway systems attractive and cheap and fed the amusement park boom. Chicago has its Cheltenham Beach, Pittsburgh its Kennywood Park, Sandusky its Cedar Point, Cleveland its Euclid Beach, and Philadelphia its Willow Grove Park. Thus did the amusement park become a centerpiece of twentieth-century popular culture.

It was a perfect embodiment of the American spirit, reflecting the increased democratic character of society, providing an almost holy joy for those who reveled in the New Jerusalem.[6] They were, John F. Kasson writes, "a valve, a mechanism of social release and control that ultimately protected existing society."[7]

How much truer would this become in the twenty-first century, when corporate sponsors made amusement and profit Siamese twins and corporate capitalism dreamed of the Global Village? American theme parks cleaned up their act and vastly increased their scope. The best example is Walt Disney World, described in the previous chapter. There are other spectacular ones, such as Sea World of California.

On the edge of San Diego, Sea World, a jewel in the crown of massive corporation conglomerate Anheuser-Busch, opened in 1964. Dubbed a marine park, it is much more, with shows, rides, demonstrations, and concessions. Every year, 4 million customers come to enjoy the park, a botanical garden, souvenir stands, food, and well-placed corporate advertising. Although the killer whales are the chief attraction (they perform several times a day), there are also sting-less stingrays, striking sharks, pettable sea stars, breeding penguins, nesting flamingos, and wallowing walruses.[8]

Humans abound too—beauty queens, Russian singers, Olympic acrobats, ballet troupes, clever clowns, doo-wop singers, and even teams of Clydesdale horses (the Anheuser-Busch trademark). All this conjures up memories of P. T. Barnum and shows how carnivals, hype, and humbuggery coincide.

Look again at Sea World. Try the gondola ride, concession stands, vendors' cars, auditorium, and multistory play park. Ponder Sea World's slogan: "It's not just a park; it's another world."

Anheuser-Busch, the baron of beers and many other things, has carnival parks spread around America. Their four Sea Worlds (three others were built to entertain over 11 million paying visitors annually) fattened the profits. These Sea Worlds are well hyped and advertised. Nothing in the park is left to chance. Continuous labor and strict management produce a steady flow of sights, sounds, and images. Nature is extolled, but market research and statistic call all the shots.

What is the role of management? To lengthen the visitors' stay and increase their spending. This is nature by the numbers. What determines the key decisions? Market research. Marketing director Bill Thomas wears a beeper that allows him to know the "pace count" at any time.[9]

Sea World's basic problem: how to create the illusion that this is not an overcrowded space while moving thousands of people through the manicured landscapes. How to arrange and control so many bodies in time and space? There may be tens of thousands of people on 150 acres of park at any given time. Engineers know seated people take up twenty-four inches each, but suppose they are carrying cameras, backpacks, and souvenirs? New problems for the Space Age!

Eating can also be a problem. People like to linger after dining, perhaps to chat with family or strangers. Can people sit down in small groups and chat leisurely, even if the meal comes from a cafeteria line? Sea World follows the McDonald's model—deep-fat frying, serving preprepared items, moving the staff of the seven restaurants on short notice. The goal: to have the customer in and out in ten minutes. Thus do the new theme parks sacrifice the person for the profit.

Seeing and touching are stressed—feeding the dolphins always rates high. The omnipresent motto sums it up: Interactive, Participatory, and Touchable. Come to Happy Harbor Playground or Cap'n Kid's World and enter the world of the sea.

The central features of Sea World parks are the Shamu shows. They pull the entire theme park together and highlight visitors' experience. Shamu, the designated name for a colorful black-and-white killer whale, has become the park's logo and registered trademark. Shamu plays different parts or, more accurately, appears as interchangeable trained animals, scripted and acting on cue. Thus is one of nature's most magnificent animals converted into a corporate commodity.

The various Shamus perform from two to five times a day in the Shamu stadium, which consists of four deep-blue pools filled with 5 million gallons of reconstituted seawater. Visitors waiting to enter can "Have Your Photo Taken with Shamu," by posing next to a glass tank (and paying for the privilege). Once inside, a loudspeaker assures them that Sea World and Anheuser-Busch are "working for a brighter tomorrow" and promises that the Shamu show will begin in approximately three minutes. Out run four trainers as the Jumbotron screen flashes "Shamu New Visions." An aerial camera zooms in from on high, focusing on a glacier and parka-clad man, James Earl Jones. The booming bass voice of Jones fills the air: "Hello, I'm glad you could join me."

After some mushy dialogue, he gets to the punch line: "Ladies and gentlemen, Shamu, the killer whale!" Then trainers and whales go through the same routine, day after day, month after month. A female trainer appears via an extreme close-up on the screen, giving a toothy grin and saying, "Each day is different, and the best part of the day is playtime." Then she trots to the edge of the tank and "plays" with a whale. As a finale, all four whales are in the pool, jumping and splashing to the theme music. Again the booming bass voice of James Earl Jones: "We hope you'll join Shamu and all of us again soon for more new visions. Good-bye."

Times change, audiences change. In 1997, it was clear that most of the customers were white females, who were not especially impressed with African-American James Earl Jones. He was out and Jane Seymour, a family television "personality" and a positive female role model, was in.

Despite all the rhetoric about transcendence and oneness, nature and the human world are quite separate at Sea World. The trick is to conceal this. "Nature" is distant and deep, like the dream world Main Street USA in Disney World. Yes, a killer whale is there—but as a merry prankster, not ready to kill. It's a touch worthy of Walt Disney. Shamu became a mediator between the audience, Anheuser-Busch, and the larger corporate world. Sea World and its many impersonators prosper.

But with the new expansion came new problems, such as traffic control and crowded highways. A recent example points this out. It involves one of the most successful park conglomerates, Six Flags. The chain started in 1961 with "Six Flags over Texas" (the six are Spain, France, Mexico, the Republic of Texas, the Confederacy, and the United States). A few years later, there was "Six Flags over Georgia," and the flags have been flying all over the place ever since.

Six Flags over America opened with a $40 million expansion over the old Adventure World in Virginia's Prince George County on May 8, 1999. Officials had expected 7,000 people on opening day, but 21,000 turned out. The 5,000 parking spaces were soon filled. Customers began parking on the shoulders of Route 214 and on the grass. Officials hoped changing the traffic pattern and enlarging the parking lot would solve the mess. It didn't. On May 23, 1999, *The Washington Post* reported that roads to the park were clogged for hours. Some were finding a spot near a church a half mile away and walking to the Six Flags gates.

Even a summary of the carnivals, theme parks, and sea worlds gives us important insights into popular culture. People are ready to be entertained, even to be deceived, if clever promoters and corporations know how to do it. They do—pushing the hype and rhetoric aside, we find a Darwinian struggle underway for markets, money endorsements, and bodies. Consumption has become a form of public action. Sell the sizzle, not the steak. Sell the dream, not the reality. Do it well, and you will become rich and famous.

In the 1990s, opposition to theme parks began to grow. Disney wanted to buy an area in Northern Virginia where the Battle of Manassas had been fought in the Civil War and graves and statues were still in place. Virginians didn't like the idea of Mickey Mouse taking over its Confederate dead and kept Disney out.

Shakespeare thought all the world was a stage. Were he alive today, he might agree with Russell Baker. He lives in Northern Virginia, which is becoming a dormitory for Washington. "All of America is becoming a traffic jam," Baker writes. "I live in Leesburg and when I drive to Washington it seems to have become a theme park."[10]

We call them theme parks but they have many other names: street fairs, Mardi Gras, yard sales, chat rooms, rock concerts, and rap sessions. What do they have in common? They are places of fun where we leave our daily woes behind us; popular culture in a colorful and flamboyant moment. And they are all expert at selling people's dreams back to them for a heavy profit.

This insight is by no means confined to the United States. The expansion of theme parks and spectacles has girdled the globe. Two large parks (Parc Asterix and Big Bang Schtroumpf) in France compete with Euro Disney in Paris. Both Anheuser-Busch and the Six Flags organizations opened parks in Spain. There is a large-scale theme park in England, sparked by Alton Towers and Blackpool Pleasure Beach. India has its Nehru-land, and Moscow its Gorky Park. There are 300 large amusement parks in the former Soviet Union.

The list goes on and on: Jaya Ancol Dreamland in Indonesia, Tivoli Park in Brazil, Ocean Park in Hong Kong, Durban Miniature Railway Park in South Africa, Rino Adventure in Mexico, Phantasialand in Germany, Toshimaen Amusement Park in Tokyo, Sea World in Australia, and Atallah Happyland in Saudi Arabia. Collecting information and brochures on the ever-expanding number has become an operation in its own right.

Still we seem to hear the voice of a small child, strapped into the back seat of a motor vehicle, asking: "Are we having fun yet?"

The Celebrity Cult

May I have your autograph?

Citizen to Celebrity

Celebrities are famous for being famous—for awhile. They shoot up out of nowhere, like a bright star crossing the heavens. Their brilliance can bewitch us, and we hope they are ours forever. They are not: like falling stars, they disappear as quickly as they appear. Then, alas, they are forgotten.

Although we generally think of celebrities in show business—movies, television, pop music, Miss America pageants—they can appear in almost any venue: sports, art, music, politics, cyberspace, Main Street, Wall Street; we hunger to touch the hem of their garments. Whoever can claim to be number one will suddenly be our one and only, for the moment.

The range of the celebrity world is very wide, but not very deep. It is often as tragic as it is romantic. Two notorious examples come to mind.

She was incredibly beautiful. On the screen, she exuded a tender warmth that made her unique and irresistible. When Norma Jean Baker became a celebrity, ogled and admired by millions, she changed her name to Marilyn Monroe. In a few years, she was an embodiment, an institution, a doctrine, a fashion idol, and a sex goddess. There wasn't anything or anyone she couldn't have. Then, at the peak of her career in her midthirties, she committed suicide. Could it have been something else? Did Marilyn Monroe murder Norma Jean Baker?

Her tragic flaw was that she wanted to be recognized and understood as herself, not idolized as a celebrity—an object to twang the male erotic nerve. She was so profoundly disturbed by the idea of not being accepted as a real person that she felt herself being destroyed, yet did nothing to resist that destruction. She is one of the tragic figures of the twentieth century.[1]

Since her death, she has lived on to haunt us in the work of pop artists—a symbol of the gorgeous, erotic, glossy embrace of cornflake materialism. This lost, illegitimate young woman who killed herself with barbiturates became a myth and died because of it. She is a monument to heroic disaster.

What she stood for was summed up in the terms "hot stuff," "some dish," and "a gorgeous piece." The key adjective for celebrities is *hot*—emotional, tactile, torrid. To be with a girl like this is to be a true man who can "make the sparks fly." An earlier generation had praised the "red-hot mamas," who had "it." Clara Bow and Mae West were sex celebrities for years, with Mae's purring tagline, "Why don't ya come up and see me some time?" During World War II, the life jacket, which inflated when a sailor was in the water, was known as a "Mae West."

When Marilyn committed suicide in 1962, she took on a new life, becoming again what she had been in life—a licensed brand name and an icon. More than 300 biographies and documentaries have featured her. She combined three essentials of the generation's cravings: sex, talent, and technicolor.

She lived her life on the edge, as did others who became celebrities—Janis Joplin, James Dean, Kurt Cobain, and Jim Morrison— death beckoned her over the edge.[2]

The most publicized celebrity auction of 1998 occurred in October, when memorabilia from both Marilyn Monroe and Elvis Presley went on sale in New York. Going on the block for Marilyn was her wedding ring from Joe DiMaggio and the skintight dress she wore to sing "Happy Birthday" to President Kennedy in 1962. Christie's sold that dress for $1 million. But the glamour and excitement of the Kennedy Era was long dead—like Kennedy and other celebrities of that period.

Marilyn Monroe's male counterpart was the handsome Rudolph Valentino. Dark and well groomed, he breathed passion. As his horse galloped over the hot desert, Valentino played such roles as "The Sheik." Otherwise respectable ladies collected his cigarette butts and hid them in their bosoms. When he died suddenly, mass hysteria swept over many American women. A cordon of police officers had to keep admirers from plucking off his buttons as his body lay in state.

But one who was hotter and more celebrated than Valentino was already on the scene: Clark Gable. He was leading man not only to Mae West and Marilyn Monroe but also to Mary Astor, Claudette

Colbert, Greta Garbo, Ava Gardner, Greer Garson, Grace Kelly, Norma Shearer, Barbara Stanwyck, Lana Turner, and Loretta Young.

Born in a small Ohio town in 1901, the big-eared youth quit school at seventeen to become a day laborer, then a bit actor known as Billy Gable. Married to a woman thirteen years his senior who had been on Broadway and knew its ways, dashing, overconfident Clark Gable's stage name was invented by his first wife. In 1924, he went to Hollywood, then to Broadway, then back to Hollywood. The special alchemy of the silver screen started to work. While Douglas Fairbanks Jr. was creating celluloid swashbucklers, Gable became the lover-adventurer, certain to get the girl and come out way ahead. He was irresistible. Instead of asking his leading lady for love, he demanded it. This wholly authentic all-American guy was by the mid-1930s a household image.

Blessed with rare strength and great endurance, he reached his pinnacle as Rhett Butler in *Gone with the Wind.* (Years later, the revamped film is still breaking box-office records around the world.) At fifty-nine, Gable went to the Nevada desert to film his ninetieth picture; Marilyn Monroe was his leading lady. He was her fantasy-father. Shortly afterward, he died of a heart attack; four months after his death, Gable's only son was born to his fifth wife.

Marilyn Monroe and Clark Gable are something more than celebrities. Though dead, they live on in virtual reality, doomed to be revived on countless old movie channels and in second-run movie theaters.[3]

Texas was in the world limelight again in 1990 when an ex-hippie named Johnson burned an American flag, after having gathered television reporters to catch the action. The networks put it on national news, and all hell broke loose. You would have thought he had burned the Constitution or assaulted President George Bush.

When the courts said Johnson was protected by the First Amendment, President Bush suggested a constitutional amendment. Does Old Glory, which has flown on its own since the Revolutionary War, need a constitutional amendment for protection? But never mind—the flag flies everywhere in 2001. Patriotism is our secular religion.

In January 1994, President Clinton made his first major trip to troubled Europe and all of the world covered the historic meetings. But many Americans were watching another story—the Bobbitt trial in Manassas, Virginia.

By severing her husband's penis, Lorena Bobbitt had created an ir-resistible media event. Sixteen satellite-uplink trucks and hundreds of reporters invaded the quiet village. T-shirts, posters, and buttons were on sale (sporting wry slogans such as, "Lorena for Surgeon General").

Over 2,000 stories about the event soon appeared. Lorena was fea-tured in *Vanity Fair* in a sexy bathing suit. A radio station gave away Slice soda and cocktail wienies. In Lorena Bobbitt's native Ecuador, a feminist group threatened to castrate a hundred American men if she served any time. CNN, carrying the trial live, doubled its ratings and was flooded with complaints when it switched to the Russian summit. Bobbitt-mania had become America's fad of the moment.

Who can say how certain events grab the public's imagination and sweep through the media like wildfire? Of the thousands of stories in-volving millions of people, why do one or two make it to the top? And once there, why do they disappear so quickly? What part do human nature, modern culture, and the media play in all this?

Each new top story has its own twist and personality. Consider the flare-up surrounding Tonya Harding, an American ice skater in the 1994 Winter Olympics. Now that she has moved on into oblivion, we might ask: was her story a parody or a tragedy? She was accused, and later convicted, of being involved in a plot to damage the legs of her arch ri-val, Nancy Kerrigan, thus enhancing Tonya's chances of winning the gold medal and all the acclaim and endorsements that would follow.

Instead, she tried to short cut the path to celebrity and ended up a good example of another American platitude: Crime does not pay. The story has an ending worthy of a Greek tragedy. Pleading inno-cent, despite all the evidence and near conviction, she still skated in the Olympics. She was photographed wearing a T-shirt with the in-scription: NO COMMENT. She was going for the gold.

It was not to be. She faltered and failed on the ice, then broke down (to quote George Vecsey in *The New York Times,* "from collective na-tional disbelief, betrayed by her laces"). Tonya Harding personified our worst fears, the old Broken Shoelaces Nightmare.[4]

She showed no grace in defeat. Our last view of her at the Olym-pics was looking down at the ice rink from the viewer's stand where a triumphant Nancy Kerrigan was winning a silver medal. Tonya was crying, out of breath, hooked up to a breathing machine.

Tonya's fifteen minutes of fame were over. She was no longer the person of the moment, and the reporters and television crews quickly left, as they had with O. J. Simpson. No more hourly updates on television, no more rallies with posters and flowers. Her fame had gone with the wind.

One cannot gloat over anyone's misfortune, and I do not intend to be Tonya Harding's judge or jury. But I do blame the media for creating a pseudoevent, exploiting it, and then forcing it down our throats.

A pseudoevent is manufactured news, staged not to inform but to entrap. It is the way our media managers spoon-feed a news-hungry nation and make mountains out of molehills. The quickie titillates but does not educate; tabloid journalism thrives on quickies.

In this instance, CBS seems most culpable. Having sponsored the American television coverage, CBS was determined to increase interest and suspense—via Tonya Harding. Pulling out every stop, the network gave Harding far more time than she deserved; they even sent her over to Norway with CBS's Connie Chung, presumably to catch every word, every sigh. The climax was an in-depth interview in which Harding would tell all—on CBS. It was the television parody of the year. When the interview was held, Harding was so offended by the questions that she took off her microphone and left the studio. Finally even poor Tonya was fed up. So was America.

We have a long history of pseudoevents and manufactured tearjerkers, and they continue in our New Age. How we agonized over whether Liz Taylor should marry for the sixth (or was it the seventh) time! We had to know how Oprah Winfrey lost sixty pounds. Could she keep it off? She could and did. In 2000, a slick new ad-filled publication—*O: The Oprah Magazine*—was the flavor of the month. The founder and editorial director was Oprah Winfrey, of course. A series of tear-outs featured her smiling face and many new ventures. The theme of her July 2000 issue was "Live in the Moment! It's Our Mission." A special section is called "Phenomenal Women," and an upbeat article by then-first lady Hillary Clinton fitted the theme. Is it true, as the media speculated, that Oprah is the richest woman in America? Ah, celebrity!

Although television talk shows and sports stadiums create instant celebrities (can you name the outstanding play in last year's Super Bowl?), the silver screen remains the best breeding ground for celebrities—especially if we include the smaller screen in our living room, the television screen. The annual Oscars create each year's new celebrities. If a film wins several Oscars—as *Titanic* did in 1997—not only the actors and directors but even the sunken ship can become famous.

The movie or television camera can bring stardom not just to people but to animals (we all remember Morris the cat and Lassie—oldies remember Rin Tin Tin or the Lone Ranger's horse, Silver), fabricated models (the Ziegfeld girl, Hugh Hefner's bunnies), places (Las Vegas's Strip, New York's Times Square or the Southern plantation).

The much-glamorized plantation peaked in popularity in the nineteenth century, when cotton was king. If Tara, in *Gone with the Wind,* created in fiction and materialized in Hollywood, is the main example, many others exist. Look at the tourist brochures from Southern states or from cities touting historic homes around Charleston, Savannah, Biloxi, New Orleans, Tallahassee, or Richmond. The glamour didn't die.[5]

There are lavish amusement parks such as Carowinds in South Carolina, Dollywood in Tennessee, or Six Flags over Georgia; a rack of the latest sex-and-slavery paperback novels; Colonel Sanders and his fried chicken; hundreds of "Old Plantation" motels and restaurants; or the phenomenon of a sequel to *Gone with the Wind* (as well at the unparalleled publicity given to the 1976 television rerun of the film). The plantation of the antebellum South has become a central image—however inadequate or inaccurate—of what the South has been and, for many, still is. It has achieved celebrity status.

As for popular music, Tin Pan Alley for many years took us to the plantation to enjoy beautiful belles, honeysuckle, mint juleps, sunny skies, and a life of leisure. Three good examples from the early twentieth century: "Away Down South in Heaven," "Anything Is Nice If It Comes from Dixie Land," and "You're Living Right Next Door to Heaven When You Live in Dixieland."

Hugh Hefner is a male celebrity who had a longer-than-usual run—though he, too, has gone now into the long good night. Hefner not only created *Playboy* magazine and its "world," but the people to inhabit it. Working at *Esquire* as a promotion copywriter after having served in World War II, Hefner was making fifty dollars a week in 1951. Refusing a raise, he quit to start a new magazine. He got the first issue together on a bridge table in his kitchen. With no support, Hugh Hefner had only $7,000 when he published the first issue of

Playboy. It wasn't dated, since he feared there might never be a second. Within a decade, with a circulation of over 2 million and a notorious reputation worldwide, the man and the magazine were global celebrities. What was his secret?

In Russia, the leading satirical magazine, *Krokodil,* provided one answer. The editors praised *Playboy* because Hefner's imagination was "indeed inexhaustible." Meanwhile, Italy, Germany, and France arranged for their own foreign editions of *Playboy,* edited and printed in Milan, Paris, and Munich. By 1970, a typical holiday issue of *Playboy* had 350 pages. In America, more money was spent buying it at newsstands than had ever been spent during a thirty-day period for any event in the field of paid entertainment.

"The Playboy Model"—actually a stereotype—caught fire in a nation weaned on austerity but ready for hedonism. Hefner was willing to "let it all hang out"—well, almost all—viewing the world through the eyes of a sophisticated, urbane, affluent, promiscuous, mature bachelor. This goal, scholars have suggested, is "what most Americans have long desired as a perfect style of life."[6]

The real celebrity was not Hefner, but the *Playboy* rabbit. (Similarly, Mickey Mouse, and not his creator, was the message.) The rabbit, an ever-present symbol for Hefner, was always dressed in expensive, fashionable clothes, off to enjoy such "in" activities as yachting, skin diving, nightclubbing, or racing foreign sports cars. Sexy girls, scantily clad, were always nearby, but they didn't seem to unnerve him. His eyes remained half-closed in a bored fashion; his mouth turned up slightly at the corners, reflecting smug self-satisfaction. Here, at last, was a rabbit of the world.

Playboy was more than mere diversion and fantasy. Every issue taught the readers symbols, styles, and rituals of a real playboy; the attitudes, beliefs, and gestures that are required. The key was "cool but active sophistication."

To give substance to their reveries, men bought keys for *Playboy* Clubs in various American cities. While the magazine appealed largely to a college-age audience, the Clubs served an older clientele—men who didn't mind paying to ogle "bunnies" who served as waitresses and hostesses. A lucky few could go right to Hefner's Chicago home and watch "bunnies" swim nude in his great glass pool. In this world, clock and calendar were redundant. Night could be day,

Tuesday could be Saturday, if one had the cool and the courage to control his environment.

To be a celebrity in Playboyland one had to be multidimensional; up on the latest authors and theories; equally at home at diplomatic receptions and hippie beer bashes. The whole process was full of wish fulfillment and reinforcement. Here was a way to make the scene, to be the talk of the town.

Hugh Hefner's star faded in the early 1980s. Hard-core pornography was becoming more readily available, and the spicier approach passed him by. In addition, a powerful antipornography movement swept across America, and *Playboy's* advertising plunged over 60 percent in 1985.

What saved *Playboy* was Hefner's level-headed and shrewd daughter Christie, who extended the *Playboy* brand to television, built a catalog division selling videos, CDs, and DVDs, and (in the early 1990s) brought the company into pay-per-view. Widescreen entertainment took over where publishing had faltered. In 1995, Hefner acquired Spice Entertainment, a soft-porn pay-per-view, which helped too. By 1997, operating income was up 66 percent, stock price up 70 percent.[7]

By then, Hugh Hefner seemed like a figure from another world with his notorious bunnies and much-publicized orgy room in his quasi-baronial Chicago manse. Christie doesn't see much of her father these days; she's too busy making money, setting the pace for Oprah.

National culture is being replaced like the horse and buggy when the automobile arrived, a synthetic substance that exists in the media. "Entertainment" is never just entertaining, being chock-full of attitude-forming information. Ads both sell and shape. Not the illusion of progress but the illusion of technique ensnares us. Not our jobs but the texture of our personalities is endangered by the lifestyle.

The new American imago is couched not in terms of causes or events but in images picked up by our constant involvement in vicarious activities of the human race all over the world. In this sense, our celebrities are exported, on film and paper, all over the world. They, in turn, are affected by and sensitive to their global audience.[8]

Mass media (especially television and block-buster films) have greatly increased the visibility of entertainers and inflated their importance. Publicists know that the best way to succeed is to put entertainers on a pedestal that overshadows rational objects of respect and affection. The line between hero, artist, and salesman has blurred.[9]

Nineteenth-century robber barons grabbed natural resources and staged "The Great Barbecue." Today, we have television and show business robber barons who go beyond the old truism that business is business—now show business is show business.

These techniques affect politics, art, journalism, criticism, and education. Image making is revealed in almost everything we do, say, or see. Television is chewing gum for the eyes. The question is no longer "Do you like me?" but "Do you like my shadow?" Like the people in Plato's allegorical cave, we mix illusion and reality, mistaking the shadows for ourselves. We turn from the three-dimensional emancipator toward the two-dimensional entertainer.

The boom in professional sports (especially football, basketball, and hockey) has created scores of new celebrities. Professional sports is a carousel world where movement, music, lights, and hysteria hypnotize. Here is something we can all observe, interpret, and judge. We can immerse ourselves emotionally and viscerally in sports, which will play an increasingly important role in popular culture and celebrity making.

Not only players but sports themselves come and go—changes in fads and styles are complicated. We know little at this time about measuring the changing audience, the evolving aesthetic, and the heroic climate. Easy come, easy go. A new sign and image is conjured up somehow out of the subconscious. People under thirty usually accept the urban world forced upon them—not the world that Daniel Boone pioneered or Henry David Thoreau eulogized, but the world of neon light, billboards, comic strips, and strippers. The television commercial is the new lingua franca. The unreality of the environment is what makes it seem so real.

Pop style, from which celebrities emerge, makes of the phony an epiphany. Shallowness, repetition, and frustration are all built into the model. Andy Warhol today might be the best-known artist in the world. People laughed when Warhol said that someday everyone would be famous for fifteen minutes. After all, Warhol was a trendy lightweight who came up with clever phrases: "I want to be a machine." "I like to be bored." Once cryptic, he became cultic. Painter, photographer, filmmaker, social arbiter, celebrity, Andy found the theme that defined a generation: passive disenchantment. As for popular culture, he ate the whole thing.

He might have done much more: with the opening of the Andy Warhol Museum in Pittsburgh in 1994, critics began to see him in a different light and with a new appreciation. He created an art that would be meaningless to anyone who didn't know it was made from and about photographs. But the photograph may supply the credibility to the twentieth century that Greco-Roman images did for the Renaissance. If the antiquities provided one age with beauty, photographers provide our age with truth. "He turned to photographs of stars," David Sylvester wrote in London's *Independent* on Sunday, May 22, 1994, "as the Renaissance turned to antiquities, to find images of gods."10 Who were his gods and goddesses? The pantheon of pop culture: Marilyn Monroe, Elizabeth Taylor, Jackie Kennedy, Elvis Presley—and Warhol himself.

Warhol's love of repetition and standardization were mirror images of our popular culture. He said he was painting this way because he wanted to be a machine.11 He noted that in the United States the richest consumer buys the same things as the poorest: Everybody drinks Coke.

Warhol followed the dictum of that most famous and elite or modern architects, Mies van der Rohe: Less is more. He invites us not only to look at his work, but also to contemplate it. In so doing, Warhol moves us beyond pop to Zen. And he couched it all in a single phrase: Fifteen-Minute Culture.

What then to make of all this? Are celebrities pivotal—even essential—to popular culture? Why the sudden explosion in the celebrity cult? Have they taken the place of our heroes? Are they now at the heart of the American dream? This much is certain: media exposure—especially television commercials, which can turn a great basketball player such as Michael Jordan into the television ad super star—favors celebrities over heroes. Was the black heavyweight boxer who began as Cassius Clay and then became Muhammad Ali a celebrity or a hero? Alternately, he was a pseudopoet, buffoon, world champion, and special presidential envoy to Africa. Ali defied the old categories.

Nothing better demonstrates the increased power and persuasiveness of electronic media than a comparison of blonde goddess celebrity of the 1950s, Marilyn Monroe, to her successor in the 1970s,

Farrah Fawcett. She is the ultimate hype. Coming to Hollywood from Texas in 1966 (she was chosen most beautiful freshman at the University of Texas), Farrah was shaped by publicist David Mirisch, agent Dick Clayton, talent coach Renee Valente, and hairdresser Hugh York. With a baroque hairstyle and a toothy smile, Farrah took off. A spot on a detective series called *Charlie's Angels* exposed her to millions; Farrah had developed "now" talents, such as karate, and she wore no bra. Contracts were hastily negotiated for dolls, deodorants, posters, clothes, public appearances, books, autograph parties, television guest shots, magazine covers, cosmetics conferences, and T-shirts. Having starred in *Charlie's Angels* for one season, she got movie contracts, modeling contracts, and products contracts. Farrah left her television series with agents and managers. She had attained the American dream: She was a celebrity.

This means being everywhere, being beautiful, and being admired by all. You saw Farrah Fawcett everywhere because she was a celebrity and vice versa. Her face, hands, hair, and breasts sold everything because they included her. America was obsessed with her because America knew her; she was the most well-known person of all well-known people. She was famous for being famous—for a little while.

Making celebrities is a national obsession. Since 1974, three major magazines (*People, Us,* and *Celebrity*) have been created to fuel the celebrity boom. They update earlier publications such as *Photoplay, Modern Screen, Motion Picture,* and *Modern Movie*. Favorite topics never change: everyday life of the stars; unhappiness and infidelity of the stars; sex and the new morality.

How many celebrities are there? It is hard to say. Some are gone before you can count them. Earl Blackwell and Cleveland Amory compiled a *Celebrity Register* with 2,200 brief biographies. Their criterion for inclusion is simple. All you have to do is weigh press clippings.

Sometimes someone who seems to be a genuine hero ends up a celebrity—Charles Lindbergh, for example. Some become celebrities merely by being born: England's Prince Charles or Canada's Dionne quintuplets. Certain names denote wealth or power in their own right. Who would challenge a check signed by a Carnegie or Rockefeller, for example?

People have become celebrities by climbing up the sides of buildings or jumping over canyons on motorcycles. There are even those who become celebrities merely by associating with celebrities. Then they can go on television talk shows and let the world see them. Oprah, Jay, Conan, or Dave will host the event. Then their phones will start ringing, and they will be offered the chance to sell panty hose, sleeping pills, and shaving lotion. Who knows how high their stars may rise? Or when new celebrities will pop up and replace them?

Students of popular culture ponder this and realize that any new age is in some way a replay of the old. The Greeks thought that there was nothing new under the sun, and Indian philosophers have long maintained that the best way to understand culture is to think in circles. Does all this apply to celebrities?

How will our celebrities thrive in the newly emerging Global Village? Will they appear and disappear at different times and in different places? Will they be part of a vast global junkyard? Are we becoming, as Walter Ong suggests, part of the exterior activities everywhere?[12]

Other intriguing questions arise. Can the mass media move celebrities around like figures on a chess board? Will the lines between hero, celebrity, and salesperson merge?[13]

The nineteenth-century robber barons grabbed our natural resources and became both clebrities and moguls. Business is business. Now show business is business. By their celebrities shall ye know and note them.

The popular imagination is plagued by extravagant expectations. We expect anything and everything. Masters of entertainment industry work day and night to oblige: a television spectacular every week, a literary masterpiece every month, a new celebrity every season. The 1976 bicentennial was a national orgy of celebrities and celebration.

Celebrities are part of the American daydream, suspended between the long shadows of Rousseau and Darwin. We are eternally drained by our allegiances to natural man, on the one hand, and to naturalistic man, on the other. Pioneer-believer at the same time we are pioneer-brute, we see every log cabin as a potential Shangri-La, knowing that the land is dark and bloody ground. We want both at the same time. The double want can never be satisfied and turns out to be a lasting crucifixion. The nails that bite the flesh from the outside turn out to be inside. Self-destruction is self-generated.

The most ephemeral field, by everyone's admission, is popular music. Rock groups are hardly in before they are out. As a group ritual, the rock concert persists, but the faces of those staging it change constantly.14 *Billboard,* the industry's chief trade journal, predicted in June 1975 that no major trend threatened. Wrong. Suddenly, disco burst on the scene, by 1977 virtually owning *Billboard's* record charts. *Saturday Night Fever,* a movie released in December 1977, made the prizewinning statement about the new rage:

> With a racially and ethnically-integrated cast and musical soundtrack as a backdrop, the hero and the heroine (John Travolta and Karen Lynn Gorney) meet, dance, pair off, dance, flirt, dance—all on the urban disco floor. . . .15

Soon disco was the dominant background music on television programs, commercials, and movie sound tracks. An estimated 10,000 new dance clubs opened, with spotlights, flashing colors, costumes, high-volume music, and special effects (such as laser beams and fog machines). Had we finally found a dance form in which everyone could be a celebrity?

On the sidelines, fans of former celebrities recalled how fickle Dame Fortune is. Take the case of the king himself, Elvis Presley. His 250 million records sold and thirty-one popular movies seemed to guarantee him a lifelong adulation. As it turned out, life was not to be long. At forty-two, Presley was dead, apparently of a drug overdose. A host of imitators scrambled to fill his shoes.

Can astronomers, who themselves are becoming celebrities at the beginning of the twenty-first century, cast any light on our problem? I think they can.

A new school of much-celebrated astronomers now believes that somewhere out there—far, far away, beyond a new universe which they "discovered" in 1999—is a black hole of unimaginable size and depth. Into it, suns, moons, and planets simply disappear. Like the Big Bang, their popular tag for the scientific theory of creation, we have a mystery. How can stars and planets just disappear? Where do they go?

I dare not suggest an answer, but I will draw a comparison. Our celebrities are like those stars (in fact, that's what we call them). When they disappear from the talk shows, CNN and new television ads, do they too end up in a black hole?

From Humbuggery to Hype

There's a sucker born every minute.

P.T. Barnum

Humbuggery and hype are alive and well in the third millennium. Seldom discussed or denounced, they are fast-spreading viruses influencing our popular culture.

No one knows where the term *humbug* originated. Appearing in English writings in the 1750s, humbug points to a hoax, fraud, or deception. Many encountered it when Scrooge spat out his disclaimer of Christmas in Charles Dickens's *A Christmas Carol:* "Bah! Humbug!"

Fewer recall that Dickens's Mr. Bottom uses it in the first chapter of *The Pickwick Papers:* "He had merely considered him a humbug in a Pickwickian point of view."

We find humbug in many other passages of literature. George Bernard Shaw used it in his song, "My Irish":

> And as far as angels' laughter
> In the smelly Liffy's tide
> Well, my Irish daddy said it,
> But the dear old humbug lied.

America's master of humbuggery was Phineas T. Barnum (1810-1891). Others denied their humbuggery—Barnum flaunted his, calling himself "The Prince of Humbugs." This father of modern public relations wrote many books explaining and justifying his ways. In this he has had no equal.[1]

Barnum began his career by purchasing and exhibiting Joice Heth, a black woman alleged to be 160 years old and George Washington's nurse. Immediate success allowed him to buy Scudder's Museum in New York City. Six years later, he renamed it Barnum's American Museum, full of oddities, freaks, exotic animals, curios, and dioramas. Later there was much more: Tom Thumb, "The Midget Marvel;" Jenny Lind, "The Sweet Songbird from Europe;" and New Yorkers' first live hippopotamus. Soon Barnum was rich and famous.

There was more to Barnum than humbuggery. In East Bridgeport, Connecticut, he developed a model industrial and workers' community. He followed a strict moral code of showmanship, gave the public all it paid for, kept his shows free from all indecencies, and led a completely respectable personal life. Many humbug followers of Barnum can make no such claims.

In 1871, at sixty-one, Barnum made the leap that would guarantee his fame. He bought a circus, billed it "The Greatest Show on Earth," and started making it just that. By adding a second and even a third ring, Barnum delighted and awed the public with more entertainment than they could absorb. In 1881, he joined up with his rival, James A. Bailey. Barnum and Bailey became the ham and eggs, coffee and cream, hot dog and mustard, of the entertainment world. It carries on in the twenty-first century, as Ringling Brothers Barnum and Bailey Circus.

I can still remember when their circus train came into Roanoke, Virginia, during my boyhood. We got up at dawn to watch the animals unloaded from their cages—real lions and tigers—then paraded through town to the fairgrounds, as the steam calliope belted out circus music. Few childhood events gave me such a thrill. This was, indeed, the greatest show on earth.

Of course, there were great shows and humbugs earlier and everywhere. New studies show that hucksters, self-promoters, and swindlers flourished in earlier centuries, especially the eighteenth and nineteenth.[2] Some of the leading artists of the twentieth century, such as Marcel Duchamp, Andre Breton, and Salvador Dalí gave us antiart art and ironic playfulness, tinted with humbug. Their tradition flourished in the United States with such people as the artist-prankster Joey Skaggs. His notorious and outrageous humbuggery included packaging the "Roach Hormone," a miracle drug to cure acne and arthritis; and "Portafess," a mobile confessional booth which he set up at various political convention sites. He even advertised a fictitious canine bordello where, for $50, your male dog could be serviced by "Fifi," a pedigreed French poodle.

Perhaps you think no one would take people like Skaggs seriously? Look at the ads running in newspapers and on television screens—white-coated "authorities" promise to cure whatever ails you from cramps to cancer, restore your hair, reduce your cholesterol, increase your sexual vigor, and harness the mysterious forces of life. What happens to such postmodern people? Many of them get rich. They never run out of suckers.

* * *

The world of Barnum never really faded away, but it did move from the tent to the movie house and television screen. Hollywood took over in the early twentieth century and moved forward with super-movies, giant pageants, and visual extravaganzas. This suburb of Los Angeles got a new nickname, Tinseltown, as movie moguls replaced earlier small-time tricksters. They invented a new name for their medium, the magic screen, and perfected the "star" system, still a cornerstone of popular culture.

The spectacular rise of the movies at home and abroad is a colorful and well-known story.[3] With maximum sunshine, mild temperatures, varied terrain, packaged glamour, and a fine labor market, Hollywood attracted talent from around the world. It still does.

Peep shows turned into movies in the 1890s. The first one-reeler, a "real movie," was Edwin S. Porter's *The Great Train Robbery* in 1903. In 1912, Adolph Zukor imported a four-reeler, *Queen Elizabeth*, from England for $18,000 and made $80,000 in return. The era of the feature film was off and running.

In 1914, Cecil B. DeMille, Jesse Lasky, and Samuel Goldwyn produced *The Squaw Man*. In 1915, D. W. Griffith released the innovative and controversial *The Birth of a Nation*. New studios and films followed, led by Adolph Zukor, William Fox, Samuel Goldwyn, and Louis B. Mayer. The names of early "stars" such as Charlie Chaplin, Rudolph Valentino, Gloria Swanson, Lillian Gish, and Tom Mix became household names. They helped create a worldwide market. Hollywood's Golden Era got underway. Ballyhoo triumphed and is still with us.

The origin of the word *ballyhoo* is obscure, but the meaning is now part of popular parlance: blatant, extravagant advertising or publicity; clamor or outcry. Among the many recent books reflecting Hollywood ballyhoo are: Geoff Gehman, *Down But Not Quite Out in Holly-weird: A Documentary in Letters of Eric Knight* (Scarecrow Press, 1998); Alan Betrock, *Bikinis and Lingerie: A Pictorial Guide to Pin-Up Magazines* (Shake Books, 1998); Hans J. Wollstein, *Vixens, Floozies, and Molls* (McFarland, 1998); Seriden McCloud, *Hollywood Lovers: The Raunchy Revelations of Tinseltown's Rich, Famous, and Beautiful People* (Orion Group, 1998); and John M. Wilson, *Inside Hollywood* (Writer's Digest Books, 1998). "Fan magazines" (now called fanzines), television pitchmen, and used car salesmen are often masters of ballyhoo.

Like all golden ages, Hollywood's didn't last. In popular culture, nothing causes failure like too much success. With it comes complacency, extravagance, and arrogance. New technology creates new audiences and ballyhoo. New ideas force old ones into decline and finally oblivion.

Grown fat and rich from decades of domination, Hollywood's movie studios were not prepared for the advent of television after World War II. Suddenly, millions of people were staying at home to watch the "magic box," free entertainment, instead of going out and paying to see movies. When a series of court decisions judged the major Hollywood studios to be trusts in restraint of trade, movie revenues and prospects plummeted. Wider screens, richer colors, new lenses, and stereophonic sound helped, but the "great days" had passed.

Many fine films were made overseas. Signing new contracts with television productions helped movies to retrieve some of their old power. By 1980, computers, VCRs, and compact discs were growing ever stronger.

In *Understanding Media: The Extensions of Man* (1964), Marshall McLuhan called television an extension of our central nervous system, which would affect the totality of our lives. He was right. So was anthropologist Margaret Mead, who knew that we can now see history being made and not remade in Hollywood: space flights, inaugurations, natural disasters, wars underway, all come live to our homes through television.[4] This presentation of actuality outmoded edited views of reality, arranged by filmmakers and writers. Television would change the whole nature of humbuggery and ballyhoo. A new popular form of television blossomed in 2000, "reality television." This genre attempts to show how people will "really act" under extreme pressure—but with multiple cameras on them. It was still show biz, bogus reality.

Ballyhoo, like humbug, is fluid and adaptable. Herman Melville used the term in his 1847 novel *Omoo:* "Steer clear of this ballyhoo of blazers as long as ye live." Today, the word best applies to bombastic nonsense in the media and politics and money scams.

Ballyhoo flourishes at the point where materialism, capitalism, and new technology intersect, conjuring up images of ringing bells, flying flags, parades, bared bosoms, and wild sex. Favorite adjectives are sensational, tremendous, and gorgeous.

Harry Haun writes of "Broadway Ballyhoo" in *Playbill* (March 31, 1997); Don Shewey of "Ballyhoo and Daisy, Too" in *American Theatre* (April 1, 1997); K. E. Grund on "Ballyhoo or Breakthrough?" in *Endoscopy* (February 1997); Rochelle Stanfield on "Ballyhooing the Bachelor's Degree" in *National Journal* (May 1997). *Playboy* put out a special issue on "Ballyhoo Boo-Boo and Boondoggling" in July 1995. The list goes on and on.

Ballyhoo is not confined to Hollywood, Broadway, and the entertainment empire. It invades all aspects of our lives, having found a fertile home in the new technology. We wonder how it got started. We can be so mesmerized by externals that deeper lasting changes go unnoticed. This has been true for centuries.

HYPE

Give the people light and they will find their way.

Thomas Jefferson

Give the people hype and they will lose their way.

Marshall Fishwick

America, land of the red, white, and blue, has undergone dramatic color changes. We have lived in one lifetime a series of cultural changes in America, each marked by trendy new slogans and popular best-sellers. Other alarming things have occurred: the selling, tricking, glutting, malling, and trashing of our homeland. We are finally seeing that all these labels are subsets of the mother gerund: hyping. First, we shall try to define it, then ask how to expunge it. Is there hope after hype?

* * *

A popular term extending humbug and ballyhoo is hype. Short for "hyper," a prefix implying excess and exaggeration, it flourishes in our New Age, day and night, flowing like a mighty river. We are confronted by banner ads, mass murders, frightening headlines, and media hyping of shopping, travel, entertainment, and kitsch. The pixels roar, demanding your attention. Here, there, everywhere, ads pop up like weeds or prairie dogs. An era of fear-mongering, sometimes headed by televangelists, Greenpeace, Consumers Union, diet gurus, health care planners, and doom-sayers of all persuasions. All hype.

Save time and money on the Internet? Want to buy a Hermès tie directly from France? Steve Homer tried it. Search engine Altavista.com turned up 788 new sites with key words *Hermes* and *tie*. After four hours of searching, the best he could do was get the phone number of a shop in Texas that might carry Hermès. Poor Steve had been hyped.

Following up on my computer, I searched around and made a startling discovery: there are over 800 "hype" entries, covering a massive range of topics, ideas, and situations. "Hype" has become an overused bit of jargon, a cliché that has lost clear or coherent meaning.[5]

Thomas Jefferson wrote: "Give the people light and they will find their way." We can write a new version: "Give the people hype and they will lose their way."

Hype has a partner, glut. We swim, flounder, and sink in it. The World Wide Web has unlimited space for advertising and is always hype-heavy. Radio and television operate with finite space and air time. At key times on television, such as the during Super Bowl, a thirty-second ad can cost $1.6 million. Has the Super Bowl become our super hype, in the land of superpower, superdome, and superstar? Is football taking on the role of organized religion, with sports fans (short for "fanatics") becoming pilgrims in the new crusades to Super Bowl? Instead of the Sunday service we have the Sunday game. Your "offering" is a high-priced ticket.

The game is only the eye of the storm. Tidal waves come first in books, magazines, television specials, and endorsements. Only a limited number can sit in the stadium; but millions can watch on television, which allows you to see the "magic moments" on instant replay time and again. A miracle!

The extent of the hype is noticeable when one studies the clock. Pre-game and postgame activities consume 20 percent of the television time, advertising another 15 percent, between plays and halftime another 40 percent. Much of the remaining 25 percent scoreboard time goes for huddles, decisions, and penalties. During the four-hour telecast, there is less than ten minutes when the football is actually in motion. The over-hyped Super Bowl has been turned into a celebration of dominant emotions and lifestyles of America.

Other sports, such as tennis, golf, and soccer, long described as "minor," have lately earned big-time hype. Women's soccer is a fine example. Between 1990 and 2000, over 100,000 girls began playing soccer. Spin doctors responded, and "soccer moms" were targeted by politicians. The climax came on July 11, 1999, when the U.S. women's soccer team defeated China for the championship. Headlines like this quickly followed:

> U.S. Women Rule the World!
> World Cup Fields New Role Models!

Bill and Hillary Clinton were among the 90,184 spectators on hand to cheer the team. But the center of attention was on player Brandi Chastain, who took off her shirt to reveal her new soccer bra to the whole world. Then she clenched both fists and let out a mighty yell. The picture ended up on the cover of *Sports Illustrated, Newsweek,* and other publications around the world. Only later did we learn that the victory shout had been carefully planned, with Nike Corporation supplying the bra. When Nike rushed a new line of sports bras into production, sales rose 25 percent in one week. Nike competitors, like Reebok and Fila, quickly produced their own versions, estimating that Chastain's seminudity would do wonders for the $230 million-a-year market. They expected "exponential growth."

Chastain had a prior contract, revealed as "in five figures"; but her agent promised to renegotiate for much more. Meanwhile, soccer equipment firms, television talk show hosts, cereal box designers, all cashed in on the soccer frenzy. Soccer has become big money and big business.

In *The Joy of Sports,* Michael Novak calls sports our natural religion and morality play. The holy trinity is still football, baseball, and basketball. Today's spectators and "fans" perform a sacramental act, which their ancestors experienced by going to church. The stadium is our new place of sanctity. Let us pay.

* * *

Internet publishing is yet another new rage, with the top publishers holding 70 percent of ad revenues and everyone else scrambling to share in the profits. The ultimate promise of the Internet is to generate television-sized audiences and still target a single individual. A new opportunity for hype?

Time-tested forms of hyping abound. Special interest groups, consultants, news analysts, radio and television ad agencies know them well. Regions, such as the "Sunny South" or the "Golden West," have long been hyped, to get millions of immigrants to leave their native lands and come to America's "streets of gold," endless boom times, and good jobs. Hype promises hope but often delivers only despair.

A hype by any other name is still a hype. Clever publicists call it disinformation, rather than information. Those who fabricate falsehoods are spin-doctors; those who believe it become pundits. Another term for what we are describing is pseudoevent.

Walter Lippman identified it in his 1922 book, *Public Opinion.* There are vast differences, he noted, in the real world outside and the pictures we have in our heads. We oversimplify in order to understand; we have false (or stereotypic) ideas of "Japanese," "African Americans," "Harvard Men," and "agitators" and many other things. We can defend our prejudices by forming easily grasped images— hence, another form of humbuggery.

When Lippman wrote this, pseudoevents had not flooded the culture. The classic analysis appeared in 1962, in Daniel Boorstin's *The Image: Or What Happened to the American Dream.*[6] Pseudoevents, Boorstin wrote, are not things that happened on their own, but were made to happen, to suit someone's needs and strategy. A pseudoevent is not spontaneous, but planned, planted, or incited. The purpose is to have it reported or reproduced; success is measured by how widely this is done. The ambiguity of a pseudoevent makes it newsworthy. Pseudoevents try to be self-fulfilling prophecies. Once out, the pseudoevent can expand indefinitely and geometrically.

Take this example: A neighbor sees a baby in its carriage, and says to the mother: "What a lovely baby!" The mother replies: "That's nothing. You ought to see the photograph!" Now the "photograph" or image, shown countless times on television, Internet, and print, takes command.

Why and how can pseudoevents overshadow real events? There are several reasons. Pseudoevents are often more dramatic, more easily circulated, and can be repeated at will. There is a driving force behind them. Time and money have gone into the making; makers want returns.

If all goes well and well-laid plans work out, pseudoevents become the standard way of "being informed," or on top of things. We want to have all the facts—and end up getting some facts plus fiction. Pseudoevents spread like an epidemic. Daniel Boorstin posits a new Gresham's law of American public life. Counterfeit events drive the real ones out of circulation.[7] Hype-masters know this and act accordingly.

New technology—ever faster, all penetrating—has made this flood of unreality omnipresent. The increased speed of printing was revolutionary but can't match electronic speed. We crossed the gulf from daguerreotype to color television in less than a century. Eastman's Kodak appeared in 1888, Edison's radio patent a year later. Motion pictures arrived, as did the first radio voice transmission, around 1900. Television entered the American home in the 1950s. The Information Revolution, based on computer technology and fiber optics, changed the world in the 1980s and has accelerated ever since.

All this was mirrored in popular culture. The dimensions and depth of the changes won't be apparent for years, but their profundity is already obvious.

Hype can be compared to a thunderstorm—the thunder of promoters, the lightning of the sound bites, the gusty wind of people spreading the word and adding to the turbulence. But hype hasn't produced a single new giant, like P. T. Barnum with his humbuggery. We do have new popular culture categories: hype masters and spin doctors. They make their living (often fortunes) by knowing when and how to hype winners, filtering them out from a vast field of losers. Their promotional tactics vary widely, and Lady Luck often determines success or failure. They try to control the flow of information, building a golden glow; winning over reporters, television anchors, and talk show hosts to their point of view; spending big money on "exclusive" parties or conferences. They have product stars, often beautiful slim young women who smile at the world from giant video screens, showing pearly-white teeth. They must be first: first to spot the hot company or product, first to release the big story to mainstream media, first to make predictions, first to strangle the competition, first to lure the audience or customer.

Hype happens. Two examples show how hype masters work. Kim Polese, an attractive young woman, CEO of start-up Marimba, is hired to hype high tech. She became a glamour figure in the industry—an industry dominated by middle-aged males. She appears in glamorous photographs, her face softly lit and airbrushed, with an alluring smile. *Time* magazine includes her in its list of the twenty-five most influential Americans. That tag became a self-fulfilling prophecy. A star in Silicon Valley politics, she is invited to visit the White House with a lobbying group. Regular meetings with Vice President Al Gore follow, as well as a chance to collaborate with him on a public school project called Education Dashboard.

Back home, she is a fund-raiser for Bill Clinton—one of a small group who later meet with visiting dignitaries such as Russian Prime Minister Viktor Chernomyrdin. What next? An Anne Klein fashion ad, running in such magazines as *Vogue* and *Harper's Bazaar?* She is famous for being famous. A clever hype master becomes a celebrity.

Few can match the soaring success of Bill Gates, whose $50 million home has become a high-tech shrine. His story has often been told and hyped, especially by Gates himself. A typical ploy occurred on August 24, 1995, when talk-show host Jay Leno hosted the product launch of Gates's Windows 95, which everyone knew about months before-hand. Over 600 reporters turned up at Microsoft headquarters for the big event. Newspapers and magazines ran 3,670 stories. Microsoft, with other Windows supporters, spent more than $1 billion marketing their product by the end of 1995.

The Gates hype has continued, even accelerated, since then. In August 1999, he was acclaimed as the first person in history to head an enterprise worth more than $500 billion. Even federal charges of illegal monopoly practices in 2000 didn't slow him down.

Hypes were described as early as 1871 in Charles Mackay's book on *Extraordinary Popular Delusions and the Madness of Crowds.* Mackay described the Mississippi Scheme that swept France in 1720, the South Sea Bubble that devastated England, and the Dutch tulip mania when fortunes were made and lost not only on a single tulip bulb, but a portion of a bulb. Others' irrational exuberance baffles us; we hardly notice our own. Consider the degree of stock market madness in our postelectronic boom and subsequent bust.

Connections between humbuggery, ballyhoo, and hype cast light on our new technology and new age. They expand with an exploding economy. After years of unprecedented prosperity, we live in a time when enough is never enough. How much do we want and expect? We are never sure just what the "more" is; but the more we think about it, the more we need it, crave it. Then, in 2000, the bubble burst and the good times evaporated.

Historians note that good times are "more times." We wanted more in 1920s and the 1950s; more became less in the Great Depression of the 1930s and the grim war years of the 1940s. We tightened up a bit, too, in the 1970s—but opened the throttle in the 1990s. We forgot the old truism: What goes up must come down. Stocks tumbled and unemployment rose as blue skies got ever more gray. Suddenly, after the surprise bombing attacks on September 11, 2001, we were in a new era, a new kind of war. We didn't know where we were going, but we were on our way.

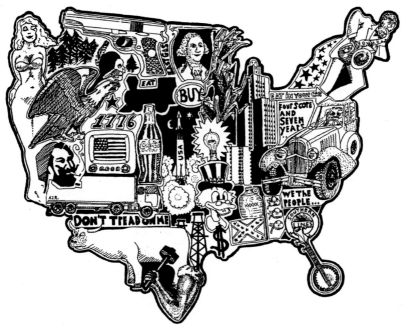

PHOTO 1. The United States can be seen as a mosaic in which images, symbols, myths, celebrities, and heroes evolve, intermingle, and overlap. The old must always make way for the new. The photos that follow illustrate how stark the contrast can be and what problems it creates. (Matthew R. Tamagni)

PHOTO 2. Every new age creates its buzzwords. Ours includes high style, gender equality, and sports. All three combine here at the Greenbrier, one of America's most stylish and expensive resorts, where tennis and golf are obsessions. (Courtesy of Robert S. Conte, Historian, The Greenbrier)

PHOTO 3. In nineteenth-century Lexington, Virginia, Michael Miley caught these four ladies looking out on the traditional Southern world that had been destroyed forever by the Civil War in which their husbands fought for the Confederacy. They are still dressed in black, the color of mourning. Compare them to the females featured in our twenty-first-century movies and advertisements. The shock of the new.

PHOTO 4. In twenty-first-century New York, another kind of war is raging: between the haves and the have-nots, the accepted and the rejected. Those who see no future in the new technocratic world resort to an ancient form of communication—sign-writing—and they leave their mark on any vacant space they can find. (Photo by Melissa J. Mineo)

PHOTO 5. Yesterday's ladies lived and dressed by strict codes, confined, of course, to class and status. This attire appears now only at costume balls and in lavish Hollywood movies. (Courtesy of Robert S. Conte, Historian, The Greenbrier)

PHOTO 6. Today's liberated women, on the other hand, reject the strict codes and restrictions of the past. They can deal with men as their feelings dictate, as this picture plainly shows.

PHOTO 7. Nineteenth-century travelers, on horseback or in stagecoaches, stopped frequently at the famous hotel in Crow, Virginia, where old-style cooking (in this fireplace) awaited them. Here, the author studies the chimney; the hotel and the guests are no more, but the massive stones remain as monuments to a popular shrine. (Photo by author)

PHOTO 8. In affluent times, when meals like this are prepared for the lords of cyberspace, cost is not the major factor. What we eat shows who and what we are. (Courtesy of Robert S. Conte, Historian, The Greenbrier)

PHOTO 9. Mrs. Charlsie Lester—eighty when this picture was taken—lived and died alone at Yellow Sulphur Springs near Blacksburg, Virginia. On this property, Confederate veterans—including General Jubal Early—retreated after Lee's surrender at Appomattox and founded the organization that still honors the fallen Confederacy. (Photo by author)

PHOTO 10. In any contemporary city, people and graffiti intermingle in what David Riesman calls *The Lonely Crowd*. (Photo by Melissa S. Mineo)

PHOTO 11. The American Constitution guarantees Americans the right to bear arms. They have been bearing them, in ever-greater abundance, ever since. (Photo by Melissa J. Mineo)

PHOTO 12. Men and women still pay to shoot guns—at clay pigeons—on the spacious grounds of the Greenbrier Hotel in West Virginia. In the nearby main hotel, a secret bunker was built in the 1950s to house Congress in case of a nuclear attack on Washington. From rifles to atomic bombs—all in a lovely sylvan setting. (Courtesy of Robert S. Conte, Historian, The Greenbrier)

PHOTO 13. This "Sketch and Scenery of Mr. Forest Springs, four mile from Christiansburg Montgomery County in a deep vallie," was drawn by Lewis Miller about 1850. (Courtesy of Robert S. Conte, Historian, The Greenbrier)

PHOTO 14. In a new century, spas and springs reflected the new affluence and splendor of an America leading the world in its economy and military strength. This is a view of the Greenbrier, not far from Mr. Forest Springs, but far apart in appearance and eminence. (Courtesy of Robert S. Conte, Historian, The Greenbrier)

PHOTO 15. In hard times, people have to eat cheap. During the Depression when this sign was erected, it meant that a family of six could eat for a dollar. (Photo by author)

PHOTO 16. A family of six in twenty-first-century New York City with a dollar to spend would starve to death. Their best bet would be to buy on the street—perhaps from this monkey. But could they hope for six hot dogs? Hardly. (Photo by Melissa J. Mineo)

PHOTO 17. Marshall Fishwick, the author, stands in downtown Cairo, Egypt, once the master of a great empire. The ancient monuments of the pyramids and the Sphinx were then the highest and most visible icons. Now that distinction belongs to 7Up and Pepsi. (Photo by author)

Surprise Attacks

May 4, 2000, dawned in much of the Western world as a balmy spring day. But for millions of Internet users, businesses, and governments, it ended in chaos and despair. A surprise e-mail attack known as the "Love Virus" assaulted computers world-wide. Worming its way in through e-mail, it cut e-mail communication as it swept through Asia, Europe, and North America. The self-replicating virus seemed to have no quick remedy; instead, it was an epidemic.

Who could resist opening an e-mail with a subject like "ILOVEYOU"? All the world loves love, for it makes the world go round. So claims popular culture, countless pop songs, movies, and more. The Beatles had it right: "All You Need Is Love." What television series could match *I Love Lucy,* or *The Love Boat?* And who could escape this virus?

Experts could only estimate how fast it spread and how much damage it caused. Reliable sources said it depleted files containing music, pictures, and programs that automate business, hitting 80 percent of the computers in Sweden, 70 percent in Germany, and 30 percent in England and the United States. Twenty countries were hit. By noon, there were seven new variations of the "love bug," causing damages ranging from $300 million to $10 billion. It gave a whole new meaning to the word *love.*

One of the intriguing aspects of this surprise attack is that it originated in a third world country—the Philippines—by a teenager who claimed he had "hit the wrong keys" and launched it by mistake. Think of the implications for future viruses: a surprise attack of devastating proportions from anyone—anywhere in the world!

* * *

June 14, 2000. The Wall Street wheelers and dealers were singing "Happy Days Are Here Again" in the morning; but soon they were singing a different tune. It would be known as "Black Wednesday in

Cyberland." The news resonated around the world. Typical headlines read:

> FBI Swoops Down on Wall Street Mob
> Wiretaps Reveal Mob Teams Up to Cheat Investors
> Farthest-Reaching Securities Fraud Ever

How was it done? Not with tommy guns and broken limbs, but on the Internet. Since at least 1995, the Bonanno, Colombo, Gambino, Genovese, and Luchese families had been infiltrating the stock market through computers. Cooperation, not competition, had linked the five families and a Russian mob group. Scores of other people, including corrupt brokers and security managers at every level, were indicted—money managers, brokers, lawyers, pension-fund officials, and even a New York City police detective, Stephen Gardell, treasurer of the Detectives' Endowment Association, allegedly received money to build a swimming pool at his home, free hotel rooms and meals at gambling casinos, and a fur coat.

The extent of the scheme, involving fraud, threats, extortion, physical intimidation, and solicitation to commit murder were incredible; the widespread implications were staggering. Arrests were made in thirteen states, but no one believed the problem had been solved.

More fraud is happening—and much more will follow. That was the message of Jeffrey Rosen's new book, *The Unwanted Gaze: The Destruction of Privacy in America* (Random House, 2000). He shows that we have lost our ability to control how much personal information is available to anyone, and how we can suffer surprise attacks from anywhere at any time. Our right to privacy and protection at home, at work, in court, and in cyberspace has been undermined by recent legal, technological, and cultural changes. The kind of deception worked by the Mafia on Wall Street can and will be worked on us all, in many different ways. Our most private papers and diaries are vulnerable. Workplace surveillance has become a way of life. New technologies for sense-enhanced searches are now routine. Not all the surprise attacks will come from "the bad guys." The U.S. government runs the Echelon, a spy network that can eavesdrop on any phone call, fax, or e-mail transmission anywhere on earth.

You thought you were in charge of your life? That no one could attack without your knowing it? Surprise!

Can and should we expect all this to change? Should we, at the very least, believe that the Mafia threat on Wall Street and the very financial life of America will be prosecuted and ended? It would be naive to think we're going to eradicate this. This is bad news for the millions who entrust their money, credit card numbers, Social Security numbers, and house mortgages to the new electronic marketplace. Surprise attacks may come at any time. We may all find the name of a preelectronic 1939 movie coming to haunt us: our security, confidence, and privacy have *Gone with the Wind.*

* * *

July 1, 2000. America was in a festive mood, only a few days before the glorious Fourth of July, the birthday of our nation. We had reached our 224th birthday—sitting on top of the world, enjoying the greatest economic boom in history. Three cheers for Old Glory! The world's leading superpower on the military, economic, and cultural fronts. Globalization is succeeding—all the world was watching our movies, drinking our Cokes, welcoming Wal-Mart's and living in the shadow of McDonald's golden arches.

That very day, the surprise attack: across the ocean, in the French village of Millau, over 20,000 angry citizens from the region were following a hay wagon en route to the courthouse, shouting, "No to McDonald's! No to globalization!"

A trial was about to begin. Ten defendants, members of the Peasant Confederation, were charged with wrecking the restaurant in Millau on August 12; the "symbolic dismantling" left the Ronald McDonald figure headless in a pile of rubble.

Faced with up to five years imprisonment and a $73,000 fine if convicted, the ten suspects were quite confident of being released. They knew their cause was just.

This protest could grow, spread, and eventually wreck the government, warned their colorful leader, Jose Bove. The surprise attack was no local matter, no passing incident. It was farm versus city, authentic food versus junk food, local versus global, France versus the United States.

As the world media covered the story, Bove, a sheep farmer and rural activist, was borne into the cheering whistling crowd on a hay wagon—a symbol of the opposition to high-tech globalization and

American domination. Some of us in America remembered the impact of seeing Martin Luther King's coffin pulled by a mule team—the past warning us not to take all recent changes on face value.

Was Bove right? Would France and perhaps many other groups and nations support his protest? A CSA-Le Parisien poll showed broad French support, including that of both President Jacques Chirac and Prime Minister Lionel Jospin.

The sacking of McDonald's in the year 2000, like the shot fired by the American patriot farmers in 1776, was a pop heard round the world. In November 1999, the global issue had been challenged when well-orchestrated antiglobalization and environmental groups besieged and closed down the World Trade Organization meeting in Seattle. Now the virus was spreading. Suddenly, back in the United States, Ralph Nader, heading the Green Party, was making dramatic inroads in the 2000 presidential elections The media labeled Millau, the small French town in southwestern France on the Tarn River "Seattle-on-the-Tarn."

Meanwhile, a strong force of French security officers surrounded the rebuilt Millau McDonald's to repel any further attacks. A new day seemed to be dawning in the Global Village. Ronald McDonald could hardly be smiling now. He has many more battles awaiting in the New Age.

* * *

July 8, 2000. A few days earlier all America had celebrated the glorious Fourth of July. There had been parades, accolades, prancing maidens, well-decorated Marines, tall ships on the East Coast, fireworks, and more rockets glaring red than Francis Scott Key, who wrote the "Star-Spangled Banner," could have imagined. Hillary and a smiling Bill Clinton got the red carpet treatment on the deck of a super aircraft carrier—Hail to the Chief!

No wonder he was smiling. In a few days, the National Missile Defense System, which he championed, was to be tested. Another triumph for techno-America (and the Democrats).

It was a $100 million gamble—and we lost.

The second failure in three missile tests since October—which shocked and surprised the missile proponents—raised the question: How many such expensive failures should we support?

Here is what happened: a decoy balloon on the rocket that lofted the warhead twenty-one minutes earlier from Vandenburg Air Force base in California failed to inflate. Meanwhile, the "kill vehicle" high over the Pacific Ocean never got a chance to perform, because it failed to separate from the booster rocket. As its engines flamed out, the rocket tumbled into the sea without receiving a signal to detach itself. Lieutenant General Ronald T. Kadish, who headed the test, said the failure of the kill vehicle was an unexpected event that was not even on his list. Surely his was the biggest unexpected surprise.

The Washington Post reported that Pentagon officials, seeing and hearing reports, were shocked. President Clinton made no comment.

Theodore Postol and other independent scientists believe the tests were rigged to cover up the intercept's inability to distinguish between the real warhead and multitudes of decoys that are quite easy to develop.

Russian military leaders immediately urged the United States to abandon the program. Our European allies breathed a sigh of relief and expressed hope that the misfire would delay the controversial U.S. effort.

A self-imposed deadline required President Clinton to decide by mid-November whether to begin construction on a multibillion-dollar X-band tracking radar system on a remote Aleutian Island, where severe weather sharply limits the building season. More great surprises await.

* * *

One such surprise came on July 15. It centered on a book written in pencil on a yellow pad by a young Englishwoman named J. K. Rowling. Her story of a young wizard named Harry Potter was becoming the fastest-selling book—of any kind—in history.

Pop went the record.

No one was more surprised than Rowling, who said she didn't think her Harry Potter books would appeal to more than a handful of readers. How wrong can you be? Her first three Harry Potter books sold 35 million copies and were printed in thirty-five different languages. But her fourth in the series, *Harry Potter and the Goblet of Fire,* became the jewel in her crown. There were 5.3 million advance copies, with 2 million advance orders. When the book went on sale at

12:01 a.m. Saturday, July 15, 2000, bookstores hosted pajama parties, hired magicians, and filled up their cash registers. Here was the triumph of hype, the legerdemain of marketing. Harry Potter was hot! Apparently the whole world wants to know what went on in the "Riddle House" in the village of Little Hangleton.

The author promises three more books in the series, so one cannot pass any final judgment. Each book follows Harry through an academic year at Hogwarts School of Witchcraft and Wizardry. This is not the place to review the remarkable story thus far or predict how it all might end. What can be said: expect the unexpected. Popular culture is moving forward with the speed of light—and pencil. Get ready for more surprise attacks.

The Electric Shocker

I grope, I probe, I listen, I test—
until the tumblers fall and I'm in.

Marshall McLuhan

"We don't know where we're going but we're on our way." That is
an apt line for the new century and millennium. Time and space are
linked as time-space in virtual reality. Everyone can be everywhere at
once. Words flood in, words wash out. We are awash in both information and misinformation. Our emotions, like our stock market, rush
up and down. Whirl is king.

Politicians and promoters call this the best of times; a vocal minority takes the opposite view. The highly-respected *Media Studies
Journal,* published as an open forum for journalists and informed
scholars, devoted a whole issue in the winter of 2000 to Campaign
2000, deploring the poor standards, overreaction, and shoddy reporting that marks our times.

Who best succeeded in deciphering these mixed signals, explaining our dilemmas, exploring our life in cyberspace? Perhaps the man
who coined the phrase *Global Village*—Marshall McLuhan. Suppose
he is what he sounds like, Tom Wolfe asks, the greatest thinker since
Newton or Darwin?[1]

I won't try to answer Wolfe's question; but I do believe that Canadian Marshall McLuhan, working in his weird, wired exhilarating
vortex, is our prince of pop-think, our electric shocker.[2]

One could not have predicted this from his early years. Born in Ed-
monton, Canada, in 1911, his family moved seven times in the first
eight years of his life. His mother left home for long periods of time
to be a stage "impersonator;" his father drifted toward "mystical psychology." Entering the University of Manitoba in 1929, Marshall developed an obsession with "great men" and decided he would become
one. During the Great Depression he worked for the government's
mosquito campaign, pouring oil on insect breeding grounds for forty

cents an hour. He hardly seemed marked either for greatness or popularity.

Then came a major breakthrough. His excellent academic record and the persistence of his mother landed him a place at England's Cambridge University. There his intellectual awakening occurred. He was introduced to the New Criticism and the works of T. S. Eliot, Ezra Pound, I. A. Richards, and James Joyce. The young Canadian left Cambridge University in 1936 to teach and earn money.

On the personal side of major events in his Cambridge years was his conversion to Roman Catholicism. For the rest of his life, he was a true believer, fortified by the teachings of the Church. In 1938, he met Corinne Keller Lewis, a Texan, whom he married; a lifetime commitment followed. Getting a leave from St. Louis University where he was teaching English courses, he and Corinne returned to Cambridge. McLuhan finished his thesis on the Elizabethan writer Thomas Nash. On the basis of this and several published articles, he got a position at St. Michael's College at the University of Toronto. There McLuhan discovered communications and Harold Adams Innis.

Innis, a professor of political economy, brought a poetic sensitivity and historical imagination to his work. He and McLuhan met daily for coffee and conversation. Innis published two major works: *Empire and Communications* (1950), in which he explored how communication shaped empires; and *The Bias of Communication* (1951), a series of essays in which he explained his major themes. He summed up what would become McLuhan's lifelong premise: "In oral intercourse the eye, ear, and brain, these senses and the facilities act together in busy cooperation and rivalry, each eliciting, stimulating, and supplementing the other."[3] McLuhan admitted later that much of his work and research was a series of footnotes on Innis.[4]

About face for McLuhan, following in Innis' footsteps; from the elite and esoteric theories of the Cambridge dons to the earthy images of a new media, television.

Television irritated him, McLuhan admitted, but fascinated his students. How could he deal with them without seeing what they saw? Few were reading or studying his favorite writers. Instead, students got much of their information from tapes and television. He began to formulate his most famous idea: The medium is the message.

What he needed now was money and leisure to develop his new ideas. The breakthrough came on May 19, 1953, when he was awarded a Ford Foundation grant for $44,250. McLuhan was off and running.

Starting with the premise that media, in whatever form, has always been a key to dominance, McLuhan decided that rather than scorning the new technology, he must study and demystify it. If print had divided us into interest groups, castes, and nations, perhaps electronic magic would unify us. We might translate our lives into a spiritual form of information, bringing the entire human family into a single consciousness, even a Global Village. Then all information would be shared and peace would prevail.

He launched a new experimental magazine called *Explorations*. It produced an embryonic McLuhan cult, which grew with the magazine's circulation. For the rest of his life, books were McLuhan's chief source of information. In a typical week, he might speed through thirty-five books, not including synopses of books prepared by his cronies. He thought we might outgrow the world of print; he himself never did.

His first opportunity to reach an American audience came in December 1955, when he spoke on communications at a Columbia University seminar in New York. He spoke to the National Council of Teachers of English (NCTE) that same month. His wide erudition, boldness, and the technique of outrageous brush-off swept through America's academic world. He became an instant academic celebrity.

I asked him to address a 1956 conference on "The Communication Revolution," sponsored by the Wemyss Foundation, held at Airlee Center outside Washington DC. He agreed to come if the sponsors provided a private plane. We did. Once there, he asked to speak outdoors. After a few minutes, he began to walk at a brisk pace. (He had very long legs). "Come, follow me," he said, setting out over the hills. Those of us with shorter legs did so, huffing and puffing and trying to absorb his wildly disconnected monologue. It was quite a memorable affair. Then he flew home.

His growing reputation as an odd but original thinker, his radical notions about the media, and a profound ferment in society all came together in a critical mass. The result was an explosion of interest in his work and a cult following that would have done honor to a hot rock group. Sensing this, McLuhan explained his success by quoting from Coleridge's "The Rime of the Ancient Mariner:"

We were the first that ever burst
Into that silent sea.

The "bursting" accelerated in 1962 with his publication of *The Gutenberg Galaxy.* McLuhan argued that the printing press changed the psyche of Western culture, leading to the visualization of knowledge and subsequently to rationalism, mechanistic science, capitalism, and nationalism. The venerable organ of the English literary establishment, London's *Times Literary Supplement,* reviewed the book and said it was breaking new ground.

What was this "new ground?" It was McLuhan's uncanny ability to reconceive history as a pageant whose inner meaning is man's metamorphosis through the media. He saw an age dominated not by political or military leaders, but money ("The Poor Man's Credit Card"), photographs ("Brothels Without Walls"), and movies ("The Reel World"). Electronic media had created a Global Village in which all information could be shared, simultaneously, by everyone. Walls between people, nations, art, and thought came tumbling down. A new world awaited us.

With this book, McLuhan's fame and fortune increased considerably. Not only was he featured in countless newspaper and magazine articles, he even appeared as himself in a Woody Allen movie, *Annie Hall.* Professors and philosophers argued with him. He had closed the gap between elite and popular culture.

Having broken into the *Time-Life-Fortune* orbit, McLuhan was able to set up to his own base at the University of Toronto: a Centre for Culture and Technology, which would investigate the psychic and social consequences of all technologies.

I visited the Centre, which is situated away from the old university buildings in a converted Victorian coach house, behind a new building on the Toronto campus. His cluttered office had green wall-to-wall carpet and an orange sign which read:

Inform All the Troops
That Communication Has
Completely Broken Down!

He was an avid Marx brothers fan. A poster of Groucho adorned his wall, alongside a rowing paddle labeled "Trinity Hall Rugger Boat, 1936." Suspended from the ceiling was this Latin inscription:

Causae Ad Invicem Cassae Sunt

The Oxbridge paddle and Latin inscription (translation: Causes of disputes are decided by the courts) are keys to a complex personality: an English gentleman working in his native Canada to vivify what he thought of as the Great Tradition. Working is the key word. No puritan ever took work more seriously. He said he kept work on the back burner, waiting for the right opportunity to pop, then push the probe further.

He lived in a spacious nineteenth-century house, located in a suburb called Wychwood Park. A log fire crackled in a large stone fireplace; shelves, stairs, and tables were weighted down with books. One was reminded of the English squirearchy; of similarities with English intellectuals and writers such as Kenneth Clark, C. P. Snow, and Arnold Toynbee. None was more complex than McLuhan. The best comparison is with James Joyce, whom he called "the greatest behavioral engineer and the funniest man who ever lived."

He invited me to his Tuesday seminar, for which he had not prepared. He simply chatted, asked me questions, threw out one aphorism after another. He was friendly but distant. His mind seemed to be roaming in far-off fields. We were all spellbound. This man was able to stimulate a stream of fresh and free thought upon our stock notions and habits. He had new understandings of a society in which the extensions of people were media controlled.

His secret weapon was a profound understanding of how culture changes with changes in mass media. We become what we behold, McLuhan pointed out. We shape our tools and afterward our tools shape us. Like the nomadic hordes wandering across the desert searching for the soul's oasis, graphic man grabs the pleasures of barbarism and gives heart and soul to a celebrity. As it turned out, that was what the world would take McLuhan to be.

In 1964, at the height of his new popularity, McLuhan published his most popular and significant book: *Understanding Media: The Extensions of Man*. There were seven chapters on media in general, plus twenty-six on specific media, including human speech, print, clocks, money, and television. The subtitle, *The Extensions of Man,* summed up his notion that every human artifact was an "outering" or extension of some human sense or portion of the body. The radio extended the voice, the automobile the foot. This was McLuhan at his most playful and original.

Now he toured the land, widely feted and toasted as the New Guru. Tom Wolfe followed him to do a profile article for *New York Magazine,* which appeared in November 1965. In it, Wolfe began with the tag line, "What If He Is Right?" which would be repeated for years afterward. This tweedy Canadian academic exerted the unself-consciousness of a seer over corporate executives.

When *Understanding Media* was republished by the MIT Press in 1998, Lewis H. Lapham pointed out in his introduction that much in it makes a good deal more sense now than it did in 1964. McLuhan forecasts the coming and meaning of MTV, the Internet, shopping malls, and e-mail long before they existed. He both anticipated and named the Global Village, which he predicted would lead either to a new international harmony or a worldwide bloodbath. He seems to have been right on both scores.

After 1968, a number of critics and communicators began to complain that despite his sudden fame and peppy puns, the Canadian Guru had misread history and even misunderstood the medium where he seemed most brilliant: television. The idol had feet of clay. They insisted that the role of content to television was crucial, just as it had been with the printing press and every other great innovation. McLuhan's ideas, some critics said, were based on wild speculation, not observation.

Fascinated with electronic media, which compressed space and time, McLuhan began to consider a world-soul. Perhaps this mystical secular image came from his conversion to Roman Catholicism in his early twenties and from absorbing the ideas of G. K. Chesterton.

His later books, quickly completed and often repetitive, didn't sell well. Former disciples began to walk, then run, away. His enemies closed in for the kill. One of them, Everette Dennis, even wrote the "Post-Mortem on Marshall McLuhan," noting that his star had fallen. Goodbye, guru. Electronic angels sing thee to thy rest.[5] Richard Schickel agreed. McLuhan's books, Schickel wrote, "are mere incidents in the larger celebrity drama that has first call on his creative energy."[6]

Spontaneity and originality have always fared badly in academe. Plainly McLuhan was, for a while, a celebrity, even a sort of entertainer. Fewer and fewer people were merely entertained by McLuhan. His faddish appeal (on which popular magazines feed) was dead. What may be remarkable is not that it faded, but how long it lasted.

What is the connection between McLuhan's theoretical books and popular culture? They were never popular with ordinary people—and were denounced by many leading critics and scholars. Few then and now can follow the convoluted path, the clever puns, and the epigrammatic obscurity that are McLuhan's trademarks. Like many famous thinkers (Descartes, Newton, Einstein, Foucault) his reputation was not built on how many read or understood him, but what others had said of him. McLuhan was a master phrasemaker who inspired clever nicknames and anecdotes.

The medium is the message, he said, then punned on it: *The Medium Is the Massage* (1967). The term Global Village clicked in the public imagination and has remained there ever since. Even disc jockeys on radio stations fell under his spell. He was the "in" oracle of electronics, pop daddy, massage man, the gee-golly guru.

McLuhan loved all this, for there was a streak of P. T. Barnum in him. As a young man he had vowed he would be a great man. We call this *hubris,* from the Greek *hybris.* He became not so much a scholar as a celebrity. That may help to explain why, like most celebrities, his star faded in his latter years. Still, what if he was right?

On September 26, 1979, McLuhan suffered a massive stroke. He eventually regained physical mobility, but never his ability to read and write. Worst of all, he couldn't speak, except for a few odd phrases. For a man who lived to talk, this was the ultimate torment.

The following June, Toronto University decided to dismantle McLuhan's Centre. There would only be a McLuhan Program, with a meager budget of $20,000 to carry on his work. Packing up before leaving the Coach House forever, McLuhan wept.

At some point in the early morning of the last day of 1980, Marshall McLuhan died peacefully in his bed.

* * *

The academic jealousy which had pursued him abated somewhat after his death. More and more people came to understand that he had dramatically changed the way we look at the world. Whenever we surf the Net, go online, tune into MTV, pop a videotape in the VCR, McLuhan is watching. Like it or not, we live in a McLuhanesque world.

His daughter, Stephanie McLuhan, produced a series of six video-tapes labeled "Video McLuhan" in 1997, covering the years from 1958 to 1979. With commentary by Tom Wolfe, they make it possible for a new generation to see and hear McLuhan in action.

We finally have a full and authoritative biography by Philip Marchand: *Marshall McLuhan: The Medium and the Messenger,* published in 1989 and reissued by the MIT Press in 1998. In the fore-word to the new edition, Neil Postman, professor at New York University and director of the department of media ecology, notes that by 1996, over one hundred students at New York University had earned media PhDs and more than four hundred, MAs. "I can assure you," he writes, "that all of them know they are the children of Marshall McLuhan. I consider myself to be one too, not quite an obedient child, but the kind who knows where he comes from and what his parents wanted him to do."[7]

McLuhan refused to join the doom and gloom school of intellectu-als that flourished in the twentieth century. The wails and predictions of Herbert Marcuse, José Ortega y Gasset, Aldous Huxley, George Orwell, Norman O. Brown, and R. D. Laing were not for him. He pre-ferred to listen to Emerson: "Never strike sail to a fear"; and to the medieval mystic who believed all would be well, and all manner of things would be well.

How will the future deal with the "Canadian Comet"? We have no way of knowing. He waxed; he waned; he died. A revival of interest followed and expands. Was he a celebrity or a seminal thinker? What makes and breaks celebrities? When do fads reappear as trends or movements? Answers to such questions lie deep, out of the range of pollsters, pundits, the Internet, and satellites.

Some interesting attempts at answers have been made. One, by the theologian Martin E. Marty, is of special interest, since it refers spe-cifically to *le McLuhanism*. In "How to tell a fad from a trend," Marty points out that no one ever thinks *he* (or she) is fooled; fads are other people's obsessions.[8] He then makes a fascinating observation:

> For one terrifying moment when McLuhanism fused with Radi-cal Theology, this mode of measuring was in jeopardy. It looked as if theology was to be done over the television or telephone....

Are we sure it isn't? Perhaps Marty is a fallen star? We can confuse a gigantic system of words with a new protean mythology. We tremble when the old disappears, then tumble again when the new takes over. The jury is not yet in on Marshall McLuhan and might not be for some time. Meanwhile, we might recall Alfred North Whitehead's observation: The nonsense of today is the sense of tomorrow.

In his last letter to me, McLuhan made a comment on nostalgia and fads. I use it as his epitaph:

> Have you forgotten that we live in an age of nostalgia and that all past fads have to be retrieved frequently? Witness *Star Wars*. Your turn may come yet!

The old McLuhan is dead, but another one is emerging. What his new status and influence will be, we cannot yet say. Tom Wolfe may have asked the right question after all: "What if he was right?"

Style

Style, not substance, will be the wave of the future.

Ralph Waldo Emerson

Emerson was right: style was the wave of his future and of ours. Why is this so? What is style?

Style: a characteristic model manner, or method of expression; skill or grace in performance, manner, or appearance. One of the keys that unlocks popular culture is style; but trying to define it need not be stylish. People who have style tend not to write or talk about it; and people who write and talk about it usually don't have much.

Yet the term *style* gets attached to everything, age after age: actors, writers, cultures, nations, periods, crafts, and dynasties. Despite all this, the word *style* eludes us. What brings a dead object to life is hidden within a living viewer or reader, not the object. But what sets the process in motion? What makes certain epochs, cultures, and people "stylish"?[1]

Certainly prominence and power help. When the Egyptians were developing a unique style which still delights us, their Pharaohs were power brokers throughout their known world. The Athenians under Pericles were a mighty factor, so that the ideas of Socrates, Plato, and Aristotle were carried far and wide. One of Aristotle's pupils—Alexander the Great—was a world conqueror, and is said to have cried when, as a young warrior, there were no more lands to conquer. Alexander had style.

The Greeks were in turn conquered by the Romans, whose empire flourished for a thousand years and who left theaters, forums, and aqueducts everywhere they went. They even made much of thermal baths, such as the one Claudius constructed in Britain. Today, England's Bath is a major structure and tourist attraction, and spas are stylish everywhere.

The ecclesiastical Gothic style long favored by the Vatican left magnificent Gothic cathedrals; one was recently completed as a national shrine in Washington, DC. At the same time, one of the popular youth cults in the 1990s called itself the "Goths."

That other powerful nations in their prime shaped style on a worldwide scale is obvious—China, Spain, France, and Great Britain. Under Queen Victoria, the British controlled almost a quarter of the world, so that "The sun never set on the British Empire." It set in a hurry after World War II, when the British lost their empire and American power and prestige took in the West. Did that result (or has that resulted) in an American style that will do the same? In popular culture, style seems bound up with fads, formulas, and model building. Style isn't something that activates the process but is instead the result of that process. Alexis de Tocqueville, the great French traveler who toured America in the 1820s, pointed this out. He thought the new nation's motley multitude would create a new style. We have been trying to verify this ever since. In a nation that long thought of itself as a melting pot but now favors the term *multicultural,* is a new style emerging in the new millennium? Can we describe it?

Back we go to crucial definitions. Just what is style—a word that glitters like gold but is as elusive as quicksilver? Who has it, and how did they get it? Where does it come from, and how does it function?

One can peruse the whole library on the subject without finding answers. Style seems to be intrinsic, not extrinsic—built into the very fabric of the art, story, film, or costume that we call "stylish" or "famous." The mental image of a culture's style is the culture itself.

Few create a new style, while many imitate it. Who can count the number of "Petrarchan" or "Shakespearean" sonnets we have endured—or those in our time who mimicked Charlie Chaplin, Groucho Marx, Madonna, or Elvis Presley?

Style setters become our models. They live on long after they die. Our visual memory acts like a drug, awakening in us new creative effort. This seems to be the secret to the ever-changing list of "top ten" songs, rock bands, best-sellers. When you're hot, you're hot, when you're not, you're not. Soon they disappear, like falling stars.

For centuries, we have thought and taught in terms of "national styles." Does America have one? If so, it is rooted in Europe, shaped largely by British life and lore, then altered constantly by world immigration and influences. In this sense, our "Founding Fathers" set the style and tone of the New Republic. Crucial figures were our first president, George Washington, and author of the Declaration of Independence, Thomas Jefferson.

Were they "truly American?" Washington wore the red coat of the British army before putting on the blue one of our revolution; and Jefferson drew heavily on Locke and other European thinkers in writing the famous Declaration of Independence. Their homes, Mount Vernon and Monticello, look more like European manor houses than frontier log cabins. As Emerson noted, we listened to the muses of Europe before declaring our independence—and long afterward too.

As a new century and millennium begin, there is a general (if sometimes grudging) agreement that America is a superpower with a superstyle that is sweeping the globe. Many even believe that, like Britannia before us, America now rules the waves, the markets, and the missiles.

If we count dollars, aircraft carriers, nuclear submarines, bombs, and bombers, that claim cannot be contested. The Soviet Union has collapsed, and other possible contenders are only beginning to emerge. We have the power. With it has come predominance in media, movies, clothing, music, and even food. Do these and other American items make for a super style? Are they our real secret weapons as we enter the next century?

Those whose power and perks have faded think it might be well so. Britain's Lord Hugh Thomas, in his 1996 book on *World History,* concludes that American dominance offers the prospect of a better world than any other that can be reasonably imagined.[2] This takes into account that the world might be compelled to copy our style of government, music, fashion, and food. There is some evidence to back his suggestion. The same month Thomas's book came out, McDonald's opened a fast-food restaurant in its 100th overseas nation.

Not all historians, and certainly not all British historians, share Lord Thomas's willingness to wait and see. In another recent study, *Europe: A History,* Norman Davies warns that a mindless materialism of a transatlantic homogenized culture could have insidious, even disastrous, consequences. Many share both views, and even more fall somewhere in between.[3]

Let us examine both the problems and prospects of an American super style. It is a complex and multifaceted puzzle, and I make no claim to be able to solve it. If we can raise questions and evoke others to do the same, we will at least have moved the argument forward.

Styles not only rise and fall, they move in cycles of renewal and exhaustion. Wait long enough and the wheel will come full circle. Clothes discarded in one decade will be the rage again a few decades later. But this axiom may be too simplistic to match reality. Because style reflects specific and immediate aspects of ever-changing culture, it never repeats itself exactly.

Style wars rage in America like star wars in science fiction. They got early scholarly attention. Van Wyck Brooks, Gilbert Seldes, Edmund Wilson, Lewis Mumford, and John Kowenhoven probed new areas, finding in America new patterns and objects not inspired by ancient tradition but imposed by the driving energies of a new vibrant culture.

Sigfried Gideon pointed out that molded wooden forms, the revolutionized elite twentieth-century art, originate as ferryboat seats in nineteenth-century America and that many highly acclaimed Bauhaus designs in twentieth-century Germany were standard equipment of American reapers and mowers after the 1850s. Elite and popular art joined in the highly successful American movement, Pop Art, in the 1960s.

Now galleries around the world feature material from supermarkets, malls, city streets, and even junkyards. Significantly, the phrase Popular Culture, which swept the world in the 1940s and 1950s, didn't appear in the authoritative *Reader's Guide* until 1960.

Not everyone was happy with the merging and melding of cultures, creating new lores and a new international style. Reporting on the 1970 International Book Fair held in Frankfurt, Germany, Peter Haertling wrote: "This has been a fair of pop singers, famous flyers, and obsolete comic strips. I suppose novels are a thing of the past."[4]

Susan Sontag went further in *Against Interpretation* (1961), claiming that the novel is dead and that interpretation is the revenge of the intellect upon art. Even more, it is the revenge of the intellect upon the world. A new style, a new lore was in the making, with new standards of beauty, taste, and meaning. From the viewpoint of this new sensibility, the beauty of a machine, a film, a painting, and the music of the Beatles would be equally accessible.[5]

The notion of cultural synthesis became a major manifesto in 1970, when Russel B. Nye published *The Unembarrassed Muse: The Popular Arts in America.*[6] This landmark 500-page volume set a new standard for comprehensiveness. It documents major cultural shifts and the gradual improvement of popular standards of performance. Russel Nye noted that the simple literalness of Tom Mix, Mary Pickford, and Edward G. Robinson had given way to symbolic performances as in *High Noon, Shane, Bonnie and Clyde,* and films by Alfred Hitchcock.

To erase the boundaries created by snobbery and cultists, which have so long divided the arts, Nye concluded, means in the long run greater understanding of them.

Now we can be glad that so fine a composer as Aaron Copeland produces his musical triumph, *Billy the Kid,* and that *Little Orphan Annie* can leap from the comic strips to the Broadway stage in high style. "One cheats himself, as a human being, if one has respect only for the style of high culture," Susan Sontag wrote. Radical in 1960, the statement sounds platitudinous forty years later.[7]

Can we speak now of a new American "style," requiring a new "lore"? I think we can. European history and art document a heroic but tragic quest for a closed system. We have followed another start, developed another style. Ours is a saga of process more than product—the process of motion into and out of cities, space, and technologies. We are forever going west and coming east, moving up and down the social ladder, throwing rascals out and voting them in.

In Old World towns and cities, buildings are clustered like sheep as if to shield and protect one another against open space. If they are destroyed, Europeans "restore" them to look old with new materials. But in America, Jean-Paul Sartre astutely observed, streets are not sober little walks closed in between houses, but national highways and interstates. The moment you set foot on them, you know you can head west for another ocean, drive north or south toward another country.

Spit on the fire and hitch up the horses! We may not know where we're going, but we're on our way!

POP STYLE

Is popular culture creating a style of its own—or does it simply beg, borrow, and steal from all other styles, a sort of intercontinental scavenger? Is there really something we can call pop style? If so, is it evolutionary, even bringing forth totally new creations?

Scholars have not felt comfortable with such a question and have ended up either ignoring it or condemning it. The newly created Donald Duck seems phony to the naturalists and folklorists and trivial or childlike to the elite. The same thing has happened with genuine folklore, used by people such as Walt Disney and clever urban graphic artists to retell and remodel the old tales and fables. Richard Dorson comments on this in his popular study of *American Folklore.* "After 1860," Dorson writes, "the homespun yarn never again became reorganized. A century later literary scholars would unearth specimens as antiquarian curiosities."8

Daniel Boorstin, writing on *The Image: Or What Happened to the American Dream,* thought pop style depended on watered-down versions of older material, tailored for a new, less well-informed audience—that is, the people. For popular audiences, the simpler the better.9

As early as 1922 (in *Public Opinion*), Walter Lippman saw an America wedded to stereotypes, much given to oversimplified patterns.10 Since then, our images have become mirror reflections of one another. One interview comments on another; one comic spoofs another television comic, as fiction, radio, film, and television merge into mutual entertainment. The illusions, Boorstin contends, give us the image of our society. Not only public relations men and women and politicians, but also journalists, publishers, manufacturers, merchandisers, and talk-show hosts devote their lives to a world full of pseudo-events.

Such events are not spontaneous but are planted or incited. They are meant to be reported and reproduced; to be given out "for future release," since they are tied in with a self-fulfilling prophecy. They are more dramatic than mere reality, since they are planned with that in mind. Selected, not encountered, they can be repeated at will. Each event spawns other such events, in geometric fashion. Hence a new Gresham's law: manufactured happenings will always drive spontaneous happenings out of circulation. Fantasy tastes so sweet that it spoils one's appetite for plain fact.

In the hand of a great writer, such as Mark Twain, William Faulkner, or Toni Morrison, plain facts are transformed into great literature. If this becomes popular—as it certainly did with these three—might it be called pop style? Are such masterpieces as *Roughing It, The Sound and The Fury, Beloved,* and Tom Wolfe's *A Man in Full* any less important or any less valid because they became popular and pivotal?

Of course, much that clutters the stage is far more ephemeral than these three authors' works. What is "popular and stylish" with the young can be in and out in the twinkling of an eye. Fashion in hair styles, clothing, and decorations is a looking glass that proves this point. Twenty years after the event, few remember the excitement Bo Derek caused with a 1979 hairstyle. It burst on the scene in the movie *10*. The movie was easy to forget—but not the hairstyle. Called cornrowing, the style had been popular with African Americans for several years. Involving meticulous braiding and ornamenting, it was an instant style craze. Crowds of white women turned up at the Harlem YWCA Beauty Shop, which specialized in cornrows. A braids-only salon named Le Braids Cherie opened in Hollywood, and the media tuned in. Soon salons in large cities (such as Pierre Michel's in New York) were charging up to $500 to set a single chic head. It was *the* look by the summer.

An age-old process within popular culture was repeating itself. Whatever a culture does or does not have, it must have a style or, more accurately, a whole range of styles. Derived from several ancient shapes and uses, the shape and contour of a story, picture, or costume, style exhibits the spirit and personality of the creator. The mental image of a person's style is the person himself.

Style is a kind of model building. We draw from a visual memory and obscure ancestral springs; this stimulates our creativity. If the products evoke a sentimental yearning for archaic styles, we apply the tag "nostalgia." Imitation is always easier than initiation.

Never formed in a vacuum, style uses words, lines, gesture, and objects with which people are familiar. For this reason, not only individuals but also regions, nations, and even continents have their own style. America's style is rooted in nonconformist Britain but is shaped by many other European styles, as well as those of aboriginal Americans. Try as they might, Europeans changed in the new environment. The land was stronger than the people—it always has been.

Through style, we parcel out space, time, mass, and energy. The law of probability applies. Of all things that can occur, those that *do* become "stylish." Style, which depends not only on logic but also on intuition, gives us surprise and delight. Expect the unexpected. That becomes the operating first principle for mannerism, Dadaism, pop, and camp. They unseat style and mock premises as did radical chic of the 1960s, redneck chic of the 1970s, and grunge in the 1990s. Who would have expected sophisticated urbane Americans to emulate the coarse backwoods redneck? Yet one found urbanites dressed in imported blue jeans and expensive Frye boots, trying for the "down-home" or "country" look. Further manifestations are the obsession with pickup trucks, dogs, country and western music, and hard liquor. There is the aping of the uneducated on CB radios, and the high ratings for such banal television series as *The Dukes of Hazzard,* movies such as *Cowboy,* and hit tunes such as "Redneck in a Rock 'n' Roll Bar." Entertainers who want to make it in the city go country.

Is he what Steve Young calls (in his song "Renegade Picker") partly hippy, partly jigger? These antistyles eventually become styles in their own right and inspire other antistyles. Those who found Dada too stuffy took to pop art; when pop criticism became too serious, the jokers invented camp.

Their thesis: when something is quite bad, it becomes, by some perverse chemistry, fascinating and irresistible. Instead of admiring only the best, why not the worst as well? Thus, the Germans made national parks out of Nazi concentration camps. The American government celebrated the centennial of its Civil War by glorifying the Rebels who had set out to destroy the Union. When does irony become absurdity?

Whatever the complications, style springs from a single source—the imagination of a sensitive person. Mozart, van Gogh, and Judy Garland had style but all died tragically. Walt Disney, Pablo Picasso, and Aristotle Onassis, on the other hand, had style and died millionaires. Success and style are not synonymous. There are hidden variables that are part of every equation.

The artist-creator in the world of popular aesthetics is servant to the culture and slave to the market. Yet room exists for the artist-reformer, sometimes as an outsider from the elite tradition, sometimes as an insider who outgrew the restrictions of a popular form. These people Fred Schroeder calls "outlaws." From studying their work, he has developed *Outlaw Aesthetics.* He speculates in this book how artist outlaws are converted to trendsetters:

> How is it that Jane Austen and Louisa May Alcott rise out of the teenage sentimental novel? How does George Gershwin rise from Tin Pan Alley, and Duke Ellington from dance-hall entertainment? How do we get from *Astounding Science Fiction* to Kurt Vonnegut, from Hopalong Cassidy to *High Noon?*[11]

Part of the answer lies with the individual genius that appeals to the popular aesthetic, which says an artwork is good because it sells, and it sells because it never places art above the audience.

In the world of mass media, individual styles are often sacrificed to "teams" of writers and producers. These style teams work together so closely that they may develop a communal style of great brilliance and authenticity. An example is Disney Studios: for half a century, this group of writers, artists, filmmakers, and promoters has turned out productions that the world has accepted as the essence of America.

All this helps to explain why American fashions are fickle and ephemeral. One must forgive fashion everything—it dies so young. Though fads and fashions are increasingly team-produced mass phenomena, they still must feed off the individual. We speak of taste— how can it be defined or confined? It is dependent on environment and the outside world in which we function. To the American frontiersman, for whom hunting meant survival, the coonskin became a fashionable symbol. Ben Franklin wore it to great advantage in the Royal Court at Versailles, where no coon had ever dared venture. His elegant lady admirers swooned for the coon.

The frontiersmen emerged in the nineteenth century on the Great Plains, and traded his coonskin cap for a sombrero. Adding a colorful neckerchief, chaps, spurs, and a six-shooter, the American cowboy became our best-known fashion plate; a quarter of all the movies made in Hollywood have been westerns. John Wayne, the Duke, carried that image well into the twentieth century, a global hero. Further west, an enterprise called Levi Strauss & Company came forth with blue jeans in the 1850s, which swept the world after the 1960s. Decades later, it is still standard uniform for men and women on every college campus in America.

"The impact of America's fashion," writes Ernestine Carter, "rests on its popular or folk fashion, Cape Cod southwestern hats, cowboy gear from boots to Stetsons, T-shirts, denim, and above all jeans."[12] America's special skill is to take European, African, and Asian ideas and absorb, adapt, and project them.

Blue jeans are now more global than American. Many are made abroad, along with much of our clothing. Most of us now function in many worlds, if not in body then on film, television, and the Internet.

We are no longer nation-bound or even earthbound. Space travel has had its effect on fashion, too.

There were changes not only in what Americans read but also in how it was written. The national "literary style" became more experimental and subjective. Changes were both external and internal. The linear block-like page gave way to a new emphasis on special type, graphics, inversions, injections, and made-up words. Those experimenting were said to have "style" and to be "New Journalists." Thus has it always been. When a singer or a writer has style, we can overlook or forgive anything. Who cares what John Denver or Barbra Streisand sings—or what subjects Tom Wolfe or Gay Talese choose?

What causes style changes? Glut, overuse, novelty, boredom. What we finally want is surprise and enchantment. We must have the new coat, the new look. Overnight, females throw away their skirts because they are too short or too long, and males rush to the barber to trim or braid their shaggy locks. How dreadful if they were to be seen out of style!

More than vanity is at stake in such changes. Dress is a necessary form of communication, sending out unspoken signals. Our dress conforms to a whole range of moral and social attitudes; we are what we wear. Out of style, out of favor. If fashion is about pleasure, it is also about danger.

Fashion, a subset of style, is a meeting point for many different aspects of our culture. To know about the style of America, we need to ponder what we see in the looking glass.[13]

One unique aspect of American fashion might be its willingness to go to the factory, football stadium, or rock concert hall to get the "look." If Europeans created the "beau," we created the "tough." And what could be tougher than grunge?

Like many terms in the ephemeral world of electronic pop culture, grunge is not easily defined. Originally it was a tongue-in-cheek term for pungent guitar noise. Centered in Seattle, bands such as Nirvana, Alice in Chains, Candlebox, and Soundgarden claimed their fame. Soon there was the grunge look: torn clothing, used or discarded items, and mismatches. Seen as "the only vital white culture in years," grunge even developed a standard uniform of its own: seedy flannel shirt, combat boots, and ripped jeans. Gradually, mix and match became mess and muddle. The establishment, so scornfully dismissed by grunge, struck back, claiming "The Great Grunge

Hoax" had ended. But in the hinterland both the music and the style lived on, into the twenty-first century.

Then it was hip-hop's turn, built on the concept of rap. Rap: to strike with a quick light blow; to utter sharply or vigorously. In pop culture, to spit out words so quickly that they sound like machine-gun fire. The accepted term for the culture surrounding rap music, hip-hop, glorifies that music, break dancing, and graffiti. It emerged in the Sugarhill Gang's seminal 1979 hit "Rapper's Delight." Dominated by African Americans, it is bluntly aggressive (as in gangsta rap) or even nihilistic. Denounced by many, it nevertheless helped shape not only street fashion and television, but even soft drink ads.

When a youth fad explodes, everyone wants to get on the bandwagon.[14] But hurry. It may leave town before you get on board. You might join the Guerrilla Girls, for example—a direct-action group of anonymous art-world feminists who wear gorilla masks when taking to the streets. The "Girls" assume names of famous women artists, attacking the establishment, with every possible device, including sarcasm. Then there are the Fat Girls, champions of the "fat acceptance movement." Led by Nomy Lamm, author of *I'm So Fucking Beautiful,* the group scorns dieting and wants to fight the evils of sizeism.

Is there meaning in what many outside our subcultures see as madness? David Muggleton tackles that question in his book *Inside Subculture: The Postmodern Meaning of Style.*[15] He can't make up his mind—is the underlying theme cultural expression or class contradiction? We wonder.

In our multicultural era, you can find a rising star for almost any idea or ism. But you must run fast to catch a falling ism or a falling star.

Black Popular Culture

Free at last!

Reverend Martin Luther King Jr.

The most baffling, intractable problem in American history centers around one of humanity's oldest institutions: slavery. It occurred many centuries before the New World was discovered, and crossed the ocean shortly after the first European settlers arrived. A Dutch ship landed African slaves at Jamestown, Virginia, in 1619. Now, almost four centuries later, as we move into the twenty-first century, the issues of race, civil rights, and integration follow us every step of the way.

A single poignant story, penned by the African-American writer Langston Hughes, provides a good introduction to this overwhelming and intractable problem.

Friends recall that during World War II, Hughes, a major figure of the Harlem Renaissance, walked into one of New York's Harlem bars and met a man known as Simple. Hughes was fascinated by him, and would use him later as his mouthpiece in exploring and explaining black popular culture. Simple, it seemed, made cranks in a war factory but didn't know what the cranks cranked.

"You've been working there long enough," Simple's girlfriend said. "By now you ought to know what makes them cranks crank!"

"Aw, woman," he said, "you know white folks don't tell colored folks what cranks crank!"

Blacks of Simple's generation, like many before him, were the invisible men. Caught between Africa and Waspland, enslaved by law then ensnared by circumstances, they were not expected to ask about the cranks that made the culture turn. Assumed to be and consequently forced to be inferior, African Americans were turned into stereotypes. When the barriers of chattel slavery were let down briefly, the stereotypes were maintained. When the slaves shuffled meekly into the plantation house on Christmas morning, historian Benjamin

Quarles points out, they were greeted by the master and the mistress and given small gifts plus a dram of liquor. Slaves were sometimes permitted to have a dance; if no fiddler was available, they would simply clap their hands. To dance Jim Crow was one of their favorites:

> Once upon the heel tap
> and then upon the toe,
> An' ev'ry time I turn around
> I jump Jim Crow[1]

When a Cincinnati white man, Thomas Rice, blacked his face in 1828, donned a porter's costume, and mimicked the blacks' shuffle, the stereotype became a standard item in popular culture. The minstrel show swept the country, with Dan Emmett's so-called melodious Ethiopian band, the Virginia Minstrels, leading the way. A mixture of shuffles, sentimental melodies, exaggerations, and tall tales, the format persisted well into the twentieth century.

Christy's Minstrels, which opened at Mechanics Hall in New York in 1846, ran almost nightly for ten years to large audiences. The end men, Mistah Tambo and Mistah Bones, fitted their lines to the times, while the songs of Stephen Foster ("My Old Kentucky Home," "Old Black Joe," "Old Folks at Home," "Oh! Susanna," and many others) won a spot in the popular imagination which they have never lost. White adaptations of black popular culture—however accurate or fair their origin—have been with us for generations.

For whites of Thomas Rice's era, it was unthinkable that black Americans had a viable culture as Euro-Americans defined that term. It would be a whole generation before white scholars and two generations before black scholars reversed such a thesis. The stereotypes, like Ol' Man River, just kept rolling along. They still do—although now there are different stereotypes. To be human is to accept popular platitudes—whosoever makes them and whatever they proclaim.

Occasionally individuals appeared who seemed to symbolize the whole situation—such as Blind Tom, a black blind man for whom even the outer world was invisible. This malformed Georgia slave could not even carry on a conversation, but he could repeat verbatim anything he heard, including piano melodies after a single hearing. "Blind Tom": musical prodigy and physical misfit, "rolled neatly into one grotesque attraction," writes Bruce Jackson. "And everyone knew that old slaves could pat time and dance and sing. . . ."2 Laws change, but age-old sterotypes and prejudices hang on generation after generation. They follow us into the new millennium.3

How does blackness relate to and influence popular culture? Probing black popular culture is no easy task. Each of the three words defies easy definition or delimitation. To say more is to risk a trap, since black comes not merely from skin color or any external factor. It is seen as a lifestyle, an angle of vision. The poet Clarence Major points to "the ancient brilliance of the abstracts of black cultures . . . the black power of our cosmological armies, the horns of our virility."4

No matter how one defines, or refuses to define, blackness, Africans have forged powerful traditions and ceremonies—popular culture in the full and best sense—and many of these are alive today. An underlying assumption that goes throughout the years is that different races are "different" people.

An early major document in that understanding was Melville J. Herskovits' *The Myth of the Negro Past,* published in 1941. He asserted that there were substantial aspects of African culture surviving among black Americans, with many Africanisms spilling over into white American culture. His thesis remains controversial. Discussions of it often become emotional. Some anthropologists point out that differences in the general pattern of the cultures of Africa and Europe were not great. Institutions common to both regions included a complex economic system based on money, markets, and middlemen; a large number of crafts; a well-developed system of government based on kings; courts of law implying specialists; a religious system with a hierarchy of priests and deities; and a common stock of folklore emphasizing popular tales and proverbs.5

Scholars continue to discover Africanisms in the New World—not only words (yam, goober, canoe, banjo, etc.) but folk tales, religious practices, and social organizations. The survival of Africanisms in America was as great as it was, historian John Hope Franklin suggests, "because of the refusal of members of the dominant group in America to extend, without reservation, their own culture to the Negroes whom they brought over."6 One should note that even in his history of black America, widely used as a text, the terms *popular culture, leisure, entertainment, folklore, jazz,* and *vernacular* do not appear in his forty-three-page index.

Until the 1960s, little had been done to summarize the black contribution either to elite or popular cultural outlets. Another "standard" text, Oliver W. Larkin's *Art and Life in America* (1949), uses the word *black* in the index only in reference to three picture titles. There are four brief sentences concerning "Negro craftsmen" but none for "Negro artists" or "Negro influence." One has a feeling that a more accurate title for this work would be *Art and Life in White America*.[7]

To produce a portrait of a collective identity is no easy thing. Life and culture (be it elite or popular) are not separated by any innate quality, only by particular standards we seek to impose. Art can never be encompassed by elitist canons of personal taste or nomenclature, but only as products of man or woman the maker.[8] And what humans can make or imagine is not restricted by their color. As toolmaker, homemaker, image maker, mythmaker, and city maker, mankind uses his and her hands, on which black culture and every other culture is based.

Hence an answer to the question, "Where does *American* black popular culture begin?" can be offered: at the place and time when black men and women began to live, breathe, and create on American soil. Much of it, by its very nature, was neither perceivable nor preserved—mainly oral, not written; casual, not formal; clandestine, not overt.

What amazes us is how much was known and passed down under these difficult circumstances. New studies are opening many new doors. Africans brought to this country were a foreign people whose customs, attitudes, and desires were shaped to a different place and a radically different life. "To be brought to a culture that was, and is, in terms of purely philosophical correlatives, the complete antithesis of one's own version of man's life on earth—that is the cruelest aspect of this particular enslavement."[9]

That so many Africans made their mark before 1900 as carvers, metalworkers, weavers, and painters suggests that (in the arts, at least) there was not a complete antithesis. Art, being a universal language, overcomes ethnic and political barriers. Diaries and travel accounts tell of early artifacts and ceremonies from the black communities. As LeRoi Jones points out, Congo Square in New Orleans (later famed as the birthplace of jazz) "would nightly rock to the master drums of new African arrivals."[10] As late as the nineteenth century, pure African songs could be heard and pure African dances seen in the southern United States. African tradition was even more deeply rooted in Haiti, Guiana, Cuba, Brazil, and throughout South and Central America. These places are, in the larger and truer meaning of the term, important parts of American culture.

There are eighteenth-century references to black American painters, sculptors, and artisans. Some of them traveled and worked abroad. *The Boston Newsletter* for January 7, 1773, solicited work for "a Negro man whose extraordinary genius reflects the best masters of London." Painters such as Joshua Johnston and Robert S. Duncanson demonstrated how well black Americans could master elite techniques. Many other blacks, whose names never got into the records, created a black popular culture which would play a dominant role in the twentieth and twenty-first century.11

This culture, rooted largely in the rural South, was not the product of any racial mystique but of concrete circumstances. "Soul food" was dictated not by choice but by necessity. So were gestures, religious forms, spirituals, dances, survival stratagies, and emotional conditionings. All this must be explored in our New Age if we are to understand the roots of black popular culture.

So must the exodus to northern cities, which began with World War I. Blacks came north not only to get the higher wages but also the greater freedom and dignity which awaited them there. The proportion of blacks in the North increased to 14 percent by 1920, ending the provinciality of place which had marked black culture for decades. But it did not end discrimination and hardship. Those who expected to find the Promised Land in the urban North would be bitterly disappointed.

They would express their hopes as well as their disappointments in their popular culture. What is ignored or undernourished in official culture thrives and grows as popular culture. That which must be baptized but has no place at the high altar will go underground.

In the 1990s, scholars were busy separating and documenting the history of ragtime, show music, minstrel, jazz, and blues—the hopelessly interwoven fabric of American life, where blacks and whites pass by so quickly that they blur together to become only grays. Their work has cast new light on popular culture and shows how many of the barriers between "white" and "black" are meaningless.

Norman Mailer discussed another race and culture merger in his article on "The White Negro." When the bohemian and the juvenile came face-to-face with the African American, the counterculture (with its hippies, beatniks, yippies, and freaks) became a reality. "If marijuana was the wedding ring," Mailer wrote, "the child was the language of Hip for its argot grave expression to abstract states of feeling which all could share. In this wedding of the white and the black it was the Negro who brought the cultural dowry."[12]

In black popular culture, the intertwining of many cultural elements (African, Latin, European, Anglo-Saxon) are involved. Long-rooted prejudices and misconceptions are disappearing: narrow concepts of society, attachment to fictions and false values, sentimentality, lack of realism.

Is there a separate black aesthetic from which black culture can and does draw? Claims and arguments are emotional and confusing. The mystique called "Negritude," black critic J. Saunders Redding points out, "embraces a heavy, indeed, overriding emotional compo-nent that is referred to as 'soul force.' But the advocates of this way of thinking have no corpus of cognitive knowledge to fall back on."[13] At the same time, the fact of blackness is not only a powerful inspiration and force for black writers but also an intense force affecting nonblack thinking and writing as well. Being black is suddenly a strength and advantage, after generations of it being a barrier and handicap.[14] The consequences of wedding art and politics, black literature, and black power have produced a new "Black Renaissance."

Two great and influential African-American leaders came out of nineteenth- and early twentieth-century America and have been the subject of discussion and debate ever since. They had very different ideas of how black Americans should proceed. The gap between them has never fully closed. Booker T. Washington and W. E. Burghardt DuBois have major roles in the story we are attempting to tell.

Booker T. Washington triumphed over many incredible hardships. His autobiography, *Up From Slavery* (1901), documents his rise. Having worked in salt furnaces and coal mines to obtain money for schooling, he graduated from Hampton Institute in 1875. Taking over the newly formed Tuskegee Institute in 1881, he created a major edu-cational institution, and became an outstanding African-American spokesman of his generation.

Accepting segregation, he urged his people to train themselves in agriculture and the trades. He did not put top priority on developing an intellectual elite, as had been the case in Haiti. He preached "the gospel of the toothbrush," stressing cleanliness and adaptability. It does not seem fair to say, as have his critics, that he accepted political and social bondage as the price of industrial progress.

He urged blacks to adopt a policy of severe and constant struggle rather than one of artificial forcing. "No race that has anything to contribute to the markets of the world," he said, "is long to any degree ostracized."[15] Events of the century seem to bear that out.

His best known speech was given at the Atlanta Exposition in 1895. Here was a man saying, in highly polished English, what Uncle Remus had said a generation before in the folk idiom: Be patient. The way to win is through steady progress and legal victories. Years later, Martin Luther King Jr. would agree and his efforts helped to bring about the end of legal segregation.

Not all African Americans agreed. William E. Burghardt DuBois, who studied at Harvard and the University of Berlin before taking up a professorship at Atlanta University in 1896, had an entirely different program. His solution was the National Association for the Advancement of Colored People, which he was instrumental in founding in 1909.

His goal was to recover all of the African-Americans' social and civil rights under the Constitution. The tone of his work was embodied in the title of the magazine he founded and edited: *The Crisis*.[16]

One of the major bastions that DuBois decided he must attack was the idolization of Booker T. Washington. Washington's mistakes, in his opinions, had led him into tragic contradictions:

1. Booker T. Washington wanted to extend African-Americans rights; but they could never defend their rights and exist without the right of suffrage.
2. He insisted on thrift and self-respect, yet counseled a silent submission that sapped the African American's manhood.
3. He advocated common schools and industrial training instead of higher learning; yet none of these schools (including Tuskegee) could remain open were it not for teachers trained in African-American colleges or by their graduates.

Booker T. Washington's career seemed to DuBois to have encouraged the disfranchisement of his own people; the legal creation of a distinct status of civil inferiority for the black; and the steady withdrawal of aid from black colleges. Nor would DuBois concede that the differences were only political. His struggle against the Uncle Remuses and the Uncle Toms was, he insisted, ideological; and he waged it unrelentingly all his long life.[17]

DuBois' hundreds of pamphlets and articles speak for themselves. In them, we find "one autobiographical essay after another reconstructing the heroic figure of a man of principle fighting a universal battle for the right against an ignorant or hostile world."[18] DuBois thinks of himself (in *Dusk of Dawn*) as "crucified on the vast wheel of time," and "flying round and round with the *Zeitgeist*." Herbert Aptheker renamed the Age Progress the Age of DuBois.

Leading white writers vied with each other to honor the militant black writer. J. Saunders Redding thought only Thomas Carlyle could match his combination of scholarship and emotional power. Henry Steele Commager thought DuBois best represented the aspirations of the African American. John Gunther compared his position to that of Albert Einstein and George Bernard Shaw.

With the civil rights movement and the black revolution after World War II, a whole new set of heroes and theories emerged on the cultural scene. A folk tension, which had once been hidden in American rural areas or in the psyche, suddenly erupted in city streets and in all the media. The popular culture of the black minority set patterns for the white majority; the new youth culture was saturated with it.

The civil rights movement of the 1960s, spearheaded by the Reverend Martin Luther King Jr., changed many aspects of black life and popular culture in America. His famous "Free at Last" speech, made on the steps of the Lincoln Memorial honoring that president who signed the Emancipation Proclamation, is a crucial event of the twentieth century: that King's birthday is now a national holiday indicates how well the man and his doctrines are remembered and accepted.

The advances and achievements of African Americans are a glory of our times. It is reflected in every aspect of American culture; social, economic, legal, educational, scientific, literary—and on and on. Gains in black America have been spectacular.

Art, a universal language, can overcome cultural and ethnic barriers. This is evident in the United States with African-American mu-

sic, dance, and folklore. For generations, Congo Square in New Orleans—later famed as the birthplace of jazz—came alive to the
master drums of Africa. Long before the Civil War, African songs
could be heard and African dances seen in the southern United States.

As Siegfried Kracauer notes in *Theory of Film: The Redemption of
Physical Reality* (1960), any nation's films are fully understandable
only in relation to actual psychological patterns of that nation.

Sports have made millionaires out of Michael Jordan, Tiger Woods,
the Williams sisters, and a host of others. Writers such as Alice
Walker and Toni Morrison are honored everywhere. Henry Louis
Gates Jr. and Cornel West hold prestigious appointments at Harvard
University, as do scores of African-American scholars and writers
in universities and foundations across the country. W. Sue Jewell
traces the remarkable progress of African-American women in *From
Mammy to Miss America and Beyond*.[19] Oprah Winfrey has become
America's most popular daytime talk-show host. Significant prob-
lems remain, and Jewell deals with them too, just as Spike Lee did in
a series of films.

Talk of a "New Harlem Renaissance" surfaced in 2000, celebrating not only its rich history and culture, but a surge of economic
growth. *The New York Times* carried a special advertising section and
official guide to "Harlem Week 2000 and the Harlem Jazz and Music
Festival." It was a great success.

Gates and West strike a very positive and hopeful note in their
book, *The Future of Race*. They write in their joint preface: "Working
together with other scholars, politicians, and activists who have developed programs, we can begin to close the economic gap that di-
vides the black community in two."[20]

They recall Dr. King's credo that none of us is free until each of us
is free—white, black, brown, red, and yellow; rich and poor; Protestant, Catholic, gentile, Jew, and Muslim; gay and straight. This
dream, and those who choose to follow it, represents the crowning
achievement and hope of twenty-first-century black popular culture.

The Most Popular War

Here was the greatest and most moving chapter in American history, an ending and a beginning.

Bruce Catton, *The Civil War*

The Civil War was the crossroads of our being and it was a hell of a crossroads.

Shelby Foote, Historian

When General Robert E. Lee surrendered the Army of Northern Virginia to General Ulysses S. Grant at Appomattox on April 9, 1865, the Civil War, in theory, was over. The bloodiest, costliest war in American history, with over 600,000 casualties, ended in stunned bewilderment. But it hadn't really ended—only phase one had closed.[1] When the bullets stopped, the discussion continued, and a new rhetorical phase began. It still rages. Civil War I simply moved into Civil War II. A new book, published in 2000, is titled *Confederate Symbols in the Contemporary South*.[2]

The new millennium resounded with the boom of both Yankee and Confederate cannons on July 3, 2000. Where? On the Gettysburg Battlefield where the crucial battle of the Civil War had been fought in 1863. As smoke swirled from two cannons, a second boom was heard—explosives placed at the base of the 393-foot National Tower of the Gettysburg Battlefield were demolishing it. Why? Because preservationists claimed it desecrated the hallowed ground of our most popular war. Secretary of the Interior Bruce Babbit led the countdown. Civil War buffs, who were staging an annual war reenactment, fired the cannon pointed at the tower.

The Civil War, a devastating military struggle, was fought with blood, shells, and shrapnel. Tens of thousands of graves, marked and unmarked, dot the American landscape; the trenches still remain, which became burial grounds for thousands more. This was the defining moment in American history. The Union was preserved.

Civil War heroes are well remembered in both the North and South. Transported to separate Valhallas, their memories are guarded by devoted descendants, organizations, and official monuments. Able historians and novelists have told their stories time and again, and the pace has quickened in the last century. It quickens now. The Heroes in Blue and Gray have begun to smack of the mythological.

When the battles stopped, popular culture set in. It has turned the Civil War into a legend and a haunting memory. What had been lost can not be forgotten. Indeed, it has moved into Phase III and is being reenacted.

We keep looking backward, putting over that monumental and decisive struggle a shining glow of romance and glory. The vitality of the dream grew in strength as the physical embodiment of it drifted into ruin and sacred memory. The Civil War has been rehashed, redefined, re-recorded, and even reenacted to meet the concerns of different constituencies in American society.

The military war was over but far from forgotten in the defeated South. The Southern Historical Society, founded in 1869 and soon joined by the Sons of Confederate Veterans and Daughters of the Confederacy, kept fanning the flames. Old men hobbled around on wooden legs, and Confederate flags still flew in private and public all over Dixie. Many still do. The same fervor gripped the North, where even the name of the struggle was different—from their perspective the Civil War was the War of the Rebellion, the War of Secession.[3]

When I was a boy in Virginia, there were a few old veterans still walking around. They were, of course, demigods, men who had been with Lee at Gettysburg and had surrendered the last battle flag at Appomattox. Respect was their due; youthful awe their reward. The last great rally and reunion of the aging Confederate soldiers was held in Richmond in 1932. It was, for the South, a special, almost sacred day. They went home to go gently back into the long good night, dreaming of the green fields they once defended so gallantly.

Naturally, I learned early that what Yankees called the Civil War was the War Between the States—though Lost Cause or War of Southern Independence was preferred. *Rebel* was an honorable, even a glorious word. Who could doubt it, seeing those marble Rebel soldiers guarding every courthouse and town square in Dixie?

That "the War" (other wars followed, but *the* War was still "ours") fascinated Yankees as well as Rebels could be confirmed by glancing at any best-seller list or movie guide. Civil War fans increased by geometrical progressions, and young recruits joined the older "buffs." "A tacit agreement exists between War authors, readers, and reviewers," historian Frank E. Vandiver noted. "They will not double-cross each other by questioning the virtue of anything written about 'the War.' The subject has a special sanctity conferred by popularity. If it's about the War, its got to be good!"4

I grew up, fought in another war, World War II, and studied at a university in the Yankee heartland (Yale) before I came to realize that there was not one but several Civil Wars; before I understood why (according to Plutarch) Pyrrhus used to say that Cineas had taken more towns with his words than he had with his arms.

Civil War I, a military affair, left us the vision of Cold Harbor, Gettysburg, Richmond, and Appomattox. Civil War II, fanned by popular culture, is still waged with print, films, and television. Best-seller lists and film festivals confirm the report from the battlefront: the Yankees and the Rebels are continuing the battle.

Some of the actual veterans of Civil War I became key players in Civil War II. On "my side of the Mason-Dixon line" three novelists were enormously popular. They have faded now, but they planted the seeds that grew into flowers later on. In any account of the most popular war, they deserve mention. Their words and images formed a kind of causeway between a bloody and realistic war and a euphoric and romantic one. My contention is not only that their works help to explain the incredible and unfading popularity of the Civil War, but that it also indicates the type of research students of popular culture must do in many other areas if they want to give factual substance to their theories. With this in mind, join me in a brief look at George William Bagby, John Esten Cooke, and Thomas Nelson Page.5

George William Bagby managed to sleep through the Battle of Bull Run. Once awakened, he fought and viewed a lot. He saw Virginia under fire and eventually under heel. Watching the new day dawn, he never forgot the old. His vindication came not by the ephemeral sword but by the enduring word.

Born on a Buckingham County plantation in 1828, Bagby volunteered for the Confederate army but was eventually discharged due to ill health. He edited the *Southern Literary Messenger* before purchasing *The Native Virginian*. As a writer, he had a mission to describe everything distinctive and without parallel in Virginian civilization. Bagby's best sketch was *The Old Virginia Gentleman*. "There was in our Virginia county life a beauty, a simplicity, a purity, an uprightness, a cordial and lavish hospitality, warmth, and grace which shine in the lens of memory with a charm that passes all language at command," Bagby claimed. "It is gone with the social structure that gave it birth."[6] Despite such romantic nostalgia, Bagby was essentially a realist in his descriptions and attitudes. He marveled that so chivalrous a group of peers as those described in Civil War novels could have produced so many scoundrels as he saw about him in his lifetime. He had a sharpness of vision that made his work fascinating to a twentieth-century writer such as Ellen Glasgow. "His sketches have always been a part of my Virginia heritage," she wrote. "The vital warmth and humanity of the writing give him a permanent place in the literature of Virginia."

Yet there is no satire in Bagby's poem about General Lee called "After Appomattox." It was as though in the rear of Lee's tent had been the Ark of the Covenant. Like most Virginians, Bagby stood in awe of the great leader, as he imagined Lee on his knees just after the surrender to Grant:

> The cries that upward went that night
> Unto the great White Throne,
> To God alone are known.
>
> Sacred throughout all coming time
> For who can tell in words sublime
> The agony of Lee?

If he couldn't tell, John Esten Cooke was willing to try. Born in northern Virginia and admitted to the bar in 1851, Cooke was an eager gentleman-novelist. His aim was "to paint the Virginia phase of American society, to do for the Old Dominion what Cooper has done for the Indians, Simms for the Revolutionary drama in South Carolina, Irving for the Dutch Knickerbockers, and Hawthorne for the Puritan life of New England."

An ardent secessionist, he turned the Confederate generals (including the Calvinistic Jackson) into cavalier knights. Between battles, Cooke managed to write *The Life of Stonewall Jackson* (1863).

Enemy forces never interfered with his literary chores or his meals. Continuing to eat from a plate near his horse until the Yankees were within two hundred yards, he would gulp down his coffee and gallop away. Southern readers warmed to such an author.

Younger and more talented than Bagby or Cooke was Thomas Nelson Page, in whose veins ran some of Virginia's best blood. Two of his great-grandfathers had been governors. His father served on General Lee's staff. Only twelve when the war ended, Thomas saw the old regime in his most impressionable years and idealized it all the rest of his life. At Washington College, where Lee had gone as President, he knew and revered General Lee. Brilliant and personable, Page turned his talents to literature and gave the phrase "before the war" a special meaning. Borrowing from Russell, Cable, and Harris, he pioneered in local-color writing, working out a literary formula which captivated the North as well as the South. This is how it went:

Take a white-haired ex-slave, yearning for "de best days Sam eber see." Have him describe the plantation Eden, stressing the justice and juleps of Old Marse, the dash and swagger of Young Marse, and the sweet perfection of Southern ladies. Throw in a few barbecues, christenings, and Christmas feasts.

Then—the war.

Out with the trumpet and the Confederate flag! Of go Old Marse, Young Marse, and all Marses in the neighborhood to lead an army of gentlemen and poor whites to daring victory against incredible odds. Young Marse dies on the field of honor. Now only Sam, young Marse's faithful dog, and Lady-Who-Will-Never-Tell keep alive his gallant memory.

Page wrote novels, short stories, and poems using this format. A typical example is "Uncle Gabe's White Folks," which appeared in *Scribner's Monthly* in 1876. In his day, dialect was popular:

> "Fine old place?" Yes suh, 'tis so
> An' mighty fine people my white folks war—
> But you ought ter a'seen it years ago
> When de Marster an' de Missus lived up dyah.

Better than anyone, Page expressed the spirit of the Old South in a way which captivated the New. He believed that his picture was accurate and fair. "In the simple plantation homes was a life more beautiful and charming than any that the gorgeous palaces would reveal," he insisted. "Its best presentation was that which had the divine beauty of truth." His books are Southern to the core.

In Ole Virginia (1887) is preeminently a Civil War II classic. Anyone who wants to understand the working of the Southern mind and the persistence of certain attitudes into the twenty-first century might read it. *The Old Gentlemen of the Black Stock, Befo' de War,* and *Marse Chan* are other favorites of Page devotees. Mark Twain poked fun at the formula by having a black woman reply to a Yankee's praise of the Southern moon: "Ah, bless yo' heart, honey, you jes' ought to seen dat moon befo' de wah!"

Page's golden memories appeared during the years known as the Brown Decades, a term coined by Lewis Mumford to describe the period between 1865-1895. Mumford states:

> No sooner had the Civil War come to a close than, as a writer in *Harper's Weekly* promptly remarked, the reaction from the tension of war showed itself "in a certain public frenzy. Enormous speculation, losses, and consequent frauds; an increase of crime; a curious and tragical recklessness in the management of railroads and steamers; a fury of extravagance in public watering places are all observable."[7]

President Grant's administration was rife with corruption. Grant's cohorts, having captured Richmond, seemed determined to take over the Washington mint as well. The greedy, lawless, and capable coupled startling audacity with immense wastefulness. Leaders of the day fought their way encased in rhinoceros hides. They had stout nippers. Gentleman Jim Fisk (1834-1872) bragged that he worshipped in the synagogue of the libertines; and when he failed in his Erie Railroad stock swindle, he announced cheerfully that nothing had been lost save honor. Southerners looked back to the happy plantation days with nostalgia.

Yet all the male writers, North and South, didn't have the impact of two women. Harriet Beecher Stowe's *Uncle Tom's Cabin,* the most widely read novel in the nineteenth century, with its powerful anti-slavery message, remained for years a supreme icon of popular culture. Another writer from Georgia pushed that book out of first place. Margaret Mitchell's *Gone with the Wind,* published in June 1936, has never lost its hypnotic hold. It was an instant best seller—50,000 copies in one day, and an average of 3,700 copies a day for the rest of that year. Over 28 million copies have been sold since then. An estimated 90 percent of the U.S. population have seen the movie at least once; millions more have seen it worldwide.[8]

Born in Atlanta in 1900, Margaret Mitchell's ancestors lived through the Civil War. "I heard about the fighting and the wounds," she later said. "I heard about the burning and the looting of Atlanta, and about everything in the world except that the Confederates lost the war."[9]

She also grew up with the emergence of the New Woman, which she remembered all her life. One can sense her ambivalence regarding this issue in the unforgettable character of Scarlett O'Hara, a continuing source of fascination for millions.

The movie version of *Gone with the Wind,* starring Clark Gable and Vivien Leigh, became the most popular movie ever made. In Japan, it has been adapted into a long-running, all-female musical. When the Berlin Wall collapsed in November 1989, it signaled the end of the Cold War, and the movie made its successful debut in Moscow. The television premiere of the movie in 1990 drew 110 million viewers. Its popularity shows no sign of waning. It is the jewel in the crown of Civil War II.

Civil Wars I and II meet head-on at preserved or recreated battlefields. At New Market, Antietam, or Gettysburg, not only can one find the place of battle, but also shops selling books, flags, replicas of battle artifacts, and lavish tour guides. Even places that never hosted a battle have large displays of Civil War literature, postcards, flags, and statues. But the best place to see the merger is at Gettysburg, where meadow meets amusement park and patriotism links up with pleasure. What a symbiosis!

* * *

As the media and the Electronic Revolution energized America, the obsession with the Civil War expanded. In addition to novelists, poets, and historians, an army of filmmakers, pop singers, rock groups, and creators of popular culture joined in. The vitality of the Civil War was confirmed when Ken Burns' eleven-hour series, *The Civil War,* shown on public television (PBS) in the fall of 1990, attracted 39 million viewers. Burns' companion book was on *The New York Times* best-seller list for six months, and thousands of schools bought videos. Even bumper stickers mirrored the excitement; one shows a griz-

zled old Confederate veteran clutching the Rebel flag and saying,
"Hell no, I ain't forgettin'!"

Charlie Daniels achieved fame with a song titled "The South's
Gonna Do It Again." Muddy Waters, Charley Pride, Merle Haggard,
and B. B. King sang old songs the old way and made millions. The
Band (featured on the cover of *Time* on January 12, 1970) caused
Southerners to stand up when they played and sang "The Night They
Drove Old Dixie Down."[10]

All these activities (best-selling books, sold-out concerts, block-
buster movies, television series, and crowded Civil War Round Tables) helped prepare the way for Civil War III—the actual restaging
and reenactment of Civil War battles, complete with soldiers, muskets, cannons, horses, and Rebel Yells. In the age of virtual reality, the
"Re-enactors' War" was reality revisited.

The idea of "doing it all again" occurred first to Union soldiers
who reveled in their victory. New Jersey veterans got out their old
uniforms, tents, and muskets, and "went to war" all over again in
1878, 1881, and 1883. Because there were no Confederates close by
to oppose them, they arranged to "fight" the New Jersey National
Guard. Everyone understood the rules. The Yankees always won.

The Southern veterans responded. There was a modest reenactment
of Petersburg's "Battle of the Crater" in 1903. Not until most veterans
had died did the first major reenactment take place.[11] In 1935, the
Fredericksburg Battlefield Park Association joined with the National
Park Service to reenact the Battle of Chancellorsville. It was a great
success and (except for the World War II years when real soldiers
fought elsewhere) reenactment has grown steadily since that time.

The Civil War Centennial in the early 1960s greatly boosted the
movement, turning National Park Service sites into virtual shrines.
Battles were refought on land and at sea. The historic encounter of the
ironclads (C.S.S *Virginia* and the U.S.S *Monitor*) was refought
twenty-two times. Local centennial committees functioned throughout the South. Headstones were placed on graves of forgotten soldiers. Lectures, plays, and exhibits flourished everywhere with popular support. The centennial reenactment of First Manassas had the
blessing of Ulysses S. Grant III (grandson of the Civil War general),
the federal government, and the state of Virginia. "Popular interest is
running high and can not now be stemmed," Grant said. "Our chil-

dren and their parents will be inspired by what Americans have done. This will give a better popular understanding of America."[12]

The restaged battle of Manassas was held five miles from the actual battlefield. Confused and frightened soldiers stumbled through swirls of smoke as a Concorde jet flew overhead from Dulles Airport—too high for passengers to see the mock battle. To make troop movements as accurate as possible, a Pentagon cartographer, Patrick Massengill, was on hand. "There's a lot of ham in these people," he said, as a Union soldier shouted, "I can't see!" then stumbled and fell into the weeds.[13]

The 125th anniversary of the battle of Gettysburg, originally occurring on July 1, 1863, was staged in 1988. An estimated 100,000 spectators came for the reenactment, as 175,000 soldiers sweated it out—a popular culture high water mark. The most popular revival has been the Battle of Manassas.

Astonished by the size and scope of reenactments, I sought more details: how can we profile the reenactors, who sponsors them, and how authentic are they? Is there a national organization, and who finances them?

Most of the performances are local, by "gypsy" units who make their own rules. All sorts of people become reenactors, for numerous reasons. They join on their own and bring their own equipment; they even pay admission charges to participate. There is no national organization, and most Southerners don't want one. "National" smacks of "Federal" and "Union"—the very things the Confederacy fought against.

Scholarly Civil War historians tend to think all of this "just popular culture," a burlesque of "the real thing." One remembers John Skow's caption for a reenactment article in *Time* magazine: "Bang! Bang! You're History, Buddy."[14]

A strong group of reenactors exists in Lynchburg, Virginia, the scene of important action during "the War." They care little for what historians say or think. They like it, pay to fight, and intend to keep going. They are dedicated amateurs, cut from the same cloth as genealogists, collectors, and antiquarians. They buy and read specialized periodicals such as *Civil War Book Exchange, North-South Trader's Civil War, Blue and Gray, Civil War News, Civil War Times,* and *Camp Chase Gazette.* Here they can find how to purchase what they need to go into battle: uniforms, caps, insignia, cartridge boxes, and a musket, which might cost as much as $400. Artillery units must procure cannons and cavalry units need horses, which might cost $1,000 per soldier.

Why do so many people spend such sums without question? They believe in what they are doing. It reaffirms their strength, and the rightness of those who gave their lives for "the Cause." For them, history is a form of communion. They come together to form a community. Professional historians, secluded in stacks or in front of computers, can hardly duplicate this. Few of us who read, teach, and write histories think of ourselves as being a "band of brothers." We don't expect to spill blood to save a wounded buddy.

There have been many other reenactments of other wars, such as the French and Indian War and the American Revolution. Much activity occurred in 1976, celebrating America's 200th anniversary. The surrender of British General Lord Cornwallis, which assured American freedom, was especially glamorous. The reenactor portraying Lord Cornwallis, surrendering at Yorktown, wore a coat with twenty fourteen-karat buttons and wielded a $15,000 eighteenth century sword.[15]

* * *

Why *read* about reenactments when you can *see* one? A large ad in *The Washington Post* announced, "A Spectacular Real-Life Civil War Battle!" to be staged the following week. What would it be like? I shut down my computer and took to the road.

June 18, 1999: On a hot day in the tiny hamlet of Brandy Station, Virginia, all hell broke loose. On the 135th anniversary of a Civil War battle once fought there, occurred the largest clash of troops in Virginia since the War ended.

Over 10,000 soldiers fought. Rifles popped, swords flashed, artillery roared, and cavalry galloped. Who could count the thousands of spectators? Something in me responded to the wild yips and yells of thousands of Confederate soldiers charging into the heart of the much larger Union forces. I could almost imagine that Stonewall Jackson was leading the charge, and no one could stop him. The Rebels drove the intruding Yankees out of their entrenchments. The battlefield was littered with fallen troops, blanketed with heavy gun and cannon smoke. Like many pro-Confederate spectators, I felt my blood tingle. The reenactment had become reality.

This virtual reality, all fun and games, seemed quite real. When the muskets cracked and the cannons roared, commanders on both sides yelled: "Give 'em hell, boys!" The news media and cameras were there; so were Civil War artists and collectors, a hundred sutlers (cooks and camp provisioners), food and drink vendors, historians and authors, lecturers, and buffs of every shape and size. Nor did the fun stop with the fighting. There was a parade, medicine shows, candlelight tours of the battlefields, and a cavalry battle. Reality blended with fantasy. For three days, Brandy Station became a nineteenth-century wonderland.

The twentieth century was there too with a twenty-four-hour toll-free information hotline and a Web site. Dozens of nearby motels had soft mattresses and hot water. Nostalgia on so grand a scale becomes news. If some of the details were a bit bizarre, such as the "authentic Confederate wedding," the setup was not. Many guests brought chairs and blankets. Lists of motels were provided. Magazines were generous sponsors (*America's Civil War, Civil War Times,* and *Columbiad*). Come one, come all—rain or shine. And they came.

Might the "Confederate wedding," staged before thousands at Brandy Station, mark a new trend in popular culture? A possible clue came a few weeks later in Monroe, North Carolina, when Cathey Heffner transformed her backyard into a replica of the movie *Gone with the Wind*. It was, she said, her "Cinderella wedding."[16]

The backyard was decorated with magnolia leaves. Six bridesmaids wore old-fashioned, hoop skirt dresses. The six male attendants were dressed in blue jeans, white shirts, and Confederate hats with the Rebel flag in the center.

At 3:00 p.m., the wedding party entered the backyard with music from *Gone with the Wind* playing. Before the official kiss, the song "Angels Among Us" by Alabama was played. After the kiss, the couple left while Elvis Presley's "An American Trilogy" played in the background. The postwedding dinner was purely Southern, with collards, barbecue, black-eyed peas, potato salad, cornbread, pink lemonade, and sweetened iced tea. The past was alive again.

Did the newlyweds head to Atlanta for their honeymoon to continue the *Gone with the Wind* theme? "No," laughed Heffner, "we have to be back at work on Tuesday."[17]

The reenactment was a proving ground for new opportunities for capitalism, in which corporate sponsors can increase their profits. The sponsors weren't only history buffs, Rebel magazines, or game players, but Primedia Inc. and their many corporate partners.

"This is the first time a corporate entity is sponsoring a re-enactment," said Don Warlick, a reenactor turned organizer who helped coordinate activities with Primedia. "We're hoping it works. . . . the hobby needs [a sponsor]. We just don't have the resources to do it."[18]

Primedia sponsored the concession stand: McDonald's was there with Big Macs. Relics, books, videos, and software were for sale. Scores of vendors were hard at work. Borders Books and Music sponsored book signings. TalonSoft offered war games software. The Military Channel offered both new and old reenactment videos ($19.95 during the event, $25 later). All in Yankee dollars! American history and capitalism made chummy bedfellows.

Some reenactors worry about the corporate intrusion. One is Kyth Banks, also known as Captain Graydog of the thirty-seventh Virginia Company when the "fighting" starts. "The problem," Banks says, "is that outfits that do mega-events get into numbers, and authenticity suffers."[19]

It cost an estimated $250,000 to stage the battle. However you look at it, that's not cheap entertainment. Whatever the sponsorship and the profit, the incredible popularity of a long-concluded war—and the psychic wounds that never heal continue. The reenactors take all this seriously. Their national network of over 30,000 sew their own uniforms, train horses for cavalry charges, and cut their hair in 1860s styles.[20]

Reenactment is no new phenomenon. Similar events have taken place over the years. The 100th anniversary of the Civil War's beginning in 1961 gave the whole movement a great boost. In 1999, over 360 reenactments took place across the nation.

Chris Atkinson, a thirty-one-year-old Richmond policeman who fought at Brandy Station, confessed to a reporter: "I'm just engulfed with it. I mean every day I think about it. My comrades-in-arms feel the same way."[21] These weekend warriors have fallen in love with war. Neo-Confederates seem to have the most passion—as well as the most nostalgia. Perhaps this explains how they tend to end up "winning" every reenactment, no matter what the history books say.

What motivates a growing number of women to sign up and join the fight? One woman who calls herself Sam, is a heart-lung operator from Jefferson, Pennsylvania. This was her tenth year on the battlefield. Why does she come? "Sometimes even I don't know," Sam admits.[22]

Is reenacting a fad, a Freudian release, a moneymaker for clever promoters, or all three? Do Southerners have, as Tony Horwitz suggests in a 1998 book on the subject, *Confederates in the Attic?*[23] These "battles" combine elements of a camping trip, a county fair, and a weekend costume party. They are "real" enough to awaken some secret savage drive. At Brandy Station, sutlers were selling artificial limbs: $7 for a hand, $11 for a foot, $20 for a leg. What does one make of this?[24]

One of the proudest of the Confederate reenactors was Pete Carter, playing an artillery unit sergeant major, who comes to reenactments every summer and brings his twelve-year-old son. This costs him about $2,500 each time, but he spends it with enthusiasm and anticipation. "For me," Carter says, "you ain't nobody if you don't know your history."[25]

The Civil War is both a catharsis and an inspiration. Rhett Butler was lying when he said, "Frankly, Scarlett, I don't give a damn." In the final analysis, he did give a damn and manned guns to defend Atlanta. We still give a damn too.

The Lost Cause hasn't really been lost, but merely transformed. Turning from slaughter to spectacle, it is, for the North, a war that made modern industrial America possible; for the South, a quick explanation for everything that's wrong with contemporary America. From the Civil War we learned something we can never forget. When the great challenge comes, most ordinary people value something more than their own lives. By their acts, they revive the famous words of Nathan Hale: "I regret that I have but one life to give for my country."

Yet when the battle is over and the smoke clears, the "enemies" join hands and sing the appropriate song: "God Bless America."

If you missed these gala encounters, take heart—following is a short list of battles being planned. The spectacular reenactment of Gettysburg in the year 2003 will take place not at Gettysburg but in New Jersey: A virtual battle in a substitute location.

2001— 140th 1st Manassas (Bull Run) held in northern Virginia

2002— 140th "Enemy at the Gates!"

— The "Seven Day's Battles" just outside Richmond, Virginia (June)

— Fredericksburg 140th near Fredericksburg, Virginia (November), with pontoon river crossings

2003— Gettysburg 140th on a new, larger site in New Jersey

2004— 140th Anniversary, "The Last Battles": Weldon Railroad, Fort Stedman, Five Forks, and Appomattox

Clearly the South *has* risen again. Perhaps we should have hung on to our Confederate money after all.

Postmodern Pop

The world changes as we walk on it.

Marshall McLuhan

"Postmodern" popped up like wild spring flowers and caught many of us by surprise. Had "modern times" really ended? If so, when and why? Was this a fad, trend, or movement? Would it infect and affect popular culture? Was it a new name for the high-tech, or was it much more?

The term *postmodern* is confusing and controversial.[1] Some maintain it was used as early as the 1870s by Britain's John Watkins Chapman and later "first" dates go up through the 1960s. The common thread is that the choice depends on the different ideals and programs spotlighted. The *Oxford English Dictionary* (1982 supplement) gave this short, simple definition: "Subsequent to, or later than, what is modern." This merely raises another question. What then is "modern?"

Modernity is the term referring to the social, economic, and scientific institutions flowering in the West during recent centuries and having worldwide influence in ours. No general agreement exists about the term *modern.* Names frequently associated with postmodernism are Marshall McLuhan, Jean Baudrillard, Jean-Francois Lyotard, Fredric Jameson, and Juergen Habermas. Concern has centered in Europe, although there are many American disciples. Most have been philosophers and literary critics.

Postmodern ideas have influenced the fields of advertising, popular music, MTV, and architecture. Has all this interested scholars in writing about popular culture or popular culture itself?[2]

I asked some committed postmodern friends for definitions, finding that there are as many definitions as there are advocates. The ingredients seemed to fit an old cliché: something old, something new, something borrowed, something blue. If there is a common thought, it would be this: we have moved beyond the old "modernity." Remember the McLuhan truism: if it works, it's obsolete.

Postmodernists express a desperate need to meet the volatile and unstable elements of the new century head-on. Descartes and his cold rationalism are dead. To some historians and critics, this smacks of the rebirth of nineteenth-century romanticism, with a dash of Buck Rogers, Star Wars, culture wars, and deconstruction thrown in. In the world of big think, startling new theories emerged: the Big Bang, black hole, chaos theory. All this as the millennium approached.

It came and went, leaving us feeling confused and empty. Y2K had been a phony concern, and many of the old problems persisted. New ones appeared. The 2000 presidential election in the United States was so close that the Supreme Court finally had to decide it by a five to four vote. Then the stock market plummeted, and talk of recession filled the air. California had an energy crisis and both Washington, DC, and New York suffered massive terrorist raids. Was this what "postmodern" had to offer?

Writers such as Henri Lefebvre argue that modernism isn't dead, no matter how we change the label. He notes that it is still self-evident in politics, art, music, science, and philosophy. Before we accept the term "postmodernism," we should ask some searching questions.[3]

SOME POSTMODERN QUESTIONS

Steve Fuller raises an essential question if one wonders how postmodern popular culture should or will become, in an essay called "Does It Pay to Go Post-Modern If Your Neighbors Do Not?"[4]

Serious doubts arise (especially among scientists) about the over-all well-foundedness of the postmodernist project. Postmodernists flourish only in intellectual environments where they are the dominant, if not the only, ideological voice, Fuller points out. That is certainly not the case with popular culture, centering on entertainment rather than abstract ideologies. Might postmodern pop be a contradiction in terms?

Cyberspace, like postmodernism, has become a growth industry. In the nineteenth century, critics said that everything that came loose went West. In the late twentieth century, everything that comes loose jumps into cyberspace—and a dozen hucksters wait there to extol and expand it. Sometimes even multimillion-dollar satellites float off into the great void. Recall the case of Galaxy IV.

Of course, enormous obvious advantages come with the new technology, and they must be given their due. It's hard to see how we can predict tomorrow's temperature, get a few rocks from the moon, reserve an airline ticket, or find out if there's water on Mars without the new gadgetry. But considering the billions of dollars it takes to accomplish these feats, one has to ask: it is really worth it? How did we get along for thousands of years without those moon rocks and the answer to Mars' water supply? When does information overload become intolerable?

These postmodern questions must await serious answers. We are standing on a new virtual Dover Beach, reminding us of Matthew Arnold's real one:

> And we are here as on a darkling plain
> Swept with confused alarms of struggle and flight
> Where ignorant armies clash by night.[5]

We must not come merely as sentimentalists, obstructionists, or die-hards. Just as Canute standing on the seashore could not halt the incoming waves, we know that our culture is committed, body and soul, to what many believe to be a New Utopia. The changes wrought in recent years are dramatic, drastic, and (in some cases) irreversible. The consequences of these changes have only begun to emerge. No one knows what they will finally be.

We don't know where we're going, but we're on our way; like the old Red Ball Express, hurtling down the track with the throttle wide open. Theories of energy, matter, space, and time are in flux. What was once simple has become incredibly complex. Everything nailed down has come loose. Information fights disinformation, smut doubles with glut. Millions of terminals send messages with the speed of light. Anything and everything goes. Data, data everywhere and not a chance to think!

Communication is becoming compunction—the linking of computers, fiber optics, satellites, and the new toy of the month. Once all the world was a stage; soon it will be a screen.

Who benefits from new technologies, mergers, and buyouts? Will a new overclass usurp much of the power? Will those unfamiliar or hostile to the new electronic wizardry become a new underclass, one that is underemployed, undervalued, and unemployable?

Revolutionary changes are always frightening, especially for those raised in the earlier print culture. We know how earlier technologies—such as the automobile, television, and nuclear power—brought grave concerns. Those concerns were justified. The automobile, television, and nuclear power plants have raised problems few if any anticipated or understood. The earlier naive euphoria has disappeared. We are perplexed and polluted; bewitched and bewildered.

We can't halt the flow of information, nor deny the many obvious technological advantages. New "wonder drugs" work: we have advantages undreamed of even a generation ago. We also have new questions.

Is bigger better? Is biggest best? Who will arbitrate and regulate the Electronic Revolution and the media. Who will protect our basic privacy? What is too slanderous, libelous, or pornographic to be available to everyone? Do our doctrines of free speech and free press fit today's world?

Where to draw the line between the silly and the significant, the truth and the hype, the new and the neurotic? Add these to our postmodern questions. Don't expect easy answers.

When an old mythology disintegrates, a new one originates—along with new heroes. To discover a new mythos, we must create and participate in it. That is what we must understand and promote. Heroes, like Proteus of old, take on all manner of shapes and guises. Our postmodern world has negated past heroes and created new environments of impersonal and invisible power—new patterns, new space, and new hype.

We find ourselves in a free fall, borrowing, bending, and mending, having lost agreement not only about former heroes, but also about leaders, methods, and the "canon." The new technology has upended the old cosmos, moving us at the speed of light from reality to virtual or hyper reality. We live in Plato's cave, isolated by celluloid, cathode tubes, and clicking computers. The foundation of traditional authority has been deconstructed. All we are left with is a pile of rubble.

From that rubble we must construct another better world. It may be more regional than global, more compassionate than competitive. The message is clear: change with the times, but never forsake our past. History must be revived and revivified. It must also be expanded to include those produced by our new emphasis on gender, race, and ethnicity.

Myths and legends that served us for centuries have disappeared in cyberspace. We must work hard to find both mission and meaning in our tumultuous time—look for and welcome new views of who we are and who we want to be. This may not be as hard as some think.

The yearning for meaning—closely tied up in our myths, legends, and folklore—is always with us. Recall one of the early lines in the first book of the Bible, the Book of Genesis (6:4.3): "There were giants in the earth in those days. . . "

The new heroes and heroines will be more than technocrats, sweepstake winners, professional athletes or get-rich-quickers. They will not depend, like so many of today's leaders, on spin doctors and doctored polls. They will tell the truth and spite the devil. They will stand for what made us "the land of the free and the home of the brave" in the first place.

Hasten the time.

Faith Takes a New Face

God Bless America!

The 1950s began in America at the peak of peace and prosperity. We liked Ike—General Dwight D. Eisenhower—and he returned the compliment. We made him president and played golf and kept the good times rolling.

Eisenhower presided over a nation with a civil religion that combined patriotism and chauvinism. After all, Ike's crusade to Europe had saved the world not only for democracy but for the Christian God who brought our ancestors to the New World in the first place. We might begin by defining civil religion.

Jean Jacques Rousseau first used the term in *The Social Contract* (1762). The basic premise: the state could only endorse God's true existence and the exclusion of religious intolerance. Our founding fathers concurred and put the separation of church and state into the Constitution's First Amendment. The public deity was concerned with law and order, not sin and salvation. This God was mentioned four times in our Declaration of Independence, and the Supreme Court protected this for generations. Civil religion grew with the nation. Puritanism, patriotism, and prosperity made a powerful tonic. Once-separated colonies became one nation, under God, and God blessed America.

The mellow mood of the 1950s was reflected in the pulpit as well as the White House. One remarkable man, assisted by a host of imitators, captured popular attention and support, and made the 1950s the high-water mark of civil religion in American history. Billy Graham became the archetypal justifier of our civil religion. He won a special, almost semisacred, spot in the pop pantheon.

Parts of this chapter have been excerpted from *Great Awakenings: Popular Religion and Popular Culture* by Marshall W. Fishwick. Copyright 1995, The Haworth Press, Binghamton, NY.

Consulted and honored by every president from Jimmy Carter to Bill Clinton, Billy Graham combined religion, mass media, and politics in a way no one in the twentieth century could match.[1] He was, he said, a Western Union boy carrying God's message. He carried it very well. He was the voice of evangelical Christianity, heard by more people than any other preacher who ever lived—a prince of popular culture.

His popularity is matched only by his incredible longevity. Popes, presidents, and pop stars' mass movements come and go. Flower children fade, and macho men disappear. But Billy Graham keeps on preaching.

Born on a North Carolina farm in 1918, raised as a conservative Presbyterian, Billy joined the church at twelve and made his "decision for Christ" at sixteen. After a short time as a Fuller brush salesman, he found a new product to sell: Christianity. He became the high pastor of the proud and mighty in a very proud land. So successful was his Sunday evening radio show on Chicago's WCFL that he took to the road, wearing loud hand-painted ties and carrying a Bible that he loved to thump. His 1949 campaign in Los Angeles changed his life and the course of popular religion. At the end of those weeks, the revival soared with the angels and the American eagles.[2]

Many credit William Randolph Hearst's order to his editors to "puff Graham." Others point to Stuart Hamblen, a cowboy singer and radio talk show host. When he announced his conversion on the radio show, crowds flocked to the Canvas Cathedral. So did Hearst's reporters and photographers. The *Los Angeles Examiner* and the *Herald Express* used banner headlines. Their dispatches, carried by Hearst papers across the country, were picked up by the Associated Press. Jim Vaus, a prominent underworld figure and wiretapping expert for gangster Mickey Cohen, was converted. An Olympic track celebrity and World War II hero, who had since become poverty-stricken, Louis Zamperini, followed shortly afterward. Both *Time* and *Newsweek* featured the "new evangelist." Headlines across the country played up the conversions. The crusade finally closed on November 20, 1949. The tent, enlarged to seat 9,000, overflowed with the largest revival audience since Billy Sunday's New York campaign of 1917.

The thirty-year-old sensation's preaching style was simple. Avoiding emotionalism, Graham followed the musical warm-ups with intense but flowing sermons heavily punctuated with quotations from the Bible and focused on contemporary public crises and personal problems. The atomic bomb became a favorite rhetorical device representing insecurities, and the spread of Communism was portrayed as an increasing crisis and threat to world affairs. Graham was and is in tune with the times. This intense trumpet-lunged prophet found the right chord and has never stopped playing it. We are living in a time when God is giving us a desperate choice: revival or damnation.

On and on he rolled. In 1952, at the close of his five-week Washington crusade, a special act of Congress enabled Graham to address a rally on the steps of the Capitol building and to have that address carried live by radio and television. He became personal friends with Lyndon B. Johnson and Richard M. Nixon. In the same year, Graham also met with President Harry Truman, attended both national political conventions, spent Christmas with American troops in Korea, and was called by President-Elect Eisenhower to meet with him privately in New York shortly before his inauguration.

By then it was obvious that although Billy Graham might indeed have only one God, he had two faiths: Christian fundamentalism and Christian Americanism. Not that he was "selling his soul" to his national religion—a notion that would and does shock him; instead, he maintains the shell of Christian Americanism in order to put life and spirit into it. By supporting civil religion, he hopes not only to combat both humanism and agnosticism but also to use it as a springboard for leading people into the evangelical faith.

We all know the old liberal joke about fundamentalism—"No fun, lots of damn, and very little mentalism." But what is happening in postmodern America and, indeed, much of the world, is no joke. The move to the conservative right isn't merely a move—it's a slide. It took over the House of Representatives in 1996 after forty years of liberal Democratic control. It will remain a powerful force in the new millennium.

What is this "fundamentalism"? What are its core values? How can we explain its powerful resurgence, political appeal, and Billy Graham's popularity?

It has hit vital spots in our present culture and raised issues that others have ignored or underestimated. Fundamentalists rush in where liberals fear to tread. Fundamentalists believe we have lost our moral moorings and must regain them now. They have tapped the mood of discontent—and out pours money, votes, and crusaders. They have filled a moral void, a zeal for neutrality that has taken it out of public life and left millions of Americans outside public confidence and cohesion.

Graham understands the challenge of humanism. He thinks that if its influence can be held in check, he will have a better chance of converting people to what is the one and only way for all humankind. This is why he strongly supports Bible reading and prayer in the public schools. They will combat humanism and increase the probability that young people will be more inclined toward accepting the evangelical faith, which Graham characterizes as "personal faith in Jesus Christ."

The success of Billy Graham's strategy is seen in the way General Dwight Eisenhower moved increasingly from a vague religion of "Americanism" to a definite evangelical faith. In December 1952, the general said: "Our government makes no sense unless it is founded in a deeply religious faith—and I don't care what it is." A month later, he joined the National Presbyterian Church. His views became more clearly evangelical as he spoke of Christ as the Son of God and of the deity of the Bible as the true creator. When Graham visited him shortly before his death, Eisenhower asked how he could know that his sins were forgiven and that he would go to heaven. Graham reminded him of the biblical answer, and Eisenhower responded that he was ready to die.

One reason for the enormous and continuous success of Graham's crusades is the simple, direct points he hammers out so that no one—not even presidents—can miss them. His own foreign policy (in an age of extreme complexity) is quite simplistic. One proposition says it all: Without God, America and the free world will probably be destroyed. But if all Americans would repent and turn to Christ, whom Graham presents as America's final hope, then "we would have divine intervention on our side." There is little doubt that in the 1950s Graham's version of Christianity included the doctrine that America was the land that God had prepared for a chosen people. Rugged individualism was considered the mark of both patriotism and spirituality.

Graham and company are media masters. Using popular shows is just one note on their extensive keyboard. Radio launched Billy as a media star; it might still be his best persona. For years, he was heard every day on radio. Those who missed his voice could ponder his words in a daily syndicated newspaper column, "My Answer"; or they could get his magazine, *Decision,* which circulates in the millions. (Exact figures are hard to come by. My own inquiry to his headquarters brought the reply "well over 6 million.") Then there are television crusades, films, videotapes, and everything electronically new and viable. Yet all these figures and media outlets don't answer the crucial question: how does the "miracle" of mass conversion take place? Watch Graham himself at work and you get at least a partial answer: a time-tested formula, meticulous, almost military-like planning, high theater, and endless follow-up. Just as it takes hundreds of unseen participants to stage a grand opera, political rally, or bowl game, so is it with a Billy Graham crusade.[3]

Since television has become his most extensive and effective ministry, and his telecasts can reach into nearly every American home, let's examine how Graham uses that hour and how he actually comes across. When Graham was interviewed by *The New York Times* in 1957, he explained precisely what he wanted. He said he would like to use old religious hymns, then a skit stressing a moral truth.

> And then an interview with a famous person such as Roy Rogers or Richard Nixon who would tell of his spiritual experience. This would be followed by a sermon. The program would be produced on the same scale as a major entertainment show.[4]

Graham's television success has been closely tied to his live crusades in both style and distribution. Graham's 1954 Greater London crusade from Harringay pioneered the use of post office land-line relays to transmit Graham's voice to rented auditoriums scattered throughout England and Scotland. For the 1957 Madison Square Garden crusade, the Bennett agency worked up a contract with ABC to broadcast eighteen Saturday night sessions on national television. The live quality was a great improvement over the 1951 telecasts, and more than 1.5 million letters, including 30,000 decisions for Christ, came to Graham. God and the tube had blessed him.

His hour on television was the master performance of a perfectionist. Everything was planned and timed to the minute. When the program began, he strode on the platform. Clasping his Bible to his chest, he walked forward, like a blond prince out of a fairy tale. Standing before his master console (custom-made by IBM), he preached for exactly thirty-six minutes, asked his listeners to make a total decision for Christ, then to come forward to his platform. Then the preacher folded his arms, bowed his head, and waited.

Not so with his well-trained team, who would quietly move down the aisles, ready to answer any question, then accompany the convert on that difficult march forward, one-on-one. Nor was the spoken decision enough. Each convert was taken into a counseling room where he or she filled out a card of personal information. This was sent to his or her local church while another copy would go to Graham's headquarters. Within the next forty-eight hours, a counselor would follow up with a visit, call, or letter. The decision made at that moment was not soon forgotten—not so long as computers and telephones responded.

The hour would be almost up. One of the most important events has not yet taken place: the call to the television watchers. Turning to the camera (watch the cue cards!) Billy would stretch out his arms (as Bernini did for St. Peter's in Rome, symbolically, when he designed the colonnade) to all the world. "You too can make the decision, if you will." He would request that you write to "Billy Graham, Minneapolis, Minnesota," and offer to send television converts the same material those who walked forward on camera received. As he gave his final benediction—"God bless you"—up went the music volume and the camera panned the podium and crowd. Then the master of ceremonies, Cliff Barrows, would come in with a voice-over, repeating the call to the television audience. A picture of an envelope to the Graham Ministry would fill the screen. Another blessing would be given and credits would be superimposed over the last shots of the arena. The hour was finished—on the last second.[5]

Graham's team had delivered once again. They know their audience and how they have reached it: mainstream popular industrial culture, geared to contemporary needs and issues. Everything said, sung, and done has been within the framework of the dominant cultural assumptions of most listeners—and the power structure of those who make political and economic decisions. Graham provides the most powerful endorsement imaginable of the status quo by defining ultimate religious and moral issues as individual, private concerns. With him, Christ and culture go together like love and marriage, coffee and cream, or Peter and Paul.

The formula has worldwide appeal. Few places have responded as well to the Graham crusade as Australia; nor was his work there cut off from mainstream America. The Global Village likes global evangelism. Graham's 1969 Australian crusade, carried by 292 American television stations, brought in a bumper crop of converts at home as well as abroad.

The use of motion pictures, though less dramatic, has had a major impact which continues to be on the rise. The Billy Graham Evangelical Association (BGEA) has produced more than three dozen feature films. New ones are always in the works. As a result of the media blitz, Graham receives more than 2 million pieces of mail annually, keeping the more than 400 employees in his Minneapolis headquarters hopping. They operate the BGEA on an annual budget of millions. Billy Graham capitalizes on every mass medium in his role of preacher to the people.

Statistics confirmed the growing strength of America's civil religion. Although 38 percent of the population attended church in 1900, that number reached 49 percent in 1940 and 60 percent in 1955. It has held steady since then. Billy Graham was the chief reason, but others helped: Norman Vincent Peale with *Positive Thinking,* Fulton J. Sheen with updated Roman Catholicism issues, and Rabbi Joshua L. Liebman with *Peace of Mind.*[6]

Civil religion took over most of our national holidays—Independence Day, Memorial Day, Labor Day, the birthdays of Washington, Lincoln, and Martin Luther King Jr. Thanksgiving involved less and less thinking and more and more eating. Both the turkey and the turkey consumers were stuffed. How best to forget one's gluttony and relax? Watch a televised football game, of course. Easter remained religious for many, although new bonnets, rabbits, and "egg rolls" (including a well-publicized one on the White House lawn) increased. Christmas was tied up in an orgy of shopping and spending. Staggering home from the mall, millions of Americans watched reruns of *White Christmas,* which became a church service at home in front of the tube. Bing Crosby's version of the title song was for years the best-selling recording by a solo artist.

Despite the title, the movie isn't religious at all. A group of former soldiers rally to save the postwar ski lodge of their old commander. Finally, young girls dressed in fairy-princess costumes dance a ballet in front of a Christmas tree. The cast is drawn from all faiths (Bing Crosby was a Roman Catholic; Danny Kaye, a Jew). Anyone is welcome, since there is no Christian doctrine or ritual. Even Frosty the

Snowman or Rudolph the Red-Nosed Reindeer would feel at home. "The Man Upstairs" would understand.

So the dream of New Israel and the Promised Land continued; we still sought the new order *(novus ordo seculorum)*, the divinely sanctioned new beginning, different from and superior to the institutions of the Old World. This conviction, emerging out of American history, was nourished by our civil religion.

Then conservative America was taken by surprise with the rise of a counterculture. The young were no longer content to "see the USA in a Chevrolet" with Dinah Shore. The American dream turned into a nightmare. Hippies and yippies scorned the industrial complex, which they thought powered the Establishment. Instead of evangelism they turned to astrology, witchcraft, cults, group sex, and even reincarnation.

A drug culture spread like wildfire and flower power was youth's answer to the firepower used in Vietnam. Draft cards were burned, riots were staged, and a new cry was heard throughout the land: "Hell no, we won't go!" One who didn't go, Bill Clinton, would later become President of the United States. Draft dodging became a way of life.

Instead of going to war, many youth went to airports, dressed in saffron robes, to beg money for Hare Krishna. Hippies and yippies turned their backs on the Establishment and the religion which was its servile minion. They would do their own thing. What was "cool" was astrology, kinky sex, celebrity fever, and calling the police pigs. Instead of civil religion, they advocated civil rebellion.

A strange assortment of rebels and prophets emerged. One, a teenage guru named Maharaj Ji, had thousands of followers, even though his own mother denounced him and would have nothing to do with "the untouchable little pudgy boy." Undaunted, Maharaj Ji announced the end of the world, rented the Houston Astrodome, and assembled his disciples to await spaceships that would take them to another planet. None arrived. His guru rating slipped, but others took his place. One, Maharishi Mahesh Yogi, promised "the secret of inner delights" and converted such celebrities as the Beatles, Mia Farrow, and the Rolling Stones. By 1975, he had a following of over 150,000 people, including 6,000 teachers, and an annual income of $20 million. By 2000 his star had faded.

Claiming that meditation teaches one how to live in a complex society, the Maharishi showed considerable business acumen and imagination. He always allowed his followers to hold traditional American religious beliefs while meditating according to the sacred Hindu format. Giving followers individual personal "mantras," which they were never to reveal, added a touch of mystery. For the more adventurous, he even held out the possibility of teaching them how to levitate and fly. No successful cases have been reported.

Cultic practice tended to give the Eastern movement a bad name—even in the East. One of the most outspoken critics was the Indian writer Gita Mehta. While the capitalistic West has busied itself marketing Coca-Cola, Mehta observed, the mystic East has been marketing Karma Cola. (Karma is the "soul" or "life matter" that inhabits all living things.) This Western fascination with Eastern lore, centuries old, has mushroomed in our time. Rudyard Kipling predicted it. In the 1990s, the Dalai Lama became a cult hero. Emerson tried to look through the Transcendent Eyeball. Working on a translation of the *Upanishads,* Aldous Huxley and William Butler Yeats had found there, "something special in ourselves." Later, rock and pop singers turned East. The youth culture found new idols in India's Ravi Shakar, the Maharishi, and innumerable religious cults. The trick to being a successful Eastern religious leader, according to Gita Mehta, is to be an Indian surrounded with increasing numbers of non-Indians. If this is impossible, then separate your Indian followers from your Western followers in mutually exclusive camps. That way, one group accepts the orgies of self-indulgence as revealed mysticism and the other group feels superior for not having been invited to attend.

One of the fastest rising imports, Zen Buddhism, made converts of Jack Kerouac, Gary Snyder, and Alan Watts. Robert Pirsig's 1974 best-seller, *Zen and the Art of Motorcycle Maintenance,* became a literary rage. The goal is to sit quietly doing nothing—stopping the activity of the "monkey of the mind." Zen developed no major preacher, since it stresses silence, not speaking. But it did influence many people and change many lives. If much of its strength was dissipated in small ephemeral cells, there were some national manifestations. One was the Erhard Seminars Training, or "EST," a mind-improvement process which by 1978 had graduated over 100,000 Americans. Werner Erhard, founder and leader, acknowledges that Zen training was important in his development of the process. He was also involved in Scientology, Silva Mind Control, humanistic psychology, and other current "self-actualization" techniques. "EST" is a sort of ultimate, demythologized simplification and rationalization of the whole popular self-transformation process into a few easy steps and concepts; the ultimate Americanization of Zen.

Eastern and Western lore made unique new combinations in figures such as Wanda Moore. Mascot of a motorcycle gang, she came to New York in 1967 to found a psychedelic hard rock "club." Then she retreated to meditate, practice Yoga, and immerse herself in occult lore. Having put together a patchwork quilt involving Indian mysticism, spiritualism, reincarnation, and out-of-body travel, she emerged at twenty-five as the New Age Wanda, psychic advisor to a throng of entertainers and musicians. Among other members of "the glamour elite" of the American occult scene were the practitioners of witchcraft—Louis Huebner, official witch of Los Angeles County, and Sybil Leek, author of *Diary of a Witch.* Many new witches emerged.

One could also contact the Booking Agent for Soul Travel (Paul Twitchell); the Rector of the Church of Satan (Anton LaVey); and the Moonies (followers of Korean Sun Myung Moon). The saffron-robed followers of Hare Krishna gyrated on street corners to the sound of cymbals and sought donations in airports. An unending parade of itinerant gurus has to come our shores, including the lady Swami Sivanda, who found British Columbia a bit cold for meditation.

Not that Jesus was ignored; in fact, he became *Jesus Christ Superstar* on Broadway and repeated his triumph in *Godspell.* The media featured the Jesus Freaks, Jesus Trippers, and Street Christians. In the age of Aquarius, Jesus was "in"—a hot item for merchants and hucksters from coast to coast.

In the twenty-first century we look back in wonder, almost disbelief, and ask, "Whatever happened to the 1960s?" They faded like the flowers in the Flower Children's hands, gobbled up and spit out by a consumer society that wants a thrill every minute and a Messiah every Monday.

Did the counterculture develop its own theology? A new civil religion? In a limited sense, yes; it seemed more concerned with narcissism than Christianity. Tom Wolfe found the apt label: the "Me Generation." As for adjectives, "trendy" and "flaky" top the list. The great youth hustle! Half the population was under twenty-five; those over thirty were not to be trusted. American youth was a nation unto itself; a billion-dollar market for clothes, records, trinkets, porn, psychedelic goods, and occult gadgets. All this peaked in 1969 at Woodstock: a modern children's crusade run amok. "Apocalypse was in the air,"

Robert Sobel wrote in *The Manipulators.* "The temptation to use the media pulpits to preach and exhort was greater than any other time."[7]

Thirty years later, much preaching from those pulpits seems distant and irrelevant to many observers, who thought we had lived through one of the sloppier myths, full of pampered children, shallow causes, and religious rip-offs. The sound and fury of the Black Panthers, Tiny Tim, Ken Kesey, and the Symbionese Liberation Army fade away, not slowly, but in the twinkling of an eye.

But not the impact of Billy Graham, chief voice of popular religion. Even in the 1950s he had quickly rejected the New Thought. Instead, he became America's Joshua, warning that the prestige of this nation would go down in our sinful land, as would the good name of God. America's prestige was at stake; so was God's. Billy Graham played a key role in civil religion, but unlike many of his contemporaries, he kept preaching the Gospel once civil religion faltered.

Always anxious to use technology in the service of God, Graham has his own Web page, online material, training centers, and Internet sites. The older devices, such as radio, film, and television have been updated and expanded. There is even a toll-free number for the Billy Graham Evangelical Association in Minneapolis, available night and day. His faith and energy never seem to wane. He has been and remains what William Martin chose as a title for his 1992 Graham biography: *A Prophet with Honor.*

The following year, Arrowood Press published *The Collected Works of Billy Graham,* and since then several excellent biographies and memoirs have appeared. Bill Deckard wrote *Breakfast with Billy Graham,* Sherwood Wirt has taken *A Personal Look at the World's Best-Loved Evangelist,* and David Frost has recorded the *Personal Thoughts of a Public Man.*[8]

In 1999, Billy Graham published *Just As I Am: The Autobiography of Billy Graham.* The 760-page book documents the splendid and consistent career Graham has had. In the final month of 1999, Charles Ashman and Sam Wellman's biographies appeared, just in time to round out the century.[9]

Graham was a sprightly eighty-two when we entered the year 2000—still an icon, evangelist, and popular idol. His son was attempting to fill his father's boots—but they seemed too large for him or, indeed, any other evangelist. The elder Graham's unique place in popular culture seemed secure. He wears well in the New Age.

The Most Popular Myth

I am the greatest!

Muhammad Ali

Myths are stories that explain who we are and how we got that way—the building blocks of popular culture. Traditional or legendary stories, they express the wishes of the people. In this sense, all myths are popular. They describe and illustrate deep structures of reality, using imagery to express the eternal in terms of the temporal. Mythology is transformed into history, history into folklore, folklore into literature and entertainment. The process continues, from one century and one age to the next. We all live by the mythology of our time.[1]

Myths spring from the realm of the unconscious—a repository of memories, impulses, and fantasies which relate to childhood. But myths go back further than this, to a deeper level of the mind, which Carl G. Jung (1865-1961) called "the collective unconsciousness." Ideas here are inborn and universal variations, so do we possess a basic psychic structure which gives us typically human perceptions, responses, and insights. This collective unconsciousness is the seedbed of popular culture.

What we think and dream on this level is common and meaningful to us as a special force. These dreams contain universal human truths—in other words, mythos.[2] Myths are common property of the demos. Joseph Campbell explains:

> Dream is the personalized myth, myth the depersonalized dream; both dream and myth are symbolic in the same general way of the dynamics of the psyche. But in the dream the forms are guided by the particular troubles of the dreamer, whereas in myth the problems and solutions shown are directly valid for all mankind.[3]

These mythic symbols and archetypes crop up in all epochs and cultures, sometimes in ways and forms that we cannot or will not recognize. Mythology is only dead for those who refuse to study the living.

Jung was convinced, moreover, that "the posture of the unconscious is compensatory to consciousness."[4] If our conscious beliefs move too far from normalcy or health, the unconscious will then communicate a symbol to the conscious, stressing what is being overlooked or ignored. When in our waking world a pathological state of imbalance ensues, or neurosis or psychosis, Jung writes, a compensating symbol will appear in fantasies and dreams.[5] No wonder so much popular culture springs from, or leads to, Disney World, the Land of Oz, prime time television, or Never-Never Land.

Not only individuals face this imbalance. Whole cultures, from time to time, veer off and activate the corrective mechanism:

> Every period has its bias, its particular prejudice, and its psychic malaise. An epoch is like an individual, with its own limitations of conscious outlook, and therefore requires a compensatory adjustment.[6]

Where are "the dreams of a culture" to be found? In its popular culture and popular arts. Are not the magicoreligious functions once served by priests now met by athletes and entertainers—by people we watch just to "kill time"? "A myth itself never disappears," writes Mircia Eliade. "It only changes its aspects and disguises its operation."[7]

What forms the mythic core in contemporary America? Is there a central myth tree with many branches? How deep are the roots, how strong the trunk? These questions cannot be fully answered in a single chapter, a single book, or indeed a series. We can suggest only beginning points for further investigation.

Can we, from myriad myths, find the most popular one? The answer depends on whom we ask—for we have a multimythology, having welcomed and acculturated more people from more places than any modern nation. Certainly "Americanization" is itself a central myth, with the flag our central symbol.

With changing times, new and old groups invent and champion new myths—in the late twentieth century, involving Native Americans, race, gender, and ethnicity. All can be seen as subsets under the myth of success, which is infinitely adaptable.[8] Of course, we didn't invent it. "Success is people," wise old Aeschylus noted twenty-five centuries ago. Nothing succeeds like success. "A minute's success," wrote the English poet Robert Browning, "pays the failures of years." If at first you don't succeed, try, try again. Observe the athlete's face as he or she wins the game or race, holds up a forefinger, and shouts "I'm number one!" Or the musician, actor, or director when the Oscars, Tonys, and Grammys are given out. As Jackie Gleason loved to say, "How sweet it is."

Success has many faces and forms. Over the centuries, the label "self-made man" resonated with American culture. How that will change in the future to accommodate the feminist viewpoint we shall have to wait and see. Women have many successes and rightly proclaim them.

The history and evolution of the self-made man in America is a wide and complex thing, involving our belief in progress, capitalism, Darwinism, the frontier, technology, and globalism. It changes with the nightly news. The first European settlers in the New World had hardly disembarked before they were told that God favored the diligent and frugal. There were no positive reassurances that such traits belonged to the elect, but there were powerful hints. Although material prosperity did not necessarily ensure God's favor, it powerfully looked that way to the mortal eye. If the workers weren't worthy of salvation, who was? Pick up thine ax and swing.

Because he embodied the essence of orthodox Puritanism in America, Cotton Mather spoke effectively about the self-made man. Precocious, ambitious, and pontifical, Mather (1663-1728) tended to associate the will of God with the monthly balance sheet. "'Tis not honest, nor Christian, that a Christian should have no Business to do," he observed. His eyes glowed with satisfaction when they fell upon Proverbs 22:29: "Seest thou a man diligent in his business? He shall stand before kings." The implication was plain enough. Thou shalt find fitting work, and in this work thou shalt succeed. Religion and activism were equated.

Mather's most imposing book was *Magnalia Christi Americana*. For pious hero worship it is unexcelled in American biography. The longest character sketch has to do with Sir William Phips, a self-made man. He took the road heroes traveled and indulged in a little piracy. Boys will be boys. At the end, Phips succeeded and even became a hero. For the New Englander seeking a moral sanction for profit making, here was a book to ponder.

Other works demonstrate even more clearly how Mather wedded Puritanism to ambition in early America. His *Two Brief Discourses* quite bluntly asserted that man must serve Christ and achieve success in a personal calling. The *Essays to Do Good* held it was every man's privilege and duty to help the Lord, but wealthy people could do the most. They were stewards, whose special ability gave them special opportunities. "Honor the Lord with thy substance; so shall thy barns be filled with plenty." One even detects the suggestion that charity itself can be a profitable business venture.

Benjamin Franklin is the best colonial example of the self-made man in America. A direct relationship is evident between the thoughts of Mather and Franklin. The Philadelphia sage adopted the life of a pragmatist. Franklin's own *Autobiography* and *Poor Richard's Almanack* (issued from 1733 to 1758, and subsequently as *Poor Richard Improved*) had a great impact on America. His homely maxims influenced the colonies more than all the formal philosophies of the time combined. Franklin's debt in both instances—to Protestant mores and particularly to Cotton Mather—is plain. Mather's *Essays to Do Good,* Franklin admits in *Autobiography,* "had an influence on some of the principle future events of my life." Yet Mather's God is unlike Franklin's God-without-thunder. The thunderbolt, which was the stern voice of Jehovah to Mather, trickled harmlessly off a kite string into Ben's Leyden jar.

Franklin knew better than to turn openly against the American Puritanical household morality. Instead, he substituted a political and economic base for the religious one of Mather. Writing from the commercial capital of the New World, as a diplomat who had distinguished himself at Versailles, he emphasized the self-made man things that belonged to his age and temperament. Never immodest, he listed his own achievements in a best-seller autobiography because he thought his life fit to be imitated. He extolled the "incontestable virtues of frugality, industry, cleanliness, resolution, and chastity." "Lose no time. Be always employed in something useful; cut off all unnecessary actions." His familiar aphorisms were popularized in almanacs which, like the Bible, were read everywhere in America. God helps those who help themselves. He that would catch Fish, must venture his Bait. Idleness is the Dead Sea, that swallows all Virtues. Be active in Business, that Temptation may miss her Aim. The Bird that sits is easily shot. Here was ample preparation for the Great Barbecue ahead for the America that was to turn inexorably to urbanism and industrialization.

The swaggering, self-conscious mood of the Jacksonian period was reflected in art, literature, and education as well as in politics. Democracy was made into a secularized religion, with the self-made man as its high priest. A poor Virginia orphan named Henry Clay, who became a Republican candidate for president, first used the term *self-made man* in a Congressional debate on February 2, 1832. Under different guises and in other connections, it had already long been understood throughout America. Such men as Clay and Andrew Jackson rose not by revolution but resolution. To a Creole aristocrat who saw Jackson for the first time he looked like "an ugly old Kaintuck flat-boatman." To most Americans, he seemed just like one of them magnified a few times. Under him the perfumed gentry trembled, the national bank collapsed, and the ambiguous phrase "equal opportunity for all" meant something. Old Hickory said that if the job was too hard for the man, you ought to get rid of the job. A fellow could vote for an executive like that and whoop at the privilege.

The new democracy was built squarely on the old morality and on the self-made-man cult. It scorned the bones of a buried ancestry and was determined to remove the political obstacles that got in the hero's way. Success was the end point. Individual success justified not only the individual but also the institutions under which that individual served. If willpower be a true criterion of the hero (as it is for the self-made man), Jackson ranks high among America's great. A story that Franklin Roosevelt told in his third Fireside Chat illustrates the point. Once a small boy was asked whether or not Andy Jackson would go to heaven. His reply was as final as it was spontaneous. "He will if he wants to," said the boy. Horatio Alger couldn't have improved on that line.

A few years after Jackson's death, a neurotic and pallid young American who reflected little of Jackson's optimism left San Francisco and moved to a village at the foot of the Rocky Mountains. In a small hut he rested and brooded, asking himself a question he dared not answer: "Am I, dear God, a failure?"

The man was Horatio Alger Jr. (1832-1899). His own story is more intriguing than most of his heroes' and reveals more about American life. Born of Yankee stock in Massachusetts, Alger was the first son of a stern Unitarian minister who was a walking blue law. He damned human activities leading to enjoyment and prescribed as remedies puritanical piety and self-denial. He passed these ideas on to his son, who was known at Harvard College as "Holy Horatio." Unhappy as a Unitarian minister, Horatio moved to New York in 1866 and found his real talent in writing juvenile books, then much in demand. They flowed from his pen. He finished one titled *Garfield: From Canal Boy to President* in thirteen days to rush it on the market before Garfield died. He went on to write 135 novels.

They were potboilers, but they sold like hotcakes. They had a huge influence on popular culture, becoming dicta for two generations of young Americans. He packaged and sold the success myth in a way unequaled in potboiler history.[9]

Alger developed a surefire formula that still rings true in our pulps and personality magazines today. Were he alive today, he would be lionizing people such as Donald Trump, Bill Gates, George W. Bush, Michael Jordan, Oprah Winfrey, and all the Oscar winners. He might even have been editor of *People* and *Sports Illustrated,* extolling the myth of success.

In 1899, Alger died quietly in a drab dormitory room. But his books continued to be reprinted and his formula copied. In 1939, on the fortieth anniversary of his death, *New York Times Magazine* recalled his enormous influence on our popular mytholgy and culture:

> His imprint on American life is still clear after forty years; our papers almost every week report the success of some "typical Alger hero" of the present.[10]

In 1944, historian Stewart Holbrook wrote that "No matter that today he is unread, Alger was a man of destiny. At exactly the right moment he put into simple words and a standard plot the hopes and beliefs of a nation, and caused them to congeal into a national character.[11]

In recent years, new material indicates that one of the major factors in Alger's life—his homosexuality—has been ignored or denied; and that a good many of the "facts" in early biographies and magazine articles were indeed fiction. Two of the best recent books describe his as a "lost life," and "a life without a hero." But was his life "lost"? And are there not heroic elements in it?

To consider him only as an apologist for capitalism and the political right overlooks his basic humanitarian impulse. Many on the political left—such as Theodore Dreiser, Jack London, Richard Wright, and Upton Sinclair, read and admired Alger as youngsters, and certainly did not end up on the political right. A. K. Loring, one of Alger's major publishers, wrote: "He has captured the spirit of America. . . . What Alger has done to portray the soul—the ambitious soul—of the country."[12]

By the 1970s, even critics who refused to take Alger seriously as a writer were willing to deal with him as a social force. A number of his books were reissued, the Horatio Alger Society expanded greatly, and first editions of his books brought high prices. The rarest of these, *Timothy Crump's Ward,* is estimated to be worth $1,000. The Alger dream persists and will stay alive as long as the American system survives.

And so, for that matter, will the "up from the ranks" success story in America. In February 1997, *Forbes Magazine* released its list of America's rich and rising. Great fortunes were being created almost monthly in the United States today by young entrepreneurs, it pointed out, who hadn't a dime a few years ago.

Alger's fast-paced dialogue and nonstop action delighted his admirers but irritated his detractors. Yet, critics had to admit, every man who was a boy before World War I probably was exposed to an Alger tale of success achieved through clean living and high thinking. Alger time and again presented his case for the American Dream.

What about the quality of his work? There opinions diverge. Literary scholars, trained in elite institutions, tend to dismiss him. Brooks Atkinson thought Alger a "prodigious hack" and "literary mechanic," but Heywood Broun called his books "simple tales of honesty triumphant." Playwright S. N. Behrman, rediscovering an Alger story he had cherished years earlier, wrote: "I don't know any comparable reading experience. It's like taking a shower in sheer innocence."[13]

In *The Lost Life of Horatio Alger, Jr.,* Gary Scharnhorst quotes these words of Nathanael West: "Only fools laugh at Horatio Alger, and his poor boys who made good. The wiser man who thinks twice about that sterling author will realize that Alger is to America what Homer was to the Greeks."[14]

Alger was one of the most widely read American writers. Some of his contemporaries acquired fame; he acquired popularity. Why is this so important? Because popularity is what people's culture is about—and why studying and understanding it, with all its dubious qualities, is crucial and rewarding.

Alger's closest rival as a writer of juveniles was a New England minister, William Thayer. Thayer's biographies of Lincoln, Grant, and Garfield flooded nineteenth-century homes; that of Lincoln went through thirty-six editions. The Thayer formula for success was simple. Be born poor. Adopt good principles. Keep fighting until you reach the top. That was all there was to it, but it was enough to get him elected to the state legislature and to provide him with a sizable income for life. *Tact, Push, and Principle* (1881) was Thayer's most influential book. As a Christian minister, he took the viewpoint that religion not only condoned but demanded success. The gospel of wealth joined the gospels of Matthew, Mark, Luke, and John for Thayer.

They did so too for a Baptist minister named Russell Conwell, who came to Philadelphia in 1851 and, in the basement of his church, founded Temple University. So far as self-made heroes are concerned, Conwell's major contribution was a speech called "Acres of Diamonds." He delivered it over 6,000 times. Work your own backyard where diamonds may well be, and don't go seeking greener pastures was his main point. In any case, "Get rich, get rich, get rich!" was the message diet on which our grandparents' souls were nourished.

The pure-and-simple hero, the kind popularized by Horatio Alger, has not been driven from the scene. The character has a new name: Tom Swift, Tarzan, Luke Skywalker, E.T., or Superman. Alger himself pales beside the production record of Edward Stratemeyer (1862-1930) and the Stratemeyer Syndicate. The publication of the first of some thirty Rover Boys adventure novels led Stratemeyer to the establishment in 1906 of the Stratemeyer Literary Syndicate, with hack writers fleshing out plots and characters devised by Stratemeyer, who had been turning out books since 1894 in the Horatio Alger style. Published under various pen names, the books included *The Motor Boys* (by "Clarence Young"), *Tom Swift* (by "Victor Appleton"), *The Bobbsey Twins* (by "Laura Lee Hope"), *The Boy Scouts* (by "Lieutenant Howard Payson"), *The Hardy Boys* (by "Franklin W. Dixon"), and *Nancy Drew* mysteries (by "Carolyn Keene").[15] Using various pseudonyms and tried-and-true adventure formulas, Stratemeyer and company produced over 1,800 books, including more than 1,500 dime novels, retitled reprints, and revised editions. No one can be sure of the total sales figures—probably over 200 million copies.[16]

My own childhood included literary trips into the worlds of Tom Swift, the Rover Boys, and the Hardy Boys. By pluck and by luck— plus by using new technology—they managed to protect maiden- hood, white supremacy, and Old Glory. Tom Swift personified "better things for better living through science." He was Horatio Alger's sturdy lad with rockets. Like the heroes of *Star Wars* and *E.T.,* and like the astronauts Tom Wolfe writes about, they had the right stuff.[17]

So did Tarzan, born in the brain of Edgar Rice Burroughs (1875- 1950)—ex-miner, rancher, and aluminum salesman. Knowing little and caring less about the real Africa, Burroughs invented his own continent where he controlled history, genetics, and language. Selling his first piece to *All-Story Magazine* in 1912, Burroughs went on to write twenty-four best-selling Tarzan novels, reinvigorating American mythology.

Tarzan, almost literally a self-made man, grew up among the wild animals of Africa, although he was actually the son of Lord Greystoke, an English nobleman. Instead of facing the problems of capitalism, he dealt with the primordial jungle. Suckled by a female gorilla, he befriended Tantor the elephant and feuded with Numa the lion. Leop- ard women, ant men, European renegades, and even men from Mars tried in vain to outwit him. He was a triumph of human brawn and in- stinct—and of a superb restatement and repackaging of the basic mo- bility myth. Celebrating his seventieth anniversary in 1982, Tarzan had a publication record that would make any man, woman, or ape envious: twenty-four novels in fifty-five languages, thirty-seven fea- ture films, scores of animated cartoons, and a major television series. Still another movie, the 1984 version called *Greystoke: The Legend of Tarzan, Lord of the Apes,* was widely acclaimed and drew large audi- ences. In light of all this, Erling B. Holtsmark considers the Tarzan series an artful and sophisticated modern epic.[18] Russel B. Nye con- cludes that "except for Mickey Mouse, Tarzan is undoubtedly the best-known fictional character in the world."[19]

With this in mind, Gary Harmon has set out to "decode Tarzan as a hero," using a structuralist analysis. Tarzan's story is mythic—a nar- rative providing a large, controlling image that gives shape and ex- pression to our collective hopes and dreams. The lost world, Utopia, and time-warp themes are all there. So, claims Harmon, is "the under- lying order that helps the mythic analyst arrive at the fundamental structure of the unconscious mind."[20] We are back to Carl G. Jung and the basic premise on which mythos is built.

Thus we can confirm for the twentieth century what was true of every previous one: people live by the mythology of their time. What they believe is more closely related to fiction than to fact. "Fictions" sometimes claim a position for historians on a par with ideas. When half-conscious beliefs spread throughout a culture, they are powerful weapons. Mythology is psychology misread as history or biography.

Misread, but never discarded. One can even argue that in contemporary America we have more myths and more variations on them than any other nation—because we have accepted and processed more immigrants. This has required us to invent and embellish symbols, slogans, deeds, and creeds. In this sense, "Americanization" has itself become a kind of ritual and a way of kindling the mythic process.

Americanized, but not homogenized. Black culture is still unique. Native Americans still perform their ancient rituals, dance their timeless dances. Italian pizza, Polish sausage, Chinese chop suey, Mexican tacos, and French fries show that even our national menu is international. The result feeds popular culture.

The Greeks had their centaurs, the medievalists their saints, the philosophers their reason, the British their empire. We have our mobility—the road going out and the ladder going up. Today, that road leads us to the moon. And tomorrow?

With such prospects before us, who can possibly believe that mythology is dead? Some portions of the American version (such as the rags-to-riches myth) were badly shaken (even destroyed) by the Great Depression. Instead of expecting millions, people were singing songs such as, "Brother, Can You Spare a Dime?" and "Can I Sleep in Your Barn Tonight, Mister?" Leading writers—John Dos Passos, Theodore Dreiser, John Steinbeck, and many others—took sharp turns to the left. They pointed out that two interlocking premises—unlimited opportunity and boundless frontier—no longer applied to millions of Americans. For two decades, the economic and political resurgence of World War II and the rosy aftermath seemed to be reviving Algerism.

The American middle class had a dream, which the newly elected President John F. Kennedy gave us (in his inaugural address): a vision of the world in which we would help the poor "break the bonds of mass misery" and "form a new alliance for progress." But only twenty years later, Daniel Yankelovich would write: "So startling are the shifts . . . between the late 1960s and the present time that social historians of the future should have little difficulty in identifying the end of one era and the beginning of a new one."[21]

Success, like a barnacle, clings to various passing ships. It finds a happy home with the flag, the Constitution, the car, the credit card, and the computer. Success is self-promoting—in our time, it likes to be online. It makes full use of the media and is favorable to spin doctors and charismatic charmers. It likes to make the evening news, be on talk shows, and find a bully pulpit in the White House.

Success never allows us to forget earlier self-made men. George Washington started as a surveyor, Thomas Edison as a newsboy, Mark Twain as a printer's devil, Andrew Carnegie as a messenger, Henry Ford as a night fireman. Billy Graham sold Fuller brushes and Ray Kroc, milkshake makers. Jesse Jackson was the illegitimate son of sharecropper parents, and Bill Clinton had to pull his way out of rural Arkansas by his own bootstraps.

Stars fill the heavens; and like the stars in our movies and on television, they soon become falling stars. We may forget names or why an individual was famous for a while, but no one ever forgets what it means to succeed—to be number one. For that is our guiding myth, as constant as the North Star.

As we move into cyberspace and the twenty-first century, our myths move at the speed of light. Suddenly, we are everywhere at once. Both inner space and outer space beckon us forward, as we unlock gene chains and find new planets and universes. We may never get there in real life—but we shall certainly have myths to explain why we should.

Global Village—Utopia Revisited?

Not in Utopia—subterranean fields—
Or some secreted island, Heaven knows where!

William Wordsworth

The Greeks reminded us that nothing is new under the sun; we only think our ideas and dreams are new. One such dream, well known to Plato, was of utopia. Derived from two Greek words (*ou* and *topos*), it means "nowhere." But it lives throughout history, and it has an alluring title today: Global Village.

Long before we knew the world was shaped like a globe, the idea of human unity, in village, city, region, or empire, flourished. Sometimes it almost seemed attainable; the Roman Empire encompassed most of the then-known world, and other great empires followed. Not only military and political but religious and literary figures, have championed functioning utopias. In the nineteenth century, when "The sun never set on the British Empire," the utopian dream was popular. In our century, former English colonies, the United States, have inherited and promoted a utopia built on electric technology and the control of cyberspace.

People everywhere have prayed "that we may all be one of one heart and of one soul, with one mind." That noble prayer has never been answered—neither has it ever disappeared. The utopian dream is a perennial one that changes but always eludes us.

We are left with ruined cities, monuments, and piles of rubble. Poets and historians know this. The English poet Shelley described "two vast legs of stone, alone in an endless desert," bearing this inscription:

My name is Ozymandias, King of Kings;
Look upon my words, ye Mighty, and despair.

Mighty ones rise and fall. Alexander the Great swept into Asia in 334 B.C. and conquered most of the civilized world in eleven years.

He was educated by Aristotle, whose teacher, Plato, wrote *The Republic,* which invented the most notable utopia. Pliny, Tacitus, and countless others have reinvented it over the centuries.

Religious leaders changed the name "utopia" to fit their dreams and creeds. Christianity, adopted by the Roman Empire under Constantine in the fourth century and later formalized in the Papacy, dominated the West, known as the Holy Roman Empire. Other religions, such as Judaism with its notion of the chosen people, Islam with Mohammed and omnipotent Allah, had their own utopias.

The chief figure in modern times, the English saint and humanist Sir Thomas More (1478-1535), wrote *Utopia* in 1515, describing a harmonious city-state governed entirely by reason. Our Global Village Utopia, half a millennium later, would be governed by corporate capitalism and a free-market economy. Is this new Utopia enveloping and energizing the whole world—or is it causing more harm than good?

The real question is not how much money is made "on the top" but the actual human consequences for the millions "on the bottom." A darker side exists to these spectacular changes. Are locality and place losing their power to give life meaning and tradition? Are humans losing control of their place, time, and roots? Are our borders, institutions, and allegiances constantly shifting in unpredictable ways? If you are not "on the move" are you "in the way" in the new Global Village?[1]

A new generation of thinkers is raising such questions. Globalization means more money and more products; but does it mean less freedom, less real security, less meaningful information? Dare we stop and question the uncritical celebration of the Global Village?

Place is something created in time and attachment, from which we draw our sense of well-being and connection. What happens when that sense and those connections are severed? When we drift from job to job, float from city to city, finding that every place is like the last place? Committed to constant change, are we a country of exiles?[2]

That change has been powered by the Electronic Revolution, cyberculture, and the creation of overnight fortunes. Power has moved from the battlefield and the steel mills to Silicon Valley and the Internet. Sparta, Rome, and Napoleonic Europe were military powers. So was Britain, when its overwhelming naval power "ruled the waves." Manpower and firepower built empires. Today, the power has shifted from ocean waves to airwaves. The dynamo driving us forward is technology coupled with consumer capitalism. America still has big guns, but it is Big Mac that is leading our attack.

Not only does the new globalism inherit the old myths, it also invents new ones. That is a major function of computers, television, films, magazines, and advertising. How all this will mix with the old mythology no one can yet say. Will it increase or decrease our hostilities? Will it bring us together or tear us apart?

The Electronic Revolution has an interesting history, much of it centered in the United States. In the eighteenth century, Benjamin Franklin performed electrical experiments that impressed the world. He linked lightning with electricity. An even greater and more consequential breakthrough came with the advent of "three Ts" (telegraph, telephone, typewriter) in the nineteenth century. The telegraph gave us a social nervous system, divorced from "muscle culture." By making information available instantaneously, it effectively ended the separation of transportation and communication. Telegraph messages were sent around Europe in the 1850s and across the Atlantic in 1866. The telephone and typewriter came soon afterward, transforming the culture. Edison's invention of the electric lightbulb soon brightened up the world. The "Wizard of Menlo Park" is the godfather of today's Electronic Revolution.

The advent of radio made possible simultaneous communication between a central authority and any number of receivers. The union of invention and progress in scientific and technical areas provided a cornucopia of new methods, devices, and systems. But nothing was as revolutionary as the computerization of the late twentieth century.

No one saw this more clearly than Marshall McLuhan.[3] His 1964 book called *Understanding Media* was a firebell in the night. Master of a new pop-hop style, full of punning and funning, he created an intellectual firestorm.

Born in Canada in 1911, McLuhan left the University of Manitoba to attend Cambridge University in England. No classmate pulling an oar in a 1936 rowing boat could have guessed that McLuhan would become the oracle of electronics, a belated Whitman singing the body electric with Thomas Edison as accompanist.

McLuhan started out as an elite classicist but discovered a different approach, and adopted it. He thought in big terms and wild generalities. The Black Age of coal, mines, and factories was ending—the White Age of electricity, jet travel, and computers was coming. The

Electronic Age is returning to oral and tribal culture, abandoned in the Age of Print. We are being hurled back into the tribal and oral pattern with its seamless web of kinship and global interdependence—a world in which the electronic extensions of everyone's nerves involve them in all other people's lives.

Writing and print technology brought about isolation and psychic alienation. Now the electronic media will hasten us back into the embrace of the group. Electronic media create a Global Village in which information can be shared simultaneously by everyone—where all walls between people, art, religions, and philosophies come tumbling down. Now the major problem becomes one of data selection and processing. For these we shall have computers and new devices as yet undreamed of.

McLuhan's poetic concept was effective and seductive. But it ignored tribalism, regionalism, nationalism, love of language, and fear of change. People are reluctant to give up their cultural cocoons.

Decades later, McLuhan's words ring true. The world continues to shrink. Cheap air travel, bargain-package tourism, fast food, fast cars, chat rooms, digital connections, and popular spectacles (world competitions for beauty, brawn, or dollars) flourish. We clone and copy everything. Copies of American rock bands and music are cheaper in Beijing or Tokyo than in Boston or Baltimore.

External intrusion into cultures creates new tensions. Instead of harmony, we have global tug-of-war. The more we invade, the stronger the backlash. With the Global Village we get *Global Paradox*— the title of James Naisbitt's 1994 book. He predicted that we will have many more culture wars in our new century.

Relations between nations and publics become more complex, fragile, even hostile. When leaders from over 100 nations gathered at the United Nations in September 2000, the message was: don't underestimate the power of history, tradition, language, autonomy. People cling to these things, despite intrusions from media on the ground and satellites in the sky. Most people will travel no more than a few hundred miles—if that far—and will be buried close to their family, where they were born. Myths have more power than media.

Globalism will invent new myths. How will they mix (if at all) with the ancient myths? Will they increase or decrease hostilities? To ask that question in places such as Bosnia, the Congo, Sierra Leone, Iraq,

Colombia, Afghanistan, and Ireland does not bode well. Will globalism cure or exacerbate their plight?

Certainly people everywhere will be bombarded by more sights and sounds than were their ancestors. Much of the invasion will be in languages they do not understand, about places they never expect to see. What effect will news from London, Washington, and Wall Street have on us? Colin Cherry, professor of telecommunication at the University of London, thinks it will not unite us, but do more to keep people apart, in emotions and attitudes, than to lead to peace and understanding. It is grossly naive, he thinks, to assume that expanding world communication necessarily leads to peace and understanding.[4]

The gap between global economy and society is growing. Unless that gap is closed, the global capitalist system will not survive. Instead of progress, we will see pillage.

The lords of the Global Village will resist all changes that are not in their financial interests. They exert a homogenizing power over ideas, culture, and trade that affects populations larger than any known in our historic past. The possible result of such power brings to mind the fate of poor Ozymandias.

Still there are great limitations to this power, much of which depends on corporate buyouts and mergers. Corporations come and go—nations and national interests endure, despite changes in names and boundaries. The central cord that ties people together is not the media but the belief that freedom consists of our ability to choose our ends for ourselves. That is the real bottom line.

True enough, technology and capitalism are sweeping the globe; yet capitalism is not only an economy but a culture with many distinctive variants. A recent book by C. Hampden-Turner and F. Trompenaars identifies *The Seven Cultures of Capitalism.* My own travels and observations lead me to believe the number is more like seventy times seven. With the new cult of diversity, the number is growing.

We can transfer money and stocks in the twinkling of an eye—a process which has wrought financial chaos in Asia and sent the world markets reeling. The continued importance of national currencies, as the European Union has discovered, undercuts dreams of globalization. The Global Village is a utopian vision; the reality is the nation, region, and locality, which still control and sustain us. Millions of messages circle the globe. Yet we yearn to give to airy nothings a local habitation and a name.

This fall, I left my Virginia Village to explore for myself the Global Village and was surprised by what I found.

My travels took me to major international conferences and a number of other spots. I met people from countries in Eastern Europe, Africa, and Asia seldom read or thought about, with citizens' names I couldn't pronounce. I was well received and accommodated; I did not feel at ease in what I thought would be the new electronic Utopia. I heard from various leaders and sociologists a word seldom used in peaceful, prosperous America: *pillage.* I checked my dictionary for an exact meaning. "The act of looting or plundering; to take booty." Are we pillaging many third world countries—taking their products and labor at near-starvation prices, only to resell for huge profits? I learned that a billion people in the world still work for less than two dollars a day. Many of their products end up in the United States.

People everywhere are being bombarded, entertained, and enticed by the new mass media. The world walks under our golden arches and watches our Hollywood movies. But have they really changed deep down? Scratch the surface of globalism and the ancient nationalism and regionalism that have held sway for centuries peek through; beneath that, the tribalism that existed when history was yet unwritten. Can and will the electronic supplant the historic? If so, at what price?

Certainly the Global Village has glamorous toys and tools. Computers, faxes, e-mail, copier machines, modems, and cable boxes are universal signs of being up to date. Everywhere people listen to CNN, talk about eating lunch at McDonald's, and know that Coke is the Real Thing. The Internet and superhighway are already overcrowded. New travelers jostle for space every day. Like it or not, we live in an age when the value of sound bites, images, and ideologies has surpassed that of material acquisitions and physical space. Good news, bad news—any news pops and crackles instantaneously. Somewhere something is happening to someone. Do you mean you haven't heard? What you know has become more salable than what you own. Call your television station if you have a story! You may end up being famous—for fifteen minutes.

Is all this uniting people or keeping them apart? Might it help explain the new cynicism that blankets the world? Could our ever-expanding communication network be affecting us emotionally, eroding ancient values and customs? Is it not naive to assume that expanding world communication necessarily leads to peace and understanding? As I write this, there are forty-three wars raging around the world. Diversity as a cultural fact is one thing, but quite something else when it becomes an ideology and an obsession. Look what "diversity" and ethnic feuding has done to Yugoslavia, Sri Lanka, the former USSR, the Middle East, and much of Africa. Or check out the decaying centers of many U.S. cities to see diversity in the raw—but don't go there alone at night.

Perhaps we have been led astray by the siren call of diversity. What we need is less diversity and more harmony. At home and abroad, diversity has been linked to separatism, imposed quotas, and victimization. Could it be that some of our electronic gurus have become so self-consciously and dogmatically "diverse" that real diversity actually diminishes?

The dramatic 1994 restructuring of Congress showed the Republicans using this possibility to great advantage. Their Contract with America put them in power. It demanded a return to local and state control. The June 12, 1995, special report by *Time* magazine featured "America's Cultural Revulsion," highlighting Senator Bob Dole's "attack on the merchants of mass entertainment." Those were the same "merchants" who have profited by touting the Global Village, with its American technology and huge distribution chains.

In *The Bias of Communication,* Harold Innis (1894-1952) points out that a stable society depends on a proper balance of time and space. We are losing it, merging the two into time-space. The air is full of electronic signals, the sky full of satellites. But most people in the world live in places where the burning question is where to find enough food to survive and how to get it. To them, time depends on the sun and the seasons. Real news comes from the village store, not CNN. To them, the media is *not* the message. The real world is what they can see, touch, and smell.

I came home with more questions than answers. We cannot assume that humanity will settle for the information highway moving inevitably into a glowing future. The Global Village will become our new home if and as it meets actual existing needs, strategies, and circumstances. It must be of, by, and for the people—not merely the lords of the Global Village, who operate on the profit motive.[5] No one nation or ideology can or will dominate. The key in the new century will be partnership, not penetration.

No doubt the world will be wired for sound—but how does it sound to the world's people? How does the new technology and the media relate to the mushrooming of racial, sexual, and cultural conflict and violence around the world? And why do America's most violent films (the Stallone and Schwarzenegger variety) make the most money all around the Global Village?

What Global Village image are we creating in the world? Does it seem more like pillage to other countries? Do we seem to be making economic colonies and markets of the world, stripping them of their ancient customs, habits, and folk ways?[6] Are we doing what the British did when their Empire stretched from shore to shore—really imperial exploitation?

These and other vexing questions demand all our skills, patience, and vision. There are no easy or quick answers. This has been a great century for humanity—and the best may yet be coming. Statistics give us reason to hope. Life expectancy in the developing world jumped from forty-two to fifty years in the past two decades. Most of us live longer and healthier lives. The literacy rate shot up from a third to a half of the world population. The "green revolution" allowed many countries, such as India, to feed themselves adequately for the first time in history. We conquered deep space and landed our man on the moon. The Cold War ended, and the Berlin Wall came tumbling down. Students travel and study abroad. And yet . . .

Theirs will be no easy job. Born of parents who had the highest divorce rate in history, saddled with debts in the trillions, massive pollution, disintegrating families and cities, and racial rancor, they will find little solace in the disappearing utopia.

Perhaps we tackled too much too quickly—the great American impatience. First of all, we must put our own house (budget, military, medical system, bureaucracy) in order. Instead of standing aside and attacking the system, we might work for change from within, demanding both public and private-sector support. We have seen the enemy, and it is us.

As for the Global Village, perhaps it was—to use the title of a movie about the Allies' unsuccessful effort to rush prematurely into Germany—*A Bridge Too Far.* Instead of thinking global, I suggest that we think regional.

A region may be defined as an area held together by a common culture—myth, language, religion, a sense of belonging. The key to a workable region is cooperation, not (as with sections or nations) hostility and antagonism. Instead of attempting to monitor and regulate the scores of "nations" now in the UN, we might work through regional councils and parliaments which would take some of the terrible pressures off the almost-bankrupt and overtaxed UN.

Our own United States provides a model. We have three overarching regions—the North, South, and West, and people are proud (sometimes too proud) to acknowledge this. But there are distinct and workable subregions within the three—New England and the Middle Atlantic in the North; Upper and Lower South; Midwest and Far West. More recently, we have spoken of "belts"—Sun Belt, Rust Belt, Corn Belt, etc. In this sense, we can say we have not one but several "Americas," regions in search of a common faith and destiny.

How might this work if we put the grid on the whole world? The overarching "regions" become obvious: Western Europe, Eastern Europe, North America, Central America, South America, Pacific Rim, Southeast Asia, Middle East, South Pacific, Northern Africa, Southern Africa. Many would want to fine-tune the list or use different labels. But the implications are clear. Western Europe has more than enough to do to make the EEC work; North America, the proposed NAFTA; the Middle East, the latest Israeli-Palestinian cease-fire. All problems eventually become global; but by attacking them first on a regional level and avoiding the utopian overexpansion, we might get much better results.

What is needed is not to restore the "good old days" of national rivalry and cutthroat competition or to revive a culture vanishing under modern conditions—conditions which make it impossible—but to grow a contemporary world culture from the old roots. The crucial problem is that each region must preserve its characteristic culture, which should also harmonize with that of its neighbors. We cannot give up our heritages with all their rich variety. They are essential for the odyssey of the human spirit.

How to match diversity with unity; patience and impatience; daydreams with reality? What is the future of our past? How will folk art fare in the electronic Global Village? Let no one think that we all live today in a problem-free, peace-loving Global Village, because we don't. We have not only scores of military wars but many culture wars to deal with. Can we solve them? In due time, perhaps.

But we must begin by putting our own house in order. Our goals should be specific, sensible, and attainable. Millions of words dealing with billions of dollars float through the air with the greatest of ease. But what do they really mean? This is the crucial question for American cultural studies.

"Nothing worth doing is completed in our lifetime," wrote Reinhold Niebuhr, "therefore we must be saved by hope. Nothing true or beautiful or good makes complete sense in any immediate context of history; therefore we must be saved by faith."

Let us hope we have the faith.

Some Final Thoughts

It ain't over 'til it's over.

Yogi Berra, New York Yankees

I end facing a paradox: I have questioned "virtual reality" in this book—yet I spend much of my life in it. I have pointed out all the imminent dangers of the high tech—yet I depend on it. American society could no longer function without computers. We have hold of the electrical wire, the current is on, and we can't let go. Ah, the ironies of our new age.

Having confessed this, I took action. I left my little well-wired electronic nest—Blacksburg, the village that *Esquire* magazine labels "Cyburbia"—and struck out into the "real world," alias the Global Village.

I met reality soon enough. Reality: long lines in crowded airports; delayed flights; airplane peanuts for lunch; narrow, crowded seats amid a bevy of screaming children—not what the travel agents and airlines promised, but certainly reality. The worst is over: getting to the airport on the interstate must have turned my last black hairs gray. The recollected rumble of the eighteen wheelers still sends shivers up my spine. No wonder they call I-81 the Ultimate Gamble.

Major conferences, research libraries, pleasure outings, and day-by-day living in Europe, Africa, and Asia proved that American problems are indeed universal; in fact, theirs are often much worse than our own. The diseased and dying stare at you with plaintive eyes. People everywhere are being bombarded, seduced, and deceived by the media, even in once-idyllic places (such as Milan, Madras, Saigon, Katmandu, Bora Bora, Colombo, Seoul, Bali, Crete, and Hawaii). They share the fruits of American popular culture.

Even the countries we have learned to hate—Iraq, Iran, Cuba, North Korea are "coming our way." English is spoken almost everywhere; the lingua franca has become lingua angla. The U.S. dollar will buy almost anything you want. The best-known and most used expression in the world is OK.

Why, then, don't I feel OK? Why do the world's upscale places look like the better sections of Manhattan or North Chicago—and the others look like South Chicago or the Bronx? Why do so many people look malnourished or diseased? Why are malaria, typhoid, and AIDS epidemic, yet often untreated and unchecked? The same rich-poor, in-out, online-out of touch, white-colored gaps that haunts us haunt most of the world.

What we miss most quickly as we move around the world are the basic items: food and drinking water. Two-thirds of the world's people wake up hungry every morning. Most of the world's water is polluted or untested. Smog is so thick over many places (Mexico City, Bombay, Calcutta, most African cities, many Latin American cities) that the sun is blocked in the middle of the day. The whole crumbling Russian empire and much of China is an ecological disaster. What happened to the billions of dollars we poured out to clean up the cities and the government? And billions more to stop the drug traffic and vicious tribal wars? Have we intervened more than we have adjudicated? Is there a black hole somewhere where much American foreign aid ends up?

So what do I conclude? Am I optimistic? Pessimistic? Uncertain? All of the above. Information rushes in faster than we can absorb or interpret it. We may sleep, but we remain online day and night, and the e-mail never stops coming. We move with the speed of light—but are we enlightened? Just where should we put our hope and our trust? In technology? Science? Politicians? Firepower? Missile defense systems? Miracle drugs?

Consider the great genome breakthrough in the summer of 2000. We were told it was as significant as our 1969 moonlanding. It would give us new hope and life, allow us to cure diseases, amend malfunctions, extend life. Now we know just what makes us human. We have discovered the 3.15-billion-letter instruction book for our cells and will usher in the New Jerusalem.

Then, only a few days later, the rude rebuttal. New scientific reports suggested that 97 percent of the human genome appears to be useless strings of nonsense and repetition, chock-full of gibberish, repetitions, and redundancies. European scientists agreed. What should we believe? Who is right? Where does truth (or rainbows) begin and end? What road shall we follow to understand and advance in our New Age?

TWO ROADS: BOTH DANGEROUS

Off on a cyberrace in cyberspace, many of the old and most of the young would give a quick answer: take the high (tech) road—get on the Net, on the Web, online. Go from bigtop to laptop to palm. Get ready for nanotechnology. This is the New Age!

Enticing but dangerous. Will we repeat the South Sea Bubble and find virtual reality always gives way to reality?

Another enticing road, less traveled, is also dangerous. It glorifies the past without realizing it *is* past, and one really can't go home again. In the brilliant and bouncy lines from Gilbert and Sullivan's *The Mikado:*

> There's a fascinating frantic in a ruin that's romantic
> Do you think I am sufficiently decayed?

Like Janus, that wise god, we must look both forward and backward and act only in the present. Seek knowledge, not information— and learn to tell the difference. Trust that greatest of mothers, Mother Nature. Her process of renewal and resurrection should comfort and inspire us. Every natural fact is a symbol of some spiritual fact. From Columbus to computers we have created new symbols and shall continue to do so. Old symbols renew themselves. The argonauts become astronauts; age-old dramas thrive in new settings. That is our human heritage.

Being human, we think in symbols. They make sense out of our pilgrimage through time, from birth to burial. To live symbolically means true freedom. In *The Philosophy of Symbolic Form,* Ernst Cassirer points out that symbolism is an essential function of human consciousness, being basic to our understanding of language, science, art, myth, and religion.

In this age of advertising, symbols are called trademarks. They overwhelm us on wrappers, boxes, billboards, labels, television, and computers. Popular culture must help interpret and evaluate these symbols. God may be dead, but new symbols are alive and well on land, at sea, and in cyberspace.

I put my faith not in the flood of information that overwhelms us, but in the wisdom of A. A. Milne's *Winnie-the-Pooh.* Winnie-the-Pooh knew nothing of chat rooms, black holes, genomes, digital revolutions, or nuclear weapons. He was interested in rubber balls, not cannonballs. Rubber balls move forward steadily until they reach something hard. Then they bounce back.

Bouncing lets you go ahead with your life, to put false moves behind you, and bounce on to a new perspective. Charles Darwin called this strategy evolution. Bounceability is adaptability. Pooh's friend Tigger knew this, and won Pooh's admiration for it. If we can bounce, we can survive.

I believe our best hope lies with our adaptability, our bounceability. We have bounced back many times before and we can do it again—at speeds that Tigger never imagined. But haste makes waste. We must not let speed destroy substance or our precious traditions and memories. Our "now" is built on lessons and wisdom from "then," including the most primal and primitive modes. Instead of discarding our past, we must "remythologize" it. Otherwise, we have no viable future.

Myths that have served and supported us for many centuries and made America great are an endangered species. But the need for myths and for greatness is still with us; mythic memories and dreams sustain us. The insights of today must express the eternal. Any sentence that contains an absolute has mythic overtones.

True places are not found on maps. No matter how far and long we travel on our interstates, we will not reach the heart of America. Nor will compasses, calculators, and computers help. When they give out, myths refresh us, drawing from deep and ancient wells.

This book has, I hope, shown how our millennial myth was degraded by the Y2K bug and two-bit politicians. That is why we have no heroes but scores of hucksters who live by sound bites and polls. Where have all the heroes gone? Driven underground by political correctness.

Academics have lost agreement not only about heroes but also about texts, teaching, and the "canon." The foundations of traditional learning and authority have been deconstructed. Can we put Humpty Dumpty together again? Yes, if we really want to. It won't be easy.

Our human gift is to be able to study and sense what has been and speculate about what will be. We must learn from the past, live in the present, and help shape the future.

That is because the future grows out of the past: we stand at the vortex where they meet, in the now. The past is always fading; the future, beckoning. Rebirth and renewal are as certain as the spring that follows winter. A new renaissance is always possible.

We have the power either to make it or miss it. Free will is the gift of the gods. The same rocket boosters that can carry probes to the planets can drop nuclear bombs on our neighbors. One road leads to expansion, the other to destruction.

In our New Age, we can either bounce forward and welcome a greater future than we have yet imagined, or fall backward to a New Stone Age.

All the tools for bounceability are on hand. We have indeed made giant leaps forward on many fronts. Bounce on, oh ship of state. If we have the will, we can find a way. Now it is up to us.

Notes

What to Make of the Millennium

1. The millennium was discussed, debated, and analyzed in thousands of articles, books, editorials, and debates. For an overview, see *Preview 2001+: Popular Culture Studies in the Future,* edited by Marshall W. Fishwick and Ray B. Browne (Bowling Green, OH: Popular Press, 1996). Mary Lee McLaughlin, a senior at Virginia Tech, wrote this paper for Dr. Fishwick's seminar in the spring of 2001.

2. Nancy Gibbs and Michael Duffy, "Two Men, Two Visions." *Time,* November 6, 2000, p. 24.

3. John Hague, *An American Mosaic* (New York: American Heritage, 1997), p. 19.

4. Barbara Grizzuti Harrison, "The Incubator of Dreams." *New York Times Magazine,* October 17, 1999, p. 101.

5. Gabriele Bartz and Eberhard Konig, *Michelangelo Buonarroti.* Koln, Germany: Konemann Verlagsgeselleschaft, 1998.

6. Ibid., p.106.

7. William Safire, "The ME Millenium: On Language." *New York Times Magazine,* October 17, 1999, pp. 40-42.

Popular Culture: The Beggar at the Gate of Our Public Schools

1. A student, Joshua Mouras, used this phrase to describe popular culture during a conversation with the author on June 7, 2001.

2. "The 100 Best High Schools," *Newsweek,* March 13, 2000, pp. 50-53.

3. Jon Krakauer, *Into the Wild* (New York, Villard, 1996).

4. Stephen Chbosky, *The Perks Of Being A Wallflower* (New York, Pocket Books, 1999).

5. Rachel Dooley, "A Decision for Tomorrow: What the Class of 2003 Receives from the Class of 2002," May 14, 2001. The persuasive essay explains which novel most deserves to remain on the course reading list.

6. Conversation with the author in October 2000.

7. C. S. Lewis, "On the Reading of Old Books," in Walter Hooper, ed., *God in the Dock* (Grand Rapids, MI, William B. Eerdmans Publishing Co., 1970), p. 202.

8. In 1995, the Commonwealth of Virginia began instituting the Standards of Learning in its public schools. Virginia teachers are expected to follow curriculum guidelines set forth in the SOLs. Student progress is then measured through regular testing. For detailed information, visit the Virginia Department of Education homepage.

9. Many students are receiving Individualized Educational Plans (IEPs) in our district. During the 2000-2001 school year, 13 percent of the student population qualified for and received special accommodation at Blacksburg High School, and the number of students meeting the criteria for special accommodations rises each year.

10. See *Educating Peter,* the Academy Award-winning HBO documentary filmed in Blacksburg, Virginia.

11. Qtd. in John Fiske, ed., *Studies in Communication* (London and New York, Methuen, 1986), p. 18.

12. William Shakespeare, *The Tempest,* in David Horne, ed., *The Yale Shakespeare* (New Haven, Yale University Press, 1955), *V.i.*

The New Gold Rush

1. Quoted by Todd Oppenheimer, "The Computer Illusion," in *Atlantic Monthly,* July, 1997, p. 4. The arguments presented here will be elaborated later in this book. Meanwhile, an excellent summary of the virus problem is Douglas Rushkoff's *Media Virus: Hidden Agendas in Popular Culture* (New York: Ballantine Books, 1994). He concludes: "I am not optimistic. Instead of extending our humanity, the new high-tech might be crippling it" (p. 108).

Folk/Fake/Pop

1. A good summary of the various approaches is found in "A Theory for American Folklore: A Symposium," in *Journal of American Folklore,* 72(285), September 1959. That same journal continues to deal with this controversial subject to the present day.

2. My summary of these matters can be found in *Seven Pillars of Popular Culture* (Westport, CT: Greenwood Press, 1985). See also Daniel Roche, *History of Everyday Things* (New York: Cambridge University Press, 2000).

3. The classic study is Henry Glassie's *Folksongs and Their Makers* (Bowling Green, Ohio: Popular Press, 1979). See also Peter Laslett, *The World We Have Lost* (New York: Scribner, 1965).

4. Richard Dorson, *Folklore Research Around the World.* Bloomington: University of Indiana Press, 1979. See also Alan Dundes, *The Study of Folklore* (Englewood Cliffs, NJ: Prentice-Hall, 1965).

5. Vance Randolph, *Pissing in the Snow and Other Ozark Folktales.* Urbana: University of Illinois Press, 1977, pp. 45 f.

6. See William Zinsser, *Pop Goes America* (New York: Harper and Row, 1966), chapter 4; and Wendy Griswold, *Cultures and Societies in a Changing World* (Thousand Oaks, CA: Pine Forge Press, 1994).

7. Marshall McLuhan, *Understanding Media.* New York: Basic Books, 1964; and Philip Marchand, *Marshall McLuhan: The Medium and the Messenger* (Cambridge: MIT Press, 1998), p. 224.

8. For more on the evolution of folk style, fake style, and pop style, see Marshall W. Fishwick, *Go and Catch a Falling Star* (New York: American Heritage, 1994); Jaques Barzun, *From Dawn to Decadence: 500 Years of Western Cultural Life* (New York: HarperCollins, 2000); and Jeffery Rosen, *The Unwanted Gaze* (New York: Random House, 2000).

Sacred Symbols

1. The classic study of icons is Leonid Ouspensky and Vladimir Lossky, *The Meaning of Icons* (Basel: Otto Walter, 1952). Two other excellent studies are Erwin Panofsky, *Studies in Iconology* (New York: Oxford University Press, 1939), and Ernst Benz, *The Eastern Orthodox Church* (New York: Anchor Books, 1963).

2. See Victor Lasareff, *Russian Icons* (New York: Unesco, 1962).

3. Max von Boehn, "Prehistoric Idols," *Dolls,* trans. by Josephine Nicoll (New York: Dover, 1972), pp. 123-135.

4. Ibid., p. 28.

5. Herbert Read, *Icon and Idea.* Cambridge: Harvard University Press, 1955, p. 17.

6. George K. Boyce, *Corpus of the Lararia of Pompeii.* Rome: American Academy, 1968; and Joseph J. Deiss, *Herculaneum: A City Returns to the Sun.* New York: Crowell, 1966.

7. David Pye, *The Nature and Art of Workmanship.* Cambridge: Cambridge University Press, 1968. I am grateful to David Gerald Orr, who has helped develop these ideas in our conversations.

8. Ray Browne and Marshall Fishwick, *Icons of Popular Culture.* Bowling Green, OH: Popular Press, 1970.

9. David Cairns, *The Image of God in Man.* London: SCM Press, 1953, p. 96.

10. J.M. Hussey, *The Byzantine World.* New York: Harper and Brothers, 1961, pp. 30-31.

11. H.P. Gerhard, *The World of Icons.* New York: Harper and Row, 1971; and David Talbot Rice, *Byzantine Art.* Harmondsworth, UK: Penguin, 1968.

12. Williston Walker, *A History of the Christian Church.* New York: Charles Scribner, 1959, p. 49. See also Thomas H. Bindy, *The Oecumenical Documents of the Faith.* New York: Methuen, 1950.

13. Claude Levi-Strauss, *The Savage Mind.* Chicago: University of Chicago Press, 1967, p. 72.

14. Ranuccia Bianchi Bandinelli, *Rome: The Late Empire.* New York: George Braziller, 1971, p. 41

15. This whole area is explored by John A. Kouwenhoven. See *Made in America* (1948), reprinted as *The Arts in Modern American Civilization* (1960).

16. The article, which appeared in the Spring 1973 issue of *American Quarterly,* pp. 67-81, contains a helpful bibliography. Quote from p. 79.

17. Linda Mizejewski, *Ziegfeld Girl: Image and Icon in Culture and Cinema.* Durham: Duke University Press, 1999.

18. Arthur Berger points this out in his article on "Soft Drinks and Hard Icons," in Marshall Fishwick and Ray Browne's *Icons of Popular Culture,* pp. 30-32.

19. Marshall Fishwick and Ray Browne, *Icons of Popular Culture,* pp. 13-28.

20. E.J. Kahn, *The Big Drink.* New York: Random House, 1960, pp. 155-56.

21. The man is Wilbur G. Kurtz Jr. and his indispensable work is summarized by Cecil Munsey in *The Illustrated Guide to the Collectibles of Coca-Cola* (New York: Hawthorn Books, 1972). See also Lawrence Dietz, *Soda Pop: The History, Advertising, Art, and Memorabilia of Soft Drinks in America* (New York: Chelsea House, 1973); and E.J. Kahn, *The Big Drink* (New York: Random House, 1960).

22. Craig Gilborn, "Pop Iconology: Looking for the Coke Bottle," in Ray Browne and Marshall Fishwick's *Icons of Popular Culture* (Bowling Green, OH: Popular Press, 1970), pp. 13ff.

23. Cecil Munsey, *The Illustrated Guide to the Collectibles of Coca-Cola,* p. 119. Recently Coca-Cola has embarked on a major expansion and diversification program, moving into such areas as movies, cable television, frozen foods, and video games. What will all this do to the iconic image of Coke?

24. Marvin Trachtenberg, *The Statue of Liberty.* New York: Viking, 1976, p. 156.

25. W.H. Huggins and Doris R. Entwisle, *Iconic Communication: An Annotated Bibliography.* Baltimore: Johns Hopkins University, 1974.

26. K.C. Knowlton's *Computer-Produced Movies* (New York: Science Press, 1965) gives an excellent summary of potential capabilities of computer-controlled displays. Since then, a plethora of books, films, and discs have carried the argument forward. Two that have been most helpful to me are: Paul Wells, *Understanding Animation* (London: Routledge, 1998), and James Watson, *Media Communication: An Introduction to Theory and Process* (New York: St. Martin's Press, 1998). Trendy but still informative is Steven Daly and Nathaniel Wice's, *alt.culture: an a-to-z guide to the 90s—underground, online, and over-the-counter* (New York: HarperCollins, 1995).

The Man and the Mouse

1. Information—oral, printed, and electronic—about Walt Disney and Mickey Mouse makes up a world of its own. The best place to start might be with bibliographies, of which Kathy M. Jakson's *Walt Disney: A Bio-Bibliography* has served me best (Westport, CT: Greenwood Publishing, 1993). See also Elizabeth Leebron and Lynn Gartley, *Walt Disney: A Guide To References and Resources* (Boston: G.K. Hall, 1978); and Glenna Dunning, *The American Amusement Park: An Annotated Bibliography* (Monticello, IL: Vance, 1985).

2. Among the recent biographies are Katherine Green's *The Man Behind the Magic: The Story of Walt Disney* (New York: Viking, 1998); Amy B. Green and Howard E. Green, *Remembering Walt: Favorite Memories of Walt Disney* (Orlando: Disney Press, 1999); Caroline E. Lazo, *Walt Disney* (New York: Silver Burdet, 1999); Steven Watts, *Walt Disney and the American Way of Life* (New York: Houghton Mifflin, 1997); and *Walt Disney: Creator of Mickey Mouse* (New

York: Enslow Publishers, 1997); Carl Fallberg, *Disney's Men, Women, and Mouse* (New York: Heimburger House, 1995).

3. This idea is fully developed by J.C. Wolfe (1999) in "Disney World: America's Vision of Utopia" in *Alternative Futures*, 2:72-79.

4. Michael Real, *Mass Mediated Culture* (Englewood, NJ: Prentice-Hall, 1977); Herbert I. Shiller, *The Mind Managers* (Boston: Beacon, 1973). The Disney enterprise has continued to expand and prosper in the twenty-first century.

5. The literature on Disney World is voluminous. Three particularly helpful studies are L.E. Zehnder, *Florida's Disney World* (Tallahassee: Pensula Publishing, 1975); Stephen M. Fjellman, *Vinyl Leaves: Walt Disney World and America* (Boulder: Westview Press, 1992); and *Project on Disney, Inside the Mouse: Work and Play at Disney World* (Durham: Duke University Press, 1995).

6. For the best study that puts Coney Island, Disney World, and the whole world of amusement parks in perspective, see Judith A. Adams, *The American Amusement Park Industry: A History of Technology and Thrills* (Boston: Twayne, 1991).

Carnivals—Old and New

1. The most comprehensive study of carnivals in America—with a brief summary of early ones abroad—is Judith A. Adams, *The American Amusement Park Industry: A History of Technology and Thrills* (Boston: Twayne, 1991). Among the trade journals, the leading weekly is *Amusement Business,* Billboard Publications, Box 24970, Nashville, TN 24970; and *Funworld,* a monthly publication of the International Association of Amusement Parks and Attractions, 4230 King Street, Alexandria, Virginia, 22302.

2. Reid Badger, *The Great American Fair: The World's Colombian Exposition and American Culture* (Chicago: Nelson Hall, 1979), Chapter 4.

3. Quoted by Judith A. Adams, *American Amusement Park Industry,* p. 41.

4. John F. Kasson, *Amusing the Millions: Coney Island at the Turn of the Century* (New York: Hill and Wang, 1978), Chapters 1 and 2. Other excellent accounts may be found in Oliver Pilat and Jo Ranson, *Sodom by the Sea: An Affectional History of Coney Island* (Garden City, NJ: Doubleday, 1941); and Robert E. Snow and David E. Wright (1976), "Coney Island: A Case Study in Popular Culture and Technical Change," *Journal of Popular Culture,* 9 (Spring), pp. 960-975. For the visually minded, there is Richard Snow's *Coney Island: A Postcard Journey to the City of Fire* (New York: Brightwaters Press, 1984).

5. Edo McCullough, *Good Old Coney Island* (New York: Scribner, 1957), pp. 112 f.

6. Judith A. Adams, *American Amusement Park Industry,* pp. 145 f.

7. John F. Kasson, *Amusing the Millions,* p. 239.

8. Susan G. Davis's full-length book about Sea World is entitled *Spectacular Nature: Corporate Culture and the Sea World Experience* (Berkeley: University of California Press, 1997). Especially valuable is Chapter 3: "Producing the Sea World Experience: Landscape and Labor."

9. Ibid., p. 79.

10. Baker wrote this letter to the editor of *The Washington Post,* May 9, 1998, p. 22.

The Celebrity Cult

1. So argues J.P. Priestly, "Marilyn Monroe," *The Saturday Evening Post,* April 27, 1963, p. 12. See also Paul Rudnik, *Time,* June 14, 1999, 153(23), p. 128.

2. See Daniel Mendelsohn, "The Drama Queens: They Paid the Price for Living on the Edge," in *New York Times Magazine,* November 24, 1996, p. 72 f.

3. Marshall W. Fishwick, *Go and Catch a Falling Star* (New York: American Heritage Press, 1994), chapter 8.

4. Ibid., p. 67.

5. See Earl F. Bargainnier, "The Plantation: Southern Icon," in *Icons in America,* Edited by Ray Browne and Marshall Fishwick (Bowling Green, OH: Popular Press, 1978), chapter 21.

6. Walter M. Gerson and Sander H. Lund, "*Playboy* Magazine: Sophisticated Smut or Social Revolution," *Journal of Popular Culture,* 31(1), summer 1997, p. 114.

7. Ronald B. Leiber, "*Playboy:* The Next Generation: Christie Hefner teaches an old rabbit new tricks," *Fortune Magazine,* March 17, 1998, 136(5), p. 46.

8. This new involvement of man with man is the central concern of Walter Ong in *The Barbarian Within* (New York: Macmillan, 1964).

9. For a detailed analysis, see Patrick D. Hazard, "The Entertainer As Hero," *Journalism Quarterly,* 39, Spring, 1962, pp. 28-40.

10. David Sylvester, London's *Independent,* Sunday, May 22, 1994, p. 24.

11. Andy Warhol, *Diaries* (New York: Warner Books, 1991), p. 20. This cryptic tag line was repeated numerous times in celebrity magazines, articles, and cartoons.

12 See Walter Ong, *The Barbarian Within* (New York: Macmillan, 1964).

13. Patrick Hazard discusses these matters in "The Entertainer As Hero," *Journalism Quarterly,* 39, Spring, 1962.

14. See Bill Owens, *Our Kind of People: American Groups and Rituals* (Livermore, CA: Working Press, 1975).

15. James von Schilling, "Disco-munity, or I'm OK, You're OK, America's OK, So Let's Dance," in *Popular Culture Reader,* (Bowling Green, OH: Popular Press, 1994), p. 260.

From Humbuggery to Hype

1. In addition to five autobiographies under different titles, Barnum wrote his masterpiece in 1866: *The Humbugs of the World.* Humbug, he asserts, is universal, be it secular, moral, or religious. The greatest humbug is one who believes that everything and everybody are humbugs. Barnum denounces impositions, money manias, swindlers, quacks, hoaxes, witchcrafts, and religious humbugs.

2. Barbara Maria Stafford demonstrates how hucksters, self-promoters, and con artists all flourished in the eighteenth century in her *Science: Enlightenment, Entertainment, and the Eclipse of Visual Education* (Cambridge: MIT Press, 1995).

3. There is a whole library about Hollywood and its scandals. Ballyhoo is a way of life in Tinseltown. Hollywood had and continues to have a major impact on world culture.

4. See Mead's article in *TV Guide* for December 6, 1969, p. 11f.

5. Hype, like humbuggery, is now an epidemic, affecting all aspects of our lives. Computers, e-mail, and the Internet have all magnified hype, which is rapidly accelerating.

6. Daniel J. Boorstin, *The Image: Or What Happened to the American Dream?* (New York: Athenaeum, 1962).

7. Boorstin, *The Image*, p. 40. See also popular magazines, such as *Time, Life, People, Cosmopolitan,* and *Sports Illustrated,* and *O,* which thrive on hype.

The Electric Shocker

1. Tom Wolfe, "The New Guru," *New York Magazine,* November 1965, p. 12.

2. There is a whole library by, about, and against McLuhan. He wrote twenty books, scores of articles, and thousands of letters, now located in various archives. In addition, there are conference lectures, student papers, videotapes—even McLuhan's appearance in *Annie Hall*. In the 1960s, during his "period of fame," magazine and news articles abounded.

The best biography, in my opinion, is Philip Marchand's *Marshall McLuhan: The Medium and the Messenger* (Cambridge: MIT Press, 1998). Marchand catalogued many McLuhan letters for the National Archives of Canada. Among recent monographs, an outstanding one is Mark Slade's *Marshall McLuhan Himself: Another Look at Understanding Media*) available on the Internet at <lakshana@bc.ca>.

Other excellent sources are:
- Miller, Jonathan. *McLuhan* (London: William Collins, 1971).
- Theall, Donald F. *The Medium Is the Rear View Mirror: Understanding McLuhan* (Montreal: McGill-Queen's University Press, 1971).
- Neill, S.D. *Clarifying McLuhan: An Assessment of Process and Product* (Westport, CT: Greenwood Press, 1993).
- Nevitt, Barrington and Maurice McLuhan, Eds. *Who Was Marshall McLuhan?* (Toronto: Stoddart, 1995).
- Grosswiler, Paul. *The Method Is the Message (Montreal: Black Rose Books,* 1998).

3. Harold Adams Innis, *The Bias of Communication,* (Toronto: Toronto University Press, 1951), p. 105.

4. Philip Marchand, *Marshall McLuhan: The Medium and the Messenger* (Cambridge: MIT Press, 1998).

5. Everette Dennis, "Post-Mortem on Marshall McLuhan," in *Mass Comm Review,* I(2), April, 1974.

6. Richard Schickel, "Misunderstanding McLuhan," in *More,* III(8), 1973, p. 79.

7. Neil Postman, "Foreword," in Philip Marchand, *Marshall McLuhan,* p. xiii.

8. Martin E. Marty, "How to Tell a Fad from a Trend." *Commonwealth,* August 22, 1969, p. 509.

Style

1. The literature is vast. The work of Heinrich Wolfflin is a prime reference, although the works of Joseph Margolis, Carl A. Friedrich, Manfred Bukofzer, Helmut Hatzfeld, and John Rupert Martin are also important. See George Kubler's brilliant study of the *Shape of Time* (New Haven: Yale University Press, 1962), read in conjunction with Meyer Schapiro's essay on "Style" in A.L. Kroeber's *Anthropology Today* (Chicago: University of Chicago Press, 1953). See also Wylie Sypher, *Four Stages of Renaissance Style* (New York: Wiley, 1955), and Thomas Munro, *Toward Science Aesthetics* (New York: Abrams, 1956).

2. Hugh Thomas, *World History*. New York: HarperCollins, 1996.

3. Norman Davies, *Europe: A History*. New York: Oxford, 1990.

4. Peter Haertling, *The New York Times,* October 11, 1970, p. 88.

5. Susan Sontag, *Against Interpretation* (New York: Farrar, Strauss, Giroux, 1966). This book was very influential and opened new vistas for popular culture in the turbulent 1960s.

6. Russel B. Nye, *The Unembarrassed Muse: The Popular Arts in America* (New York: Dial, 1970). Few books have been as inluential in popular culture studies as this one. It has become a classic.

7. Susan Sontag, *Against Interpretation,* pp. 38-39.

8. Richard Dorson, *American Folklore* (Chicago: University of Chicago Press, 1962), p. 98.

9. Daniel Boorstin, *The Image: Or What Happened to the American Dream?* (New York: Athaneum, 1962).

10. Walter Lippman, *Public Opinion* (New York: Harcourt Brace, 1922).

11. Fred E.H. Schroeder, *Outlaw Aesthetics* (Bowling Green, OH: Popular Press, 1977), p. 15. William P. Randall, *The History of American Style from l607 to the Present* (New York: Crown, 1978). In the year 2000, style is featured in many of our glossy magazines, such as *Vogue, Town and Country,* and *Country Life*. It leaps out of the Internet.

12. Ernestine Carter, *The Changing World of Fashion* (London: Weidenfeld and Nicolson, 1977), p. 580.

13. Elizabeth Wilson, *Through the Looking Glass: A History of Dress from 1860 to the Present Day*. London: BBC Books, 1989, p. 13.

14. Many more are described by Paul Sann in *Fads, Follies, and Delusions* (New York: Bonanza, 1967). See also William Pierce Randall, *The History of American Style from 1607*. New York: University Press, 1996; 1,365 pp.

15. David Muggleton, *Inside Subculture: The Postmodern Meaning of Style* (New York: Berg, 2000). This book has an excellent fifteen-page bibliography that updates the style scene.

Black Popular Culture

1. Benjamin Quarles, *The Negro in the Making of America* (New York: Collier, 1964), p. 156.

2. Bruce Jackson, "Introduction" to *The Negro and His Folklore in Nineteenth Century Periodicals* (Austin: University of Texas Press, 1967), p. xviii.

3. See Marshall Fishwick, editor, *Remus, Rastus, Revolution!* (Bowling Green, OH: Popular Press, 1974).

4. Clarence Major, *The New Black Poetry* (New York: Collier, 1969), p. 13.

5. The matter is discussed fully by William R. Bascom, "Acculturation Among the Gullah Negroes," *American Anthropologist,* XLIII(1), 1941, pp. 43-50.

6. John Hope Franklin, *From Slavery to Freedom* (New York: Knopf, 1969), p. 41.

7. Larkin's Pulitzer prizewinning study, *Art and Life in America,* was published by Holt, Rinehart, and Winston in 1949 and republished in 1960. Obviously much new data has been made available since then. I do not imply that he is a bigot, but that he reflects the zeitgeist and attitudes of his generation.

8. This point is fully developed by Melville Herskovits in *Man and His Works* (New York: Knopf, 1950).

9. LeRoi Jones, *Blues People* (New York: William Morrow, 1963), p. 1.

10. Ibid., p. 19.

11. For a summary of elite achievement see James A. Porter, *Modern Negro Art* (1943, Howard University Press, 1992).

12. The essay, which first appeared in *Dissent* (Autumn 1957) was reprinted by City Lights Books, San Francisco, California, in 1966.

13. Saunders Redding, "The Black Revolution in American Studies," in *American Studies: An International Newsletter,* IX(1), autumn, 1970, p. 22.

14. See Charles T. Davis and Daniel Walden, Editors, *On Being Black* (New York: Fawcett, 1970); Addison Gayle Jr., Editor, *Black Expression: Essays by and About Americans in the Creative Arts* (Weybright and Talley, 1970); and Addison Gayle Jr., *The Black Situation* (New York: Horizon, 1970).

15. Quoted by Francis Simkins, *The South Old and New* (New York, 1947), p. 419. See also Emma L. Thornbrough, "More Light on Booker T. Washington, and the New York Age," *Journal of Negro History,* XLIII, January 1958, pp. 34-49.

16. See especially Mary Law Chaffee, "William E.B. DuBois's Concept of the Racial Problem in the United States," *Journal of Negro History,* XLI (July), 1956; Elliot M. Rudwick, "The Niagara Movement," *Journal of Negro History,* LXII (July), 1957; and Elliott M. Rudwick, "W.E.B. DuBois: in the Role of Crisis Editor," *Journal of Negro History,* XLIII (July), 1958.

17. Documents dealing with the Washington-DuBois controversy are reprinted in Herbert Aptheker's *A Documentary History of the Negro People in the United States* (New York: Citadel Press, 1950), pp. 876-886. A bibliography of DuBois's work up to 1952 is available at the Widener Library, Harvard University. The best biography is by Francis L. Broderick (1959) (see note 18).

18. Francis L. Broderick, *W.E.B DuBois, Negro Leader in a Time of Crisis* (Stanford, CA: Stanford University Press, 1959), p. 227. The other DuBois quotations in my paragraph are also quoted on this page.

19. W. Sue Jewell, *From Mammy to Miss America and Beyond: Cultural Images and the Shaping of U.S. Social Policy* (New York: Routledge, 1993).

20. Henry Louis Gates Jr. and Cornel West, *The Future of Race* (New York: Alfred Knopf, 1996), p. 67. The race issue continues to occupy center stage, both in scholarly and popular books and magazines, in the new century.

The Most Popular War

1. Robert Creedon, *The American Civil War: The War That Never Ended.* Englewood, NJ: Prentice-Hall, 1973. For an update of this never-ending war, see *Confederate Symbols in the Contemporary South,* edited by Michael Martinez, William Richardson, and Ron McNinch-Su (Gainesville: University Press of Florida, 2000). Battles over the Confederate flag have raged (especially in South Carolina) for several years and can be easily traced on the Internet.

2. See Frank E. Vandiver, "The Civil War: Its Theory and Practice," *The Texas Quarterly,* II(2), summer 1959, pp. 101f.; and Jim Cullen, *The Civil War in Popular Culture: A Reusable Past* (Washington: Smithsonian Institution Press, 1995). His subtitle is an allusion to "On Creating a Usable Past," a famous 1918 essay by Van Wyck Brooks. See also Michael Martinez, William Richardson, and Ron McNinch-Su, *Confederate Symbols in the Contemporary South* (Gainesville: University Press of Florida, 2000).

3. For northern literary defenses of the Civil War and its outstanding historical accounts, see Robert Creedon, *The American Civil War.* See also Allan Nevins, *Ordeal of the Union,* 4 volumes, and *The War for the Union,* 4 volumes, (New York: Scribner, 1947-1971).

4. Frank E. Vandiver, "The Civil War," p. 104.

5. For more on these three authors, see Marshall Fishwick, *Virginia: A New Look at the Old Dominion* (New York: Harper and Row, 1959).

6. George W. Bagby, *The Old Virginia Gentleman.* (New York: C. Scribners Sons, 1911), p. 57. Margaret Mitchell's best-selling *Gone With the Wind* and many other later romantic tales are derived from Bagby.

7. Lewis Mumford, *The Brown Decades: A Study of the Arts in America 1865-1895* (New York: Harcourt, Brace and Company), p. 14.

8. *Dictionary of Literary Biography,* volume 9, *American Writers, 1900-1947* (Detroit: Gale Publishing, 1981). See also James D. Hart, *The Popular Book: A History of America's Literary Taste* (New York: Oxford University Press, 1950).

9. Finis Farr, *Margaret Mitchell of Atlanta* (New York: Morrow, 1965), p. 17.

10. See George Lipsitz, *Times Passages: Collective Memory and American Popular Culture* (Minneapolis: University of Minnesota Press, 1990); and Greil Marcus, *Mystery Train: Images of America in Rock 'n' Roll Music* (New York: Dutton, 1990).

11. A description of Confederate memorial services and their evolution after the surrender at Appomattox may be found in Gaines Foster's *Ghosts of the Confederacy: Defeat, Lost Cause, and the Emergence of the New South* (New York: Oxford University Press, 1987).

12. "Minutes of the Civil War Centennial Commission," March 1961, Box 20, RG79, *National Archives*, June 5, 1960.

13. John Skow, "Bang, Bang! You're History, Buddy" *Time*, August 11, 1986, p. 56.

14. Ibid.

15. Ibid.

16. *Monroe Enquirer-Journal*, Monroe, NC, June 26, 1999, p. 1A.

17. Ibid., p. 1A.

18. Steven Ginsberg, "Reexamining the Civil War . . . with Sponsors: Corporate Backers Promote Three-Day Replay of History" *The Washington Post*, June 14, 1999, Metro Section, pp. B1, B6.

19. Ibid., p. B6.

20. Ibid.

21. Gregg Zoroya, "Weekend Warriors North and South Rise Again As These Soldiers Live to Fight Another Day." *USA Today*, July 2, 1999, Section 2D, Column 2.

22. Ibid.

23. Tony Horwitz, *Confederates in the Attic* (New York: Pantheon, 1998).

24. Gregg Zoroya, "Weekend Warriors."

25. Steven Ginsberg, "Bringing Battle—and History—to Life in Virginia," *The Washington Post*, June 20, 1999, p. C4.

Postmodern Pop

1. If anything, "postmodern" is harder to track and pin down than "modern." Here, too, we face many electronic sources and the information glut. The prevailing cliché is that we have "massified." If that be true, a good introduction is the popular anthology of James Wilson and Stan Le Roy Wilson, *Mass Media, Mass Culture: An Introduction* (New York: McGraw Hill, 1998). Another favorite topic is the millennium. Ray Browne and I set forth our thoughts on that in *Preview 2001+* (Bowling Green, OH: Popular Press, 1998).

The best insights on postmodernism came years ago from Marshall McLuhan. See his book *Take Today: The Executive as Dropout* (Don Mills, Ontario: Longman Canada Limited, 1972). From there, the trail leads in all possible directions.

Of the numerous postmodern bibliographies, two particularly useful and comprehensive are included in Gary Shapiro's *After the Future: Postmodern Times and Place* (Albany: State University of New York Press, 1990), pp. 333-349; and Margaret A. Rose's *The Post-Modern and the Post-Industrial* (Cambridge: Cambridge University Press, 1991), pp. 286-297.

The use of the term postmodern has generated its own problems. As the literature grows, so does the confusion.

2. See Gary Shapiro, *After the Future*, pp. xi f.

3. Henri Lefebvre, *Introduction to Modernity* (London: Verso, 1995). His argument—that modernism is far from dead—is impressive.

4. Steve Fuller, essay 16 in Gary Shapiro, *After the Future*, pp. 273 f.

5. Matthew Arnold, *Selected Poems* (New York: Rhinehart, 1963), p. 101.

Faith Takes a New Face

1. A thorough summary of his career: Sam Wellman, *Billy Graham: The Evangelist.* New York: Chelsea House, 1999. A dozen others can be found in most libraries.

2. Billy Graham's own books provide the essential story of his career and beliefs. They include *Peace with God* (1953), *Angels: God's Secret Agents* (1962), *Is God "Dead?"* (1966), and *The Jesus Generation* (1971). They were all published and distributed by the Zondervan Press, in Grand Rapids, Michigan.

3. For more on the crusades, see Joe E. Barnhart, *The Billy Graham Religion* (Philadelphia: United Church, 1972).

4. *New York Times,* March 12, 1957, p. 8.

5. Michael Real, *Mass Mediated Culture* (Englewood Cliffs, NJ: Prentice-Hall, 1977), pp. 170-180.

6. Douglas T. Miller, "Popular Religion of the 1950s: Norman Vincent Peale and Billy Graham," *Journal of Popular Culture,* 9(1), Summer 1975: 66 f. Also Robert Haught, "The God Biz," *Penthouse,* December 1980, pp. 102-106, 250-257.

7. Robert Sobel, *The Manipulators.* New York: Anchor Press, 1976, p. 243.

8. See William Martin, *A Prophet with Honor: The Billy Graham Story* (New York: William Morrow, 1992); Billy Graham, *The Collected Works of Billy Graham* (New York: Arrowood Press, 1993); Bill Deckard, *Breakfast with Billy Graham* (New York: Servant Press, 1996); Sherwood Wirt, *Billy: A Personal Look at the World's Best-Loved Evangelist* (New York: Crossway Books, 1997); and David Frost, *Billy Graham: Personal Thoughts of a Public Man* (New York: Chariot Victor Publishing, 1997).

9. Billy Graham, *Just As I Am* (New York: HarperCollins, 1999); Charles Ashman, *Billy Graham: Adventures* (New York: William Morrow, 1999); and Sam Wellman, *Billy Graham: The Great Evangelist* (New York: Chelsea House, 1999). Graham welcomed in the new millennium, and in 2000 both he and his son were busy "Crusading for Christ."

The Most Popular Myth

1. See Wendell C. Beane and William Doty, Editors, *Myths, Rites, Symbols: A Mircea Eliade Reader* (New York: Harper and Row, 1975); and Marshall Fishwick, *Seven Pillars of Popular Culture* (Westport, CT: Greenwood Press, 1985), Chapter 7.

2. Fishwick, *Seven Pillars,* p. 65.

3. Joseph Campbell, *Hero with A Thousand Faces* (New York: World, 1956), p. 19. Campbell's pioneer work and thinking have gained significance and popularity in recent years.

4. Joseph Campbell, "Introduction," in *The Portable Jung* (New York: Viking, 1971), p. xxii. This is one of the best general introductions.

5. Ibid.

6. C.G. Jung, "Psychology and Literature," in *Modern Man in Search of a Soul* (New York: Harcourt, Brace, and World, 1955), p. 166.

7. Mircia Eliade, *Myths, Dreams, and Mysteries: The Encounter Between Contemporary Faith and Archaic Realities* (New York: Harper and Row, 1975), pp. 27ff.

8. See A. Whitney Griswold's unpublished doctoral thesis on *The American Cult of Success* in the Sterling Library at Yale University. Also see Moses Rischin, Editor, *The American Gospel of Success* (New York: Quadrangle Books, 1965).

9. Quoted in Herbert R. Mayes' *Alger, A Biography Without a Hero* (New York: Macy-Masius, 1928), p. 226.

10. *New York Times Magazine,* July 16, 1939, p. 11.

11. *New York Times Book Review,* July 2, 1944, p. 9.

12. Ralph D. Gardner, *Horatio Alger: The American Hero Era* from 1889 to 1981. The resulting volume is called *Stratemeyer and Stratemeyer Syndicate Publications* (Westport, CT: Greenwood Press, 1981).

13. Ibid., p. 7.

14. Gary Scharnhorst, *The Lost Life of Horatio Alger, Jr.* (Bloomington, IN: University Press, 1985). p. xi.

15. "Microsoft Bookshelf Online," *Multimedia Reference Library,* 1996-97 Edition.

16. In a labor worthy of Hercules, Deidre Johnson has compiled an annotated checklist of all known magazine stories, dime novels, series, and nonseries titles published.

17. Tom Wolfe, *The Right Stuff.* New York: Simon and Schuster, 1979. All Wolfe's books smack of the mythic. Is he well on his way to becoming the intellectuals' Kandy-Kolored Horatio Alger?

18. Erling B. Holtsmark, *Tarzan and Tradition.* (Westport, CT: Greenwood Press, 1981).

19. Nye, *Unembarrassed Muse.* (Mendota, Illinois: Wayside Press, 1964), p. 321.

20. Gary Harmon, "Tarzan of the Apes: A Structuralist Analysis." I am grateful to Professor Harmon for allowing me to read and to quote from his unpublished essay.

21. Quoted by John Oliver Wilson, *After Affluence: Economics to Meet Human Needs* (New York: Harper and Row, 1980), p. 101.

Global Village—Utopia Revisited?

A large and ever-expanding assortment is available of books, articles, films, and transcripts about the Global Village. On Info Track (Expanded Academic Index) for example, there are 81 recent books and 366 articles under the heading Global Village. Two comprehensive summaries are Roger Rollins, Editor, *The Americanization of the Global Village* (Bowling Green, OH: Popular Press, 1989), and Ray B. Browne and Marshall W. Fishwick, Editors, *The Global Village: Dead or Alive?* (Bowling Green, OH: Popular Press, 1999). They both have extensive bibliographies.

Four recent books have been of special help in my work: Carl Coon, *Culture Wars and the Global Village* (Amherst, NY: Prometheus, 2000); Alison Brysk, *From Tribal Village to Global Village* (Stanford, CA: Stanford University Press, 2000); Riall W. Nolan, *Building the Global Village* (New York: Dutton/Plume,

1999); and Jan K. Black, *Inequity in the Global Village* (Hartford, CT: Kumarian Press, 1999).

1. Zygmunt Bauman, *Globalization: The Human Consequences.* New York: Columbia University Press, 1998, p. 56.

2. William Leach, *Country of Exiles: The Destruction of Place in American Life.* (New York: Pantheon Books, 1999). See also James Grunig, *Decline of the Global Village* (Bayside, New York: General Hall, 1976). This book anticipates many of our current problems. For an interesting study focused on games, see Anne Cooper-Chen, *Games in the Global Village: A 50-Nation Study of Entertainment Television* (Bowling Green, OH: Popular Press, 1996).

3. The best summary of McLuhan's ideas is his *Culture Is Our Business* (New York: McGraw Hill, 1970). For a restatement of his ideas, see George Haskel and Michael Rycroft, *Space and the Global Village* (Norwell, MA: Kluwer Academic Publishers, 1998). The best summary of his life is W. Terrance Gordon's *Marshall McLuhan: Escape into Understanding: A Biography* (New York: Basic Books, 1997).

4. Colin Cherry, *World Communication: Threat or Promise?* (New York: John Wiley, 1978). See also Marshall W. Fishwick, *The Global Village: Dead or Alive?* (Bowling Green, OH: Popular Press, 1999).

5. Ben H. Bagdkian, "The Lords of the Global Village," first appeared in *Nation* for June 12, 1984, pp. 54-58. Since then giant mergers have grown ever larger. See also R.M. Soccolich, *100 Steps Necessary for Survival in the Global Village* (Astonia, NM: Seaburn Press, 1997).

6. Jack L. Larsen, *Folk Art from the Global Village* (Albuquerque: Museum of New Mexico Press, 1978); and H.J. Blackham, *The Future of Our Past* (Amherst, NY: Prometheus Press, 1996).

Further Reading

The much-heralded worldwide "popular culture explosion" has produced thousands of books, films, television programs, and monographs but no widely accepted definition. By best estimates, over a million students now study popular culture in America. Who can say how many paths they pursue? How many topics they cover? And how does the subject fare abroad?

With so broad a subject covering not only centuries but millennia, a reading list could become a large volume in its own right. *Books In Print,* for example, contains 1,590 entries under Popular Culture, with twenty-two subdivisions. Of those no longer in print, there is no end.

The central clearinghouse is the Popular Culture Association and Popular Press, both located at Bowling Green State University, Bowling Green, Ohio 43403. Their journals and press continue to produce new material, book reviews, and conference notes. Catalogs and journals are available on request.

Ames, Kenneth L. *Death in the Dining Room and Other Tales of Victorian Culture.* Philadelphia: Temple University Press, 1992.

Bacon-Smith, Camille. *Science Fiction Culture.* Philadelphia: University of Pennsylvania Press, 2001.

Bailey, Brian J. *The Luddite Rebellion.* United States, New York University Press, 1998.

Baudrillard, Jean. *The Cool Provocateur.* New York: Verson, 1998.

———. *The Ecstasy of Communication.* New York: Automedia, 1999.

———. *Forget Foucault.* New York: Automedia, 1999.

Baughmann, James L. *The Republic of Mass Culture.* Baltimore: Johns Hopkins University Press, 1996.

Bennett, D. (Ed.). *Cultural Pluralism.* London: Routledge, 1994.

Bigsby, C.W.E. *Superculture: American Popular Culture and Europe.* Bowling Green, OH: Popular Press, 1975.

Blackham, H.J. *The Future of Our Past.* New York: Prometheus Books, 1996.

Blau, Judith R. *The Shape of Culture: A Study of Contemporary Cultural Patterns in the United States.* New York: Cambridge University Press, 1989.

Brooker, Will. *Batman Unmasked: Analyzing a Cultural Icon.* New York: Continuum, 2001

Browne, Ray B. *Popular Culture Landmarks.* New York: Gale Research, Inc., 1994.

Browne, Ray B. and Pat Browne. *The Guide to United States Popular Culture.* Bowling Green, OH: Popular Press, 2001.

Burke, Peter. "The 'Discovery' of Popular Culture." In Raphael Samuel (Ed.), *People's History and Social Theory.* London: Routledge, 1981.

Callaghan, Colleen. "Looking Forward to the 21st Century." In Marshall Fishwick (Ed.), *An American Mosaic.* New York: American Heritage Custom Publishing, 1996.

Campbell, Burke. *The Naked Global Village.* New York: Random House, 1997.

Carlson, Lew, (Ed.). *American Popular Culture at Home and Abroad.* Milwaukee: New Issues Press, 1995.

Chambers, Iain. *Popular Culture.* London: Methune, 1986.

Collins, Jim. *Uncommon Cultures: Popular Culture and Post-Modernism.* London: Routledge, 1989.

Combs, James. "The Play World of the New Millennium." In Ray B. Browne and Marshall Fishwick (Eds.), *Preview 2001+.* Bowling Green, OH: Bowling Green State University Press, 1995.

Douglas, Ann. *The Feminization of American Culture.* New York: Farrar, Strauss, and Giroux, 1998.

Duffy, Dennis. *Marshall McLuhan.* Toronto: McClelland and Stewart, 1969.

Felski, Rita. *Doing Time: Feminist Postmodern Culture, Theory and Post Modern Culture.* New York: New York University Press, 2000.

Fishwick, Marshall W. *Common Culture and the Great Tradition; The Case for Renewal.* Westport, CT: Greenwood Press, 1982.

Fishwick, Marshall W. *Go, and Catch a Falling Star.* New York: Forbes, 2000; and Thompson Learning, Cincinnati, 2001.

―――. *Popular Culture: Cavespace to Cyberspace.* New York: The Haworth Press, Inc. 1999.

Fisk, John. *Understanding Popular Culture.* Boston: Unwin Hyman, 1989.

Frow, John. *Cultural Studies and Cultural Value.* Oxford: Clarendon Press, 1995.

Gates, Bill. *The Road Ahead.* New York: Viking Penguin, 1996.

Gordon, Ian. *Comic Strips and Consumer Culture.* Washington, DC: Smithsonian Institute Press, 1998.

Griswold, Wendy. *Cultures and Societies in a Changing World.* Thousand Oaks, CA: Pine Forge Press, 1994.

Grossbreg, Lawrence. *Bringing It All Back Home: Essays on Cultural Studies.* Durham: Duke University Press, 1997.

Grunig, James E. "Turning McLuhan on His Head," In Ray B. Browne and Marshall Fishwick (Eds.), *The Global Village: Dead Or Alive?* Bowling Green, OH: Bowling Green University Press, 1999.

Hall, Peter Dobkin. *The Organization of Culture.* New York: New York University, 1984.

Himanen, Pakka. *The Hacker Ethic.* New York: Random House, 2001.

Hunter, James D. *Culture Wars: The Struggle to Define America.* New York: Basic Books, 1987.

Jayaraman, Raja. "Border and Borderless Culture: A Study of the Process of Recreation and Maintenance of Ethnic Boundary in a Global Society." In Ray B. Browne and Marshall W. Fishwick (Eds.), *The Global Village: Dead or Alive?* Bowling Green, OH: Bowling Green University Press, 1999.

Jensen, Richard. "Internet 2001 and the Future." In Ray B. Browne and Marshall W. Fishwick (Eds.), *Preview 2001+.* Bowling Green, OH: Bowling Green University Press, 1995.

Jones, Joel. "American Studies: The Myth of Methodology." In Sam Girgus (Ed.), *The American Self.* Albuquerque, NM: University of New Mexico Press, 1981.

Kittleson, Mary L. *The Soul of Pop Culture.* Chicago: Open Court, 1997.

Kowuwenhoven, John A. *The Beer Can by the Highway.* New York: Doubleday, 1961.

Landay, Lori. *Madcaps, Screwballs, & Conwomen.* Philadelphia: University of Pennsylvania Press, 1998.

May, Lary. *The Big Tomorrow.* Chicago: University of Chicago Press, 2001.

McLuhan, Marshall (1911-1982).

    Between 1951 and 1995, twenty of McLuhan's books were published as well as seventeen books about him, plus scores of articles and interviews. They are all listed in Phillip Marchand's new biography, *Marshall McLuhan: The Medium and the Messenger.* Cambridge, MA: MIT Press, 1998.

    Both friend and mentor, McLuhan had more influence on my work than any other person. The most influential of three books were; *The Gutenberg Galaxy: The Making of the Typographic Man* (1962); *Understanding Media: The Extensions of Man* (1964); and *War and Peace in the Global Village* (1968).

McRobbie, Angela. *Postmodernism and Popular Culture.* New York: Routledge, 1994.

Morgan, David. *Visual Piety.* Berkeley: University of California Press, 1998.

Neal, Arthur G. "Cultural Fragmentation in the 21st Century." In Ray B. Browne and Marshall W. Fishwick (Eds.), *Preview 2001+*. Bowling Green, OH: Bowling Green University Press, 1995.

Nevitt, Barrington and McLuhan, Maurice (Eds.). *Who Was Marshall McLuhan?* Toronto: Stoddart, 1995.

Nolan, Riall W. *Building the Global Village.* New York: NAL Dutton, 1999.

Nye, Russel. *The Unembarrassed Muse: Popular Arts in America.* New York: Dial Press, 1970.

Redhead, Steve. *The End-of-the-Century Party: Youth and Pop Towards 2000.* Manchester: Manchester University Press, 1990.

Robinson, Frank M. and Davidson, Lawrence. *Pulp Culture: The Art of Fiction Magazines.* Portland, OR: Collectors Press, 1998.

Roche, Daniel. *A History of Everyday Things.* New York: Cambridge University Press, 2000.

Roszak, Theodore. *The Cult of Information: The Folklore of Computers and the True Art of Thinking.* New York: Pantheon, 1986.

Rushkoff, Douglas. *Cyberia: Life in the Trenches of Hyperspace.* New York: Ballantine, 1992.

Schechter, Harold and Semeiks, J.G. *Patterns in Popular Culture.* New York: Harper and Row, 1980.

Scribner's Reference Shelf. *Encyclopedia of American Cultural History.* New York: Scribner, 1999.

Shuman, Michael. *Towards a Global Village.* New York: LPC Inbook, 1999.

Smoodin, Eric, (Ed.). *Disney Discourse: Producing the Magic Kingdom.* New York: Routledge, 1994.

Socolish, R.M. *100 Steps Necessary for Survival in the Global Village.* New York: Seaburn, 1997.

Storey, John. *An Introductory Guide to Cultural Theory and Popular Culture.* Athens, GA: University of Georgia Press, 1993.

Storey, John. *An Introduction to Cultural Theory & Popular Culture.* 1998, ISBN: 0820319600. Athens: University of Georgia Press.

Taylor, Timothy. *Global Pop.* London: Routledge, 1996.

Thomas, Hugh. *World History: The Story of Mankind from Prehistory to the Present.* New York: Harper Collins, 1996.
Thompson, William. *Darkness and Scattered Light: Speculations on the Future.* New York: Doubleday, 1978.
United Nations Publications. *Global Outlook 2000.* New York: United Nations, 1990.
Van Elteren, Mel. "The Complexities of Cultural Globalization Revisited." In Ray B. Browne and Marshall W. Fishwick (Eds.), *The Global Village: Dead Or Alive?* Bowling Green, OH: Bowling Green University Press, 1999.
Weber, Alfred. *Farewell to European History.* Westport, CT: Greenwood Press, 1977.
Wellmann, Berry. *Networks in the Global Village.* San Francisco: Westview Press, 1995.
Wilson, Elizabeth. *Through the Looking Glass.* London: BBC Books, 1989.
Wray, Masa and Newitz, Annalee. *White Trash: Race and Class in America.* London: Routledge, 1998.
Yoder, John. *Discovering American Folklife.* New York: Books on Demand, 1997.
Zeldin, Theodore. *An Intimate History of Humanity.* New York: HarperCollins, 1995.
Zinsser, William. *Pop Goes America.* New York: Harper and Row, 1996.
Zunz, Oliver. *Why the American Century?* Chicago: University of Chicago Press, 2001.

ESSENTIAL ELECTRONIC RESOURCES

compiled by
Peter C. Rollins

News and Breaking Stories

CNN Interactive has links by story categories:
<http://www.cnn.com>

Conservative spin on the news at Town Hall:
<http://www.townhall.com/>

Historical and Cultural Organizations

The Popular Culture/American Culture Associations
<http://h-net.msu.edu/~pcaaca>

This Web site has book reviews, area chair names and addresses, program announcements, and lists of officers for the organizations. Membership form and meeting information online.

The American Studies Association
<http://www.georgetown.edu/crossroads/>

Contains the newsletter of the ASA along with information about American studies programs across the land. Past issues of *The American Quarterly* online.

The Organization of American Historians
<http://www.indiana.edu/~oah/connections>

Publishes the *Journal of American History* and has excellent research and job announcements updated on a regular basis.

The American Historical Association
<http://www.theaha.org>

Organization's detailed newsletter, calendar of events, national program. Purchase pamphlets and publications from the site.
H-NET serves AHA members.

<http://www2.h-net.msu.edu/lists>

Has over 100 Web sites and associated discussion groups from African research to Women's history—and much in between.

Special Archives of Important Documents and Histories

CLIO—The National Archives has a host of sources:
<http://www.nara.gov/>

The Library of Congress American Memory site, available from the LOC home page:
<http://www.loc.gov/>

Phil Landon's Site:

Film, literature, popular culture, history links galore.
<http://www.gl.umbc.edu/~landon/index.html>

An abundance of sources in all relevant areas of American and cultural studies by a senior scholar.

Film Links

Film & History:
<www.filmandhistory.org>

This journal has twenty-four years of its table of contents on the Web site plus discussions of recent and significant films in relation to history. Every university library should subscribe to this handy source and many around the world do just that.

Index

Order Your Own Copy of
This Important Book for Your Personal Library!

POPULAR CULTURE IN A NEW AGE

_____in hardbound at $49.95 (ISBN: 0-7890-1297-9)

_____in softbound at $24.95 (ISBN: 0-7890-1298-7)

COST OF BOOKS_____

OUTSIDE USA/CANADA/
MEXICO: ADD 20%____

POSTAGE & HANDLING_____
(US: $4.00 for first book & $1.50
for each additional book)
Outside US: $5.00 for first book
& $2.00 for each additional book)

SUBTOTAL_____

in Canada: add 7% GST____

STATE TAX____
(NY, OH & MIN residents, please
add appropriate local sales tax)

FINAL TOTAL____
(If paying in Canadian funds,
convert using the current
exchange rate, UNESCO
coupons welcome.)

❑ **BILL ME LATER:** ($5 service charge will be added)
(Bill-me option is good on US/Canada/Mexico orders only;
not good to jobbers, wholesalers, or subscription agencies.)

❑ Check here if billing address is different from
shipping address and attach purchase order and
billing address information.

Signature_____

❑ **PAYMENT ENCLOSED: $**_____

❑ **PLEASE CHARGE TO MY CREDIT CARD.**

❑ Visa ❑ MasterCard ❑ AmEx ❑ Discover
❑ Diner's Club ❑ Eurocard ❑ JCB

Account # _____

Exp. Date_____

Signature_____

Prices in US dollars and subject to change without notice.

NAME_____

INSTITUTION_____

ADDRESS_____

CITY_____

STATE/ZIP_____

COUNTRY_____ COUNTY (NY residents only)_____

TEL_____ FAX_____

E-MAIL_____

May we use your e-mail address for confirmations and other types of information? ❑ Yes ❑ No
We appreciate receiving your e-mail address and fax number. Haworth would like to e-mail or fax special
discount offers to you, as a preferred customer. **We will never share, rent, or exchange your e-mail address
or fax number.** We regard such actions as an invasion of your privacy.

Order From Your Local Bookstore or Directly From
The Haworth Press, Inc.
10 Alice Street, Binghamton, New York 13904-1580 • USA
TELEPHONE: 1-800-HAWORTH (1-800-429-6784) / Outside US/Canada: (607) 722-5857
FAX: 1-800-895-0582 / Outside US/Canada: (607) 722-6362
E-mail: getinfo@haworthpressinc.com
PLEASE PHOTOCOPY THIS FORM FOR YOUR PERSONAL USE.
www.HaworthPress.com

BOF00